Talking about people

A multiple case study on adult language acquisition

EUROPEAN STUDIES ON
Multilingualism

Aims and Scope

The series seeks to promote the dissemination of empirical research evidence on the use of more than one language in Europe. The focus is on majority and minority language use at the level of individual and society, and derives from the interdisciplinary approaches of linguistics, psychology, sociology, anthropology, and education. Processes of language acquisition, language shift, language loss and the consequences of multilingualism for such areas as education and language policy are taken into account.

EUROPEAN STUDIES ON
Multilingualism 1

TALKING
ABOUT PEOPLE

A multiple case study on adult language acquisition

Peter Broeder
University of Tilburg,
The Netherlands

SWETS & ZEITLINGER B.V. AMSTERDAM / LISSE   PUBLISHERS

SWETS & ZEITLINGER INC. BERWYN, PA

ACKNOWLEDGEMENTS

This book talks about people: Mahmut, Ergün, Abdullah, Osman, Mohamed, Fatima, Hassan, and Husseyn, who allowed their language and living experiences to be observed over two-and-a-half years. I owe a lot to them; without them this study would not have been possible.

I would also like to express my sincere thanks to all those friends and colleagues who contributed to this study through invaluable comments and discussions.

The research for this study was supported by the Arts Faculty of Tilburg University (the Netherlands), the European Science Foundation (Strasbourg, France), and the Foundation for Linguistic Research, which is funded by the Netherlands Organization for Scientific Research (NWO).

Parts of this study have been published elsewhere, or will be in due time. "Praten over mannen en vrouwen" ('Talking about men and women') in *Tijdschrift voor Taal-en Tekstwetenschap* (Broeder 1989b) is incorporated in Chapter 6 on 3rd role pronominal reference. "Possession in a new language", to appear in *Applied Linguistics* (Broeder 1992) is incorporated in Chapter 8. Preliminary analyses were published in Broeder (1989a,1990).

Library of Congress Cataloging-in-Publication Data
(applied for)

Cip-gegevens Koninklijke Bibliotheek, Den Haag

Broeder, Peter

Talking about people : a multiple case study on adult language acquisition / Peter Broeder. - Amsterdam : Swets & Zeitlinger. - (European studies on multilingualism, ISSN 0926-6461 : 1)
Ook verschenen als proefschrift Tilburg, 1991. - Met lit. opg. - Met samenvatting in het Nederlands.
ISBN 90-265-1211-2
NUGI 941
Trefw.: tweetaligheid / taalverwerving ; etnische minderheden.

Cover design: Rob Molthoff
Cover printed by Casparie, IJsselstein
Printed in the Netherlands by Offsetdrukkerij Kanters B.V., Alblasserdam

© 1991 Swets & Zeitlinger B.V., Amsterdam/Lisse

ISBN 90 265 1211 2
NUGI 941

CONTENTS

Contents

NOTATION CONVENTIONS

Transcriptions

In the sequences capitals are only used to mark beginning of utterances. In addition, simplified, i.e. more readable versions of the transcription conventions in the ESF project are used:

'+'   indicates unfilled pause

'*'   non-target language words are put between asterisks: *word*

'"'   quoted speech is indicated by "quote"

'/'   indicates a speaker's self-interruption or self-repair

'\'   indicates the interruption of one speaker by another

'^'   indicates notable intonation rise

'_'   indicates notable intonation fall

'< >'   comments on the situation, the interlocutors, etc.

'<..>'   indicates that some parts of the sequence are not given

'[ ]'   simultaneous speech, one pair of brackets corresponds with another pair in the speech of another speaker

English transliteration

For clarification purposes the transliteration of Dutch is a combination of word-for-word transliteration and standard English. Dutch minimal feedback items are rendered as follows:

agreement;   *hm* = 'um', *hmhm* = 'uh-huh'

filler;   *uh* = 'er', *hm* = 'erm'

tag-like question; *he?* = 'eh?', 'right?'

Non-target language words are translated and put between asterisks: *turkish word*. The orthographic representation of Moroccan Arabic is derived from Harrell (1962).

CHAPTER 1

INTRODUCTION

This chapter introduces the area of investigation of the present study on adult untutored language acquisition: talking about people. First, the referential domain and the encoding devices are discussed briefly. Next, the general aims and research questions are specified. Finally, a European Science Foundation research project is introduced. This ESF project provided the data base and framework for the present study.

1.1 TALKING ABOUT PEOPLE

The subject of this study is the process of untutored language acquisition in adults and the focus is on Turkish and Moroccan immigrants during the first three years of their stay in the Netherlands. In this period they started to learn Dutch as a second language without any formal tuition.

The perspective on language acquisition taken in this study can be characterized as an approach which (1) starts from a concept-oriented referential domain, and which (2) focusses on the systematics of encoding devices (i.e. the form-function relationships) in learner varieties of a target language.

1.1.1 REFERENTIAL DOMAIN

A concept-oriented approach starts from a language-independent semantic and cognitive domain (cf. Von Stutterheim & Klein 1987). All successful verbal communication requires reference to the domains of people, space, and time. Basic types of person and spatio-temporal reference are studied from cross-linguistic, psychological and developmental points of view (see for example Rauh 1983, Jarvella & Klein 1982, Lyons 1977, and Miller & Johnson-Laird 1976).

The conceptual domain this study deals with is "people". Talking about people involves "the act of referring". Although intuitively it is fairly obvious which referential domain corresponds to the label "people", a precise definition is complex.

According to Lyons (1977:436-452), people, together with animals and things, are so-called first order entities. In contrast to second and third order entities, first order entities can be said to "exist". Second order entities "occur" and they include events, processes and states-of-affairs such as "the sunset". Third order entities are abstract propositions such as "love" and "peace". First order entities are relatively constant to their perceptual properties, are located in a three-dimensional space and they are publicly observable. In short: something is a first order entity if it "exists and can be referred to" (Lyons 1977:445). The domain of people is a subset of first order entities and restricted to human beings.

Successful reference to people means that "the referent is sorted out of a set of possible alternative referents" (Perdue 1984:139). The communicative role which a referent fulfils is important. There is a fundamental difference between "first person reference" (i.e. reference to the speaker), "second person reference" (i.e. reference to the addressee), and "third person reference" (i.e. reference to the person who is neither the speaker nor the addressee). In particular the origin of these traditional terms is illuminating. The classical grammarians conceived of a language event as a drama in which only the speaker and the addressee are actually participating: the principal role is played by the first person, the subsidiary role by the second person; third persons are negatively defined in that they do not correlate with any positive participant role (cf. Lyons 1977:638). Following this distinction we will talk about first role person reference (henceforth: 1st role reference), second role person reference (henceforth: 2nd role reference), and third role person reference (henceforth: 3rd role reference).

1.1.2 ENCODING DEVICES

Every language has numerous devices for the encoding of person reference. Between languages there are remarkable similarities and differences in the construction and differentiation of the set of possible referring expressions. In many languages the encoding of reference to people is done through nouns and pronouns. Nominal reference involves a set of proper names and more or less complex nominal groups (e.g. *Ahmet, my brother, my neighbour's sister*); pronominal reference is based on an exhaustive list of frequently used and predominantly monosyllabic word forms (e.g. *I, you, he*, etc.).

The historical development of languages suggests that the functional distinction between pronominal and nominal reference is not absolutely clear-cut (cf. Lyons 1977:179). Nevertheless, in most languages each of them corresponds with a distinctive way of successfully sorting out a referent from a set of possible alternative referents. Globally speaking, pronominal devices constitute the unmarked encoding of person reference, whereas nominal devices constitute the marked encoding. This certainly holds for the encoding of 1st and 2nd role reference. For these two types of reference the encoding through pronouns is usually adequate, because from the situational context it is clear who are the speaker(s) and addressee(s). Also for 3rd role reference, although to a lesser degree, pronominal devices constitute the unmarked encoding. Referents have to be established nominally in the discourse, but for maintenance of reference encoding through pronouns is adequate (e.g. *Ahmet goes to his sister in Turkey. He hasn't seen her for two years*).

1.2   AIM AND SCOPE

Adult learners of a second language (henceforth: L2) will be familiar with a set of concepts through their first language (henceforth: L1), but they will not be familiar with the specific ways in which a comparable set of L2 concepts is organized and encoded through linguistic devices of the L2. With respect to the conceptual domain of temporality, recent studies on L1 and L2 acquisition provide empirical support for the importance of Slobin's claim of "Thinking for speaking" (see Slobin 1987 and Bhardwaj et al. 1988 for further references). The language which we learn as a child is not a neutral coding system of an objective reality. Each language is a subjective orientation to the world of human experience, and this orientation affects the ways in which we think while we are speaking (Slobin 1990). Communication in a specific language implies a specific ordering of cognitive concepts. The language acquired during childhood has firmly entrenched itself and will affect the acquisition of other languages at a later age.

Especially during the early stages of language acquisition, learner varieties necessarily consist of a restricted set of linguistic devices which learners have to use as efficiently as possible in daily interactions with native speakers of the target language. The questions relevant to this study are: how do adult language learners start out encoding person reference, how does their repertoire develop, and why do they make the choices they make?

The assumption is that the variety of the target language used by the learner is a dynamic and unique system that partly coincides with and partly differs from the target language. Learner varieties are systematic not only in their internal organization, but also in the order of various stages that can be distinguished. The systematics of learner varieties are reflected in form-function relationships.

Central aims of the present study are the description and explanation of the learner's preferences in the encoding of talking about people. The basic research questions can be specified as follows:

I   Which linguistic encoding devices are used for talking about people in L2-Dutch varieties of Turkish and Moroccan adults?
II   Which developmental patterns can be found in subsequent stages of language acquisition?
III   How can learner preferences be explained?

The present study is a follow-up on the European Science Foundation project entitled *the Ecology of Adult Language Acquisition* (Perdue 1984). This ESF project provided the framework for the present study. The area of investigation, person reference, derived from the theoretical perspective taken in the ESF project and the focus is on those Turkish and Moroccan adults who played a central role in that project as second language learners of Dutch.

1.3 THE ESF PROJECT

From 1982 to 1987 an international research project was initiated under the auspices of the European Science Foundation (ESF) in Strasbourg. This project was carried out simultaneously in Great Britain, Germany, the Netherlands, France and Sweden. It focussed on processes of spontaneous (untutored) second language acquisition in adult immigrants in Western Europe. The ESF project is different from most previous studies in that it has both cross-linguistic and longitudinal dimensions. With respect to the cross-linguistic dimension the relatively young tradition of second language research has so far had a rather strong Anglo-Saxon bias. It is an American diet in which English is most commonly the source or the target language (cf. Ellis 1985:74). In the ESF project, however, five target languages (L2) and six source languages (L1) were combined in the following way:

L2:	Swedish	French	Dutch	German	English
	/\	/\	/\	/\	/\
L1:	Finnish	Spanish	Arabic	Turkish	Italian	Punjabi

The selection of these source and target languages was based on two criteria (see Perdue 1984:29-31). First, the chosen source languages belong to the major immigrant languages in the five Western European countries under consideration. Secondly, it should be possible to make a linguistically interesting comparison as four of the five target languages are Germanic, and three of the six source languages are non-Indo-European. With respect to the longitudinal dimension of the ESF project Klein & Perdue (1988:5) pointed out that research on second language acquisition by adults almost exclusively has a cross-sectional design. Conclusions about the process of language acquisition are mostly based on a comparison of different language learners at different stages of L2 acquisition. Longitudinal studies that focus on the L2 acquisition process of the same learners over a longer period of time are scarce (exceptions being Schumann 1978a, and Huebner 1983 for instance). The longitudinal design of the ESF project was as follows: over a period of two-and-a-half years each month audio/video recordings were made of four adult language learners (informants) for each source-target language pair (Total = 10x4 = 40 informants). Each informant took part in a variety of language activities. The data collection resulted in an extensive and varied computer-stored corpus of language data. A detailed description of the design and aims of the ESF project was given in Perdue (1984).

The ESF project focussed on the "analysis" and "synthesis" tasks language learners are confronted with (cf. Klein 1986:63-109). The analysis task consists of segmenting the available input into meaningful units and bringing the resulting information in line with the situational context of the utterance. This task was dealt with in two studies included in the ESF project: *Ways of Achieving Understanding* (Bremer et al. 1988) and *Feedback in Adult Language Acquisition* (Allwood 1988). The synthesis task consists of turning meaningful units (sounds, words, etc.) they have learned into understandable speech. Specific studies were made of the learner's problem of arranging words to form larger units of speech: *Utterance Structure* (Klein & Perdue 1988), and of locating the objects or events they talk about: *Spatial Reference* (Becker et al. 1988) and *Temporal Reference* (Bhardwaj et al. 1988).

In the ESF project substantial analyses were carried out for the conceptual domains of space and time. However, person reference was only touched on to a limited extent: at the word level pilot studies were carried out on the acquisition of pronouns (Broeder, Extra & Van Hout 1986 and Broeder et al. 1988:86-113), and at the discourse level some analyses were carried out for the establishment and mainte-nance of person reference in narrative discourse (Klein & Perdue 1988).

1.4   OUTLINE OF THE PRESENT STUDY

Any study on language acquisition must be selective in the number and type of infor-mants and in the amount and variety of data to be collected. First of all, a choice has to be made between a longitudinal and a cross-sectional research design. In the former, the language behaviour of one and the same informant or group of infor-mants is observed for a certain period at specific intervals. In the latter, one sample of language behaviour of a specific group of informants is compared simultaneously with other samples of other groups (at a less or more advanced level of language proficiency for instance). In contrast to cross-sectional studies, where the time factor has actually been eliminated, longitudinal studies can give a real picture of language development over time. Within both types of research design it is possible to make statements about sequences. A cross-sectional design will allow statements on the order of accuracy (or difficulty) of a given series of expressive devices, whereas only a longitudinal design will allow statements on the order of acquisition. In many cross-sectional studies it has been tacitly assumed that an observed order of accuracy reflects a non-observed order of acquisition. In other words, synchronic data have been interpreted diachronically. It should, however, be borne in mind that such an interpretation is based on assumptions, the validity of which will have to be tested empirically. The dominance of cross-sectional over longitudinal studies on language acquisition derives from the fact that longitudinal research is by definition time-con-suming (and therefore often expensive), and cannot easily be applied to large num-bers of informants.

Given the primary interest of in-depth, micro-analytical insights into processes of language development over time, this longitudinal study will be based on a large amount and variety of data, and on a limited number of informants rather than the reverse. The same informants will be followed over time from the first stages of their

L2 acquisition over a period of almost two-and-a-half years at intervals of approximately one month. The outcome of this study could serve as a basis for further research involving larger and more representative samples of informants.

This study focusses on those four informants who played a central role in the ESF project as L2 learners of Dutch: the Turks Mahmut and Ergün, and the Moroccans Mohamed and Fatima. For these core informants all interactional data that were collected will be analysed. Cross-learner and cross-linguistic comparisons are made through analyses of L2-Dutch of two Turkish adults (Abdullah and Osman) and two Moroccan adults (Hassan and Husseyn). These shadow informants also participated in the ESF project, but with these informants data were collected but not analysed. Their learner varieties have not yet been investigated in previous studies. In addition, some analyses will be presented for L2-German by four Turkish and four Italian adult immigrants.

The area of investigation of the present study is the acquisition of linguistic means for reference to person at word and discourse levels. At the word level the study will focus on pronominal reference (i.e. the use of subject, object, and possessive pronouns) and the encoding of the possessive relationship, while at the discourse level it will focus on the establishment, shift and maintenance of person reference.

The study is structured as follows: Chapter 2 deals with different perspectives in the study of language acquisition, Chapter 3 describes the data base and the informants. The subsequent chapters present a number of analyses of the learner varieties with respect to the encoding of talking about people.

Chapter 4 is a detailed account of pronoun systems in spoken Dutch, in Turkish, and in Moroccan Arabic. This description of target/source language systems results in a set of predictions about L2 acquisition processes in adults.

In Chapters 5 and 6 these predictions are tested for 1st/2nd role reference and for 3rd role reference respectively. At the end of Chapter 6 the findings on the acquisition of pronominal reference will be related to processes of child/adult language acquisition and to pidgin/creole languages.

In Chapters 7 and 8 the analytical perspective starts from functionally defined domains (i.e. a function-form perspective). The focus is on the establishment, shift and maintenance of person reference (Chapter 7), and on the encoding of the possessive relationship (Chapter 8).

In Chapter 9 the findings are put into a broader perspective; the preferences of our adult learners will be discussed in terms of specific learner type characteristics and source/target system characteristics of language development.

CHAPTER 2

THE STUDY OF LANGUAGE ACQUISITION

This chapter presents a brief account of a number of prominent theories in the study of language acquisition: (1) Contrastive Analysis and Creative Construction, (2) Functionalism and learner varieties, and (3) Chomsky's Universal Grammar. Some implications for the present study are derived from this overview.

2.1 CONTRASTIVE ANALYSIS AND CREATIVE CONSTRUCTION

Theories which have traditionally dominated in studies of L2 acquisition are Contrastive Analysis and Creative Construction (see Robinett & Schachter 1983, James 1980). A moot point was the precise role of L1 as the source language in the acquisition of L2 as the target language. A central question related to this was to what degree L1 acquisition works in the same way as L2 acquisition. Traditionally, studies of contrastive analysis and creative construction were typically product-oriented and directed at morpho-syntactic form characteristics (McLaughlin 1987:59-69).

Contrastive analysis
   Contrastive analyses of languages form the basis of traditional accounts of second language acquisition. Rooted in the general framework of behaviourism, L1 acquisition is viewed as the internalization of a finite set of linguistic patterns (habits) through imitation and reinforcement. Linguistic patterns are operationalized according to structuralist models (e.g. Bloomfield 1935, Lado 1957), and languages are described in terms of independent levels (e.g. phonology, morphology, syntax) with an emphasis on the detailed description of surface features. In this tradition of behaviourist and structuralist ideas L2 acquisition is conceived of as the transfer of L1-based habits. Similarity between L1 and L2 patterns will result in positive transfer, difference in negative transfer (or interference). It was not until the late 1960s that contrastive claims about L2 acquisition were investigated empirically (cf. Ellis 1985:7). Evidence provided by error analyses of learner language data and longitudinal observations of L2 acquisition dealt a mortal blow to contrastive analysis.

Creative construction

The findings of a number of error analysis studies contradicted the contrastive analysis hypothesis that L1 should be seen as the most important determining factor in the acquisition of L2. A comparison of a large diversity of grammatical morphemes (i.e. function words and/or morphologically marked word endings) in the language use of learners revealed that L2 learners with different source languages made similar types of errors, the majority of which reflected the influence of the target language. In the 1970s not only error analyses but also a number of longitudinal studies of L2 learners became available. These studies provided empirical support for striking similarities between the "routes" followed by L1 and L2 learners (e.g. Hatch 1978). Eventually the types of errors and the order patterns found in L1 and L2 acquisition resulted in the theory of creative construction (cf. Dulay & Burt 1975). In this view, language acquisition is determined by (1) "innate mechanisms" and (2) the structure of the target language. Guided by their innate competence language learners formulate hypotheses about the target language in order to resolve the mismatch between their input and output.

The theories of contrastive analysis and creative construction were traditionally seen by their advocates as being mutually exclusive. However, nowadays there is a general consensus that they are not. In a number of so-called process-oriented L2 studies (see McLaughlin 1987:69-79 for an overview) it is generally assumed that there are similarities as well as differences between L1 and L2 acquisition. L1 is one of the sources of knowledge that L2 learners will use, either consciously or not, in acquiring perceptive and productive abilities in the target language (see Klein 1986:25, and Gass & Selinker 1983).

2.2 FUNCTIONALISM AND LEARNER VARIETIES

Cental to a large variety of recent studies on language acquisition is the idea of functionalism. Some overviews of functionalism such as Bates & MacWhinney (1981,1987), Hickmann (1987), and Tomlin (1990) have recently made some basic assumptions and problems explicit.

Functionalism focusses on how language is used in interaction. These studies deal with "possible mapping relations holding between linguistic form and semantic or pragmatic functions" (Tomlin 1990:159). At an explanatory level attempts are made to show that recurrent form-function mappings or systemic changes (historical/developmental) are due to "general constraints on possible grammars which arise from the naturally occurring circumstances of human discourse interaction and the cognitive processes associated with them" (Tomlin 1990:159).

Recent process-oriented studies on L2 acquisition in which the influence of functionalism clearly makes itself felt centre around the notion of learner variety (see Tarone 1988, Davies, Criper & Howatt 1984, and in particular McLaughlin 1987:59-81, for further references). In this view language acquisition is seen as a process in which the learner proceeds through a number of stages. In these stages a variety of repertoires of linguistic devices of increasing complexity is used. The variety of the target language used by the language learner is considered to be a dynamic and unique system that partly coincides with and partly differs from the source and the target language systems (cf. McLaughlin 1987:69). An essential characteristic of learner varieties is that they are systematic in two respects: there is (1) an intrinsic systematicity in the organization of a learner variety at a specific moment and, (2) a transitional systematicity in the development over time from one learner variety to another (cf. Klein 1986:29). The systematic variation of the learner variety is reflected in its form-function relationships. Acquiring a language not only means being able to use the linguistic forms of that language, but also the ability to express the functions fulfilled by those forms in the target language. As Long & Sato (1984) point out, a methodological implication of this is that both "form-to-function" and "function-to-form" analyses are needed in order to unravel the intricate process of language acquisition.

A number of studies focussed on analogies reported between learner varieties and pidgin/creole languages. A pidgin is a rudimentary and limited contact language and it is always a non-primary language of its users. It develops in multilingual settings under conditions of severely restricted input (cf. Andersen 1983). A creole language is a native language acquired by children of pidgin speakers (cf. Andersen 1983). A detailed account of the process of pidginization and creolization in terms of language acquisition is given by Andersen (1983), McLaughlin (1987:109-132) and Mühlhäusler (1986). Well-known is Schumann's *Acculturation Model* (1978a), which addresses the question why, unlike L1 learners, L2 learners often fail to achieve complete control of the target language. The assumption is that the early stages of untutored L2 acquisition are determined by the degree of social distance (e.g. equality between groups, mutual attitudes) and psychological distance (e.g. cultural difference between the learner and the target language group). Schumann (1978a and 1978b) suggests that the same type of social/psychological distance brings about the formation of pidgin languages. The degree of distance determines the input (i.e. the amount of contact) and the function of the target language (i.e. communicative, integrative, or expressive). With great social/psychological barricades the learner varieties get pidginized at an early stage of L2 acquisition; developmental changes towards the target language system get stuck at the level of a restricted learner variety with an intrinsic systematicity, its only purpose being to fulfil basic functions of communication. When these barricades persist, "pidgin" learner varieties get fossilized.

Andersen (1979, 1983) expands Schumann's pidginization hypothesis by focussing on the learner's internal (cognitive) processing mechanisms. In his *Nativization Model* Andersen proposes a number of principles which would account for the (re-)construction of form-function relationships in pidgin/creole languages as well as learner varieties. As Andersen (1987) remarks himself, Slobin's operating principles specified for L1 acquisition (e.g. Slobin 1973,1985) have been of considerable influence. An example is the "one-to-one principle", well-known by different names and specifications. Andersen (1984:77) describes this principle as follows: "an interlanguage system should be constructed in such a way that an intended underlying meaning is expressed with one clear invariant surface form (or construction)". Andersen (1984) uses the word "meaning" to refer to semantic relationships such as possession, agentive or definiteness. By "form" he means grammatical morphemes as well as word order.

The idea of pidginization as an aspect of developing learner varieties (or grammars) was taken up in the Heidelberger project on "Pidgin-German" (see Klein & Dittmar 1979 for further references to this project). This was a cross-sectional project studying the untutored acquisition of German by Italian and Spanish immigrant workers. The Heidelberger project is a closely related predecessor of the ESF project on untutored adult language acquisition (see Perdue 1984).

2.3   CHOMSKIAN UNIVERSAL GRAMMAR

Ever since the early 1960s Chomskian theories have influenced ideas in fields varying from language acquisition to psychology and computing. One of the well-known elements of Chomsky's theory of language is the distinction between competence and performance, standing for "the speaker/hearer's knowledge of his language" and "the actual use of language in concrete situations" respectively (Chomsky 1965:4). In the 1980s, Chomsky introduced a comparable and related distinction: different approaches to language were subdivided into those focussing on Externalized language (E-language) and those focussing on Internalized language (I-language). According to Chomsky (1986a:36-37 and 1988:19-21), I-language approaches see language as "an individual phenomenon, a system represented in the mind/brain of a particular individual" whereas E-language approaches see language as a "social phenomenon". In these approaches language is a "product of behaviour [..] understood independently of the properties of the mind/brain". The theory of Universal Grammar (henceforth UG), initiated by Chomsky, deals with I-language. Two basic questions within UG theory (cf. Chomsky 1986a:3) are: (1) What constitutes knowledge of language? (2) How is knowledge of language acquired? These questions are directed towards the nature and origins of I-language, respectively.

What constitutes knowledge of language?
    Knowledge of language is the competence of a language possessed by a mature adult native speaker. This knowledge has two components: (1) the built-in core grammar, the UG, and (2) language specific knowledge that has been learned. The UG consists of a number of principles and parameters. In the adult grammar each parameter is set to the fixed value that corresponds with the target language.

    The aim of UG theory is to spell out a description of language which coincides with the knowledge of language as a mental construct. The grammar is psychologically real and underlies actual language use. Evidence for the internal representation of the grammar is arrived at by testing the grammaticality of single utterances.

The current generative framework which describes UG is called Government/ Binding theory (Chomsky 1981) and consists of a set of interrelated subtheories (or modules). Each subtheory specifies a number of principles and parameters. A well-explored subtheory is X-bar theory, which is directed towards the hierarchical structure of phrases (Chomsky 1986b). This subtheory includes a principle which states that in a specific language phrasal heads (e.g. the P in a PP or the V in a VP) always occur on the same side. The setting of the corresponding head parameter is either head-initial, as in English (e.g. *Peter drinks milk* and *a man like my father*) or head-final, as in Turkish (e.g. *Peter süt içiyor* 'Peter milk drinks' and *babam gibi bir adam* 'father-my like a man').

How is knowledge of language acquired?

UG finds its justification in the intriguing fact that first language acquisition is successful despite the nature of the input of the target language available to the child. Basic characteristics of the input presented to the child are the following (cf. White 1989:5):

- The "poverty" of the stimulus; the target language is underdetermined; some knowledge of language is not obvious and not explicitly taught (e.g. knowledge that the head parameter applies to a PP in the same way as to a VP).
- The "degeneracy" of the data; children are confronted with performance data which may contain mistakes, inaudible elements, slips of the tongue, etc.
- "Negative" evidence; how do children find out what is not possible in the target language, i.e. which utterances are not grammatical?

With a view to these input characteristics, advocates of UG claim that there is a logical problem (also called a learnability problem, as in Pinker 1984). The distance between on the one hand the target language made available to the child, and on the other the complexity of the language knowledge acquired by the mature adult can only be bridged if there is an in-built mental system, called the UG. This "innate language acquisition device" constrains what is possible in the target language. Language acquisition is acquiring the knowledge of how a number of principles apply to the target language and discovering the appropriate value for each parameter (e.g. that English is head-initial).

After initial scepticism about the shift in the generative enterprise (i.e. the shift from transformations to principles and parameters) UG-oriented research on L2 acquisition is now mushrooming (see Cook 1988 and White 1989 for recent overviews). Also in adult L2 acquisition the learner is confronted with the learnability problem. A moot point is the degree and nature of the accessibility of the UG when the adult learner is acquiring the new language. Three positions can be distinguished in UG-oriented studies:

(1) Direct access to UG; as far as the setting of parameters is concerned the L2 learner starts from scratch, both values of each parameter are accessible. As White (1989:49) notes, very few UG-oriented L2 researchers subscribe to this "pure" UG hypothesis.

(2)   Indirect access to UG; the L2 learner uses UG principles and parameters, but
        this use is affected by principles and parameters operating in the L1 system.
        Different variants of this position can be obtained through Flynn (1989),
        White (1989), and the contributions in Gass & Schachter (1989).
(3)   No access to UG; the assumption is that UG is no longer available to the
        adult L2 learner. Consequently, L2 acquisition should be explained through
        general learning mechanisms and cognitive strategies which are not unique to
        language. This position is taken in Clahsen & Muysken (1986,1989), and Bley-
        Vroman (1989).

Although Chomsky's UG theory has provided new insights into our knowledge of
language, it is important to bear in mind that it is a theory of grammar. Cook
(1988:189) hits the nail on the head when he says that UG might play "a central and
vital part in L2 learning, but there are many other parts". In addition, UG theory is
directed to I-language. One should be very careful in making claims about aspects of
UG such as parameters, principles, accessibility through performance data, i.e. about
E-language (cf. White 1989:58). Some critical notes on UG theory are pointed out by
Klein (1990) and Carroll & Meisel (1990) in a special issue of *Studies in Second
Language Acquisition*.

2.4   CONCLUSION

This study takes a functionalist and process-oriented perspective on language acquisition while bearing in mind those aspects of the theories of contrastive analysis and
creative construction on which there is a general consensus.

In building the structure of the target language, the adult learner can make use of
full knowledge of his first language and expand his knowledge of the target language
he is learning. In the former case, this knowledge may lead to successful or un-
successful language transfer. However, it would be naive to assume that the first language will have no effect, or that it is the only determinant of the acquisition
process.

Second language acquisition is based on a whole range of intermediate stages. A
salient feature is the fact that it results in quite different stages of target language
proficiency. Some learners reach a near-native variety, whereas others will never go
beyond a small vocabulary of words and a few syntactic or idiomatic constructions
(i.e. their variety gets fossilized). This phenomenon presents a strong contrast to first
language acquisition.

The acquisition processes can only be inferred from discrepancies between
learner and standard varieties of the target language. In particular, the intrinsic and
transitional systematicity reflected in form-function relationships might reveal the
acquisition process. In this respect, notable differences between varieties of a target
language used by different learners might emerge. This does not preclude, however,
that the same "laws" are obeyed (cf. Klein 1986:49).

CHAPTER 3

INFORMANTS AND DATA BASE

The aim of this chapter is to provide information on the socio-biographical characteristics of the informants focussed on in the present study and to give an account of
the data base that has been used in the analysis.

3.1   INFORMANT CHARACTERISTICS

The informants in the present study took a central part in the ESF project men-
tioned in Chapter 1. They were asked to participate in the project because they met
best the criteria spelled out for the "ideal informant" (cf. Perdue 1984:276):

> "when they joined the ESF project their ages varied from seventeen to twenty-
> four. They had no Dutch-speaking spouse and no children of school age. They
> had received little education in Turkey or Morocco. Their language profi-
> ciency in Dutch was very low at the start and during their participation in the
> project they learned Dutch as a second language spontaneously, i.e. without
> substantial formal tuition".

In the present study two groups of L2 learners of Dutch will be distinguished:
(1)   The core informants are two Turkish and two Moroccan adults who played a
       central role in the ESF project. The analyses carried out within the ESF pro-
       ject and reported on in the final volumes (see Chapter 1) are mostly based on
       their learner varieties of Dutch.
(2)   The shadow informants are two Turkish and two Moroccan adults who also
       participated in the ESF project. However, no analyses were made of their
       learner varieties of Dutch.

In addition some analyses will be presented for a native speaker of Dutch:
(3)   The native speaker is a Dutchman who took part in a number of language
       activities similar to those of the core/shadow informants.

Finally, for a cross-linguistic comparison, also some L2-German varieties will be considered:

(4)   Four Turkish and four Italian adults who participated in the ESF project as L2 learners of German.

In order to trace informant characteristics which may be determining factors in the pattern or rate of acquisition, a detailed socio-biographical profile is given for each of the four core informants; for the other informants basic socio-biographical charac- teristics are summarized. Detailed information on these informants can be found in the final volumes of the ESF project, in Perdue (1984:275-290), and in particular in Edwards & Levelt (1987).

3.1.1 CORE INFORMANTS

The Turkish core informants are Ergün and Mahmut. The Moroccan core infor- mants are Fatima and Mohamed.

Mahmut

Mahmut was born in a small town 150 km from Ankara, Turkey. He attended primary school and then worked as a mechanic. At the age of nineteen he went to the Netherlands to join his wife, who had been living there for about four years. He joined the project nine months after his arrival. Mahmut first lived with his parents-in-law. However, at the beginning of the data collection period he moved to a rented house next door to his parents-in-law. During the first year of his stay in the Nether- lands he was unemployed. After a year he found a job in a meat factory on a ten- month contract. This contract has been renewed since. His contacts with native speakers were limited to Dutch colleagues, authorities, hospital staff and doctors (in the third cycle he was in hospital for a week, suffering from a liver problem and he regularly saw his doctor), and people in second-hand car markets (as a former mechanic he was very interested in cars). Mahmut often reflected on his second lan- guage proficiency. He was fully aware of his shortcomings in Dutch, but also knew that owing to his family responsibilities (after a stay in the Netherlands of one-and-a- half years his daughter was born) he was unable to attend a target language course.

Ergün

After five years of primary school Ergün started working as a mechanic in Turkey. At the age of seventeen he left Turkey and joined his parents in Tilburg, who had been living in the Netherlands for some years. Soon after his arrival he attended a target language course for two hours a week for a period of five months. His attendance was rather irregular and at the beginning of the data collection period his command of Dutch was judged to be very limited. After five months he found a job as a factory worker on a temporary basis. Afterwards he was alternately employed and unemployed. At the time of the first session in the ESF project, Ergün had been living in the Netherlands for about eleven months. He was still very much a teenager at this stage. His contacts with native speakers resembled Mohamed's, one of the Moroccan learners of Dutch. Being a youngster and living with his family, he enjoyed life very much: visiting friends, going to discotheques, playing football in a mixed Turkish/Dutch team, and meeting Turkish and Dutch friends. After two years, because of many parental rows, he moved to Groningen, a city in the northern part of the Netherlands. He started working there as a car-wrecker at a breaker's yard. Given the fact that there are not many immigrants living in Groningen, Ergün's contacts with native speakers of Dutch increased even more.

Mohamed

Mohamed was born in Casablanca. After primary school he attended secondary school for only two years. Afterwards he was trained to become a mechanic, but this activity did not lead to a diploma. At the age of nineteen he and most of his family left Morocco to join his father, who had been living in the Netherlands for almost fourteen years. Soon after his arrival he found a job as a factory worker, which he remained throughout the data collection period, only temporary interrupted by a short period of unemployment. He joined the ESF project eight months after his arrival. As a youngster, living in a small town near Tilburg with relatively few immigrants he soon had lots of contacts with native target language speakers, from authorities to customers in discotheques and bars. The relation with his parents detoriated over time. He regularly stayed with his uncle for a while. After a year-and-a-half he moved in with his Dutch girlfriend at her parents' place. At the end of the data collection he was living with another Dutch girl. He had not taken part in any language course at all.

Fatima

In Kenitra, a town in Western Morocco, Fatima attended primary school for only two years, after which she received sewing and knitting lessons. For some years she was a successful seamstress. She had a little shop and taught other women. At the age of twenty-four she married a Moroccan who had been living in the Netherlands for twelve years. She joined him in Tilburg. At the time of the first encounter in the ESF project Fatima had been living in the Netherlands for one year and her proficiency in Dutch was almost zero, although she had taken part in a voluntary training course for migrant women for two hours a week, and continued to do so. This was a very basic course and had a primarily social function. She had a part-time job as a cleaning woman in the kitchen of a motel with other Moroccan and Turkish women. Her contacts with native speakers of Dutch were very limited, except for a short period at the end of the first year of her stay in the Netherlands when her husband was abroad. Her son was born when she had been in the Netherlands for two years.

Basic socio-biographical characteristics of the core informants at the time they joined the ESF project are summarized in Table 3.1.

Table 3.1: Basic socio-biographical characteristics of the core informants

| | Turkish | | Moroccan | |
	Mahmut	Ergün	Mohamed	Fatima
Sex	male	male	male	female
Year, Place of birth	1962, Kirşehir	1964, Ankara	1961, Casabl.	1956, Kenitra
Residence Source Country (SC)	Ankara	Ankara	Casablanca	Kenitra
Schooling SC	5 years	5 years	7 years	2 years
Employment SC	mechanic	mechanic	none	seamstress
Age on arrival in Holland (TC)	19	17	19	24
Session 1 (months after arrival)	9 months	11 months	8 months	12 months
Residence TC	Tilburg	Tilburg	Oisterwijk	Tilburg
Schooling TC	none	Educ. centre	none	Comm. centre
Employment TC	fact. worker	fact. worker	fact. worker	kitchen maid
Marital status	married	single	single	married
Staying with	wife	Turkish family	parents	husband
Skill in other languages	none	none	some French	none

On the basis of the socio-biographical profiles of the core informants some tentative conclusions can be drawn with respect to the degree in which propensity factors may have determined their acquisition of Dutch. Some remarkable differences can be observed, especially between Fatima and Mahmut on the one hand, and Ergün and Mohamed on the other.

Fatima and Mahmut had the fewest contacts in Dutch. If they had any, these contacts were mostly in rather formal situations like conversations with representatives of institutions, doctors or policemen. Mohamed and Ergün on the other hand had more informal contacts with Dutchmen in their free time. They had Dutch girlfriends and met a lot of Dutch peers in the disco, the swimming pool, etc.

A second difference was that Mahmut and Fatima both expected their stay in the Netherlands to be only temporary. They both wished their child to learn Turkish/Arabic because of their expectation to return to their home countries. Most of their family members were still in the home country as well. Mohamed and Ergün had no household of their own. They had both been separated from their fathers for a long time, as they lived in their home country with their mother while their father was working in the Netherlands. Family reunion in the Netherlands resulted in serious conflicts with their fathers and in their wish to become independent and build up a position of their own in the Netherlands.

As becomes apparent from these observations the perspectives for the acquisition of Dutch were more favourable for Mohamed and Ergün than for Fatima and Mahmut. During the period of data collection in the ESF project also differences in attitudes between the informants became apparent, and intuitively one is tempted to connect certain attitudinal characteristics to the rate or success of second language learning. A general difference emerged between the Moroccan informants and the Turkish informants. Fatima and Mohamed seemed to be more reluctant to take turns and talked less freely than the Turkish informants. The responsibility for initiating and maintaining interactional topics was put in the hands of the native speaker of Dutch. In contrast, the Turkish informants were more at ease and showed more involvement in the interactions. A detailed analysis of the way in which the four core informants participated in the interactions with the native speakers of Dutch can be found in Broeder & Roberts (1988).

3.1.2 SHADOW INFORMANTS

Basic socio-biographical characteristics of the shadow informants at the time they joined the ESF project are summarized in Table 3.2.

Table 3.2: Basic socio-biographical characteristics of the shadow informants

| | Turkish | | Moroccan | |
	Osman	Abdullah	Hassan	Husseyn
Sex	male	male	male	male
Year, Place of birth	1963, Trabson	1962, Kirşehir	1964, Casabl.	1957, Casablanca
Residence Source Country (SC)	Trabson	Kirşehir	Casablanca	Casablanca
Schooling SC	5 years	8 years	8 years	9 years
Employment SC	farmer	various	none	broker agent
Age on arrival in Holland (TC)	17	19	18	24
Session 1 (months after arrival)	12 months	12 months	7 months	14 months
Residence TC	Tilburg	Tilburg	Oisterwijk	Tilburg
Schooling TC	Educ. centre	Educ. centre	Educ. centre	Comm. centre
Employment TC	none	none	none	fact. worker
Marital status	single	single	single	married
Staying with	parents	parents	parents	wife
Skill in other languages	none	none	some French	some French

In many respects the core and shadow informants are quite similar. Moreover, they are all fairly typical adult Turkish and Moroccan immigrants living in the Netherlands who acquire Dutch as a second language for the most part in a untutored way. Note that in the ESF data base (see Feldweg 1991) Hassan is known as Hassan K., and Husseyn is known as Hassan M.

3.1.3 THE NATIVE SPEAKER

Gerald, a native speaker of Dutch acts as a control informant in the present study. With respect to a number of background characteristics he belonged to the social environment of the core and shadow informants. It is a reasonable conjecture that he used a variety of Dutch the core and shadow informants were confronted with. Gerald is twenty-seven years old, grew up in Tilburg and lives together with his wife. He attended secondary school for four years and received some formal schooling in English. As he said himself, it was a difficult learning task and he only achieved little proficiency in English. During the daytime he works in a distribution centre for bicycles.

3.1.4 GERMAN INFORMANTS

In the present study a sidestep is made with four Turkish and four Italian L2 learners of German who where followed during the first three years of their stay in Germany. The value of this excursion was of course the cross-linguistic perspective. An important reason however was that during the ESF project the Dutch research team and the German research team had extensively discussed the data collection procedure of one specific activity, i.e. the film retelling *Harold Lloyd at the Station*. As a result the audio-recordings made of this language activity are excellent for a cross-linguistic comparison.

Basic information on the Turkish and Italian learners of German is summarized in Table 3.3 and Table 3.4 respectively.

Table 3.3: Basic socio-biographical characteristics of the Turkish learners of German

	Ayse	Yasar	Cevdet	Ilhami
Sex	female	male	male	male
Year, Place of birth	1966, Bafra	1966, Istanbul	1966, Yozgat	1965, Yozgat
Residence Source Country (SC)	Trabson	Istanbul	Yozgat	Yozgat
Schooling SC	8 years	8 years	9 years	8 years
Employment SC	none	none	none	glazier
Age on arrival in Germany (TC)	15	26	15	17
Session 1 (months after arrival)	16 months	7 months	7 months	14 months
Residence TC	Eppelheim	Heidelberg	Walldorf	Heidelberg
Schooling TC	MBSE course	MBSE course	MBSE course	MBSE course
Employment TC	laundry help	-	furniture fact.	fact. worker
Marital status	single	-	single	single
Staying with	Turkish family	-	his father	his father
Skill in other languages	some English	none	none	none

Table 3.4: Basic socio-biographical characteristics of the Italian learners of German

	Angelina	Alese	Marcello	Tino
Sex	female	male	male	male
Year, Place of birth	1961, Salerno	1960, Raffanali	1959, Monopoli	1963, Taranto
Residence Source Country (SC)	Salerno	Raffanali	Monopoli	Taranto
Schooling SC	8 years	15 years	10 years	8 years
Employment SC	none	none	turner	none
Age on arrival in Germany (TC)	20	21	22	19
Session 1 (months after arrival)	12 months	10 months	10 months	11 months
Residence TC	Heidelberg	Heidelberg	Heidelberg	Heidelberg
Schooling TC	none	basic course	none	navy
Employment TC	housewife	-	waiter	pizerria help
Marital status	married	-	single	-
Staying with	husband	-	family	-
Skill in other languages	basic English	some Eng. + Fr.	basic Eng. + Fr.	basic Eng. + Fr.

Of course the search in the ESF project for L2 learners of German was made with the profile of the ideal informant in mind (see above). Detailed socio-biographical characteristics of the German informants can be found in Becker et al. (1988) and Bremer et al. (1988).

3.2 LANGUAGE ACTIVITIES

For each core and shadow informant in the Netherlands data collection took place over a period of 27 months starting in September 1982 and ending in December 1984. Apart from summer holidays and other interruptions, there were regular intervals of 25-35 days between each moment of data collection, resulting in 27 two-hour sessions per informant. The first sessions were held 7-14 months after their arrival in the Netherlands. In these sessions a variety of language activities took place which varied in the degree of control (cf. Perdue 1984:174-178). The basic types of language activity are the following:

(1) Free conversation marked by loosely structured dyadic interactions between an informant and a native speaker of Dutch. The latter was sometimes a member of the Dutch research team, sometimes a project-external native speaker. In some sessions conversation topics were suggested to the native speaker beforehand, however, these were not obligatory. Whenever a topic was suggested for all informants (which was the case for instance, when radio/tv programmes were discussed or travelling in Turkey/Morocco), props like travel guides, maps, radio/tv magazines, and photographs were used. The length of these language activities was approximately ninety minutes.

(2) Play scenes were pre-structured formal interactions in which the informant was asked to play a specific role, such as applying for a job, or asking for a house. The role of the official (e.g. personnel chef, housing official) was played by a project-external volunteer, a project-internal researcher, or a professional. The informant was given a task to be fulfilled (e.g. "your wife is expecting a baby within three months and therefore you urgently need better housing accommodation"). The length of these language activities was approximately thirty minutes.

(3) Film scenes consisted of retelling/commenting on several videoclips derived from silent movies (i.e. Harold Lloyd movies or Charlie Chaplin movies) or from a movie about a Dutch racing cyclist. The script was mostly as follows: The informants watched the videoclip three times, after which they were asked to retell its content. Occasionally, e.g. when the informants' retelling missed crucial parts of the content of the videoclip, some additional questions were asked by the researcher. The length of these language activities was approximately twenty minutes.

(4) Finally, the informants were asked to fulfil a number of experimental tasks. These tasks were strongly pre-structured in order to get highly comparable data. The informants had to translate words, name pictures, fill in verbs, etc.

In the present study all the interactional data of the core and shadow informants that were collected and computer-stored provide the basis for the analysis. This means that only the experimental tasks will not be used.

The data collection with the core and shadow informants was cyclically organized: the 27 sessions were divided into three cycles of nine sessions each. Therefore the informants could be observed three times in the same language use situation. Table 3.5 shows how the data collection in the ESF project was organized, i.e. which language activities took place in which sessions.

Table 3.5: Language activities over time (27 sessions)

CYCLE 1	2	3	Conversation	Film scene	Play scene
s1	s10	s19	Socio-biogr. information	-	-
s2	s11	s20	same	-	-
s3	s12	s21	-	The Cyclist	Post office, Job interview Stage direction (only in s3)
s4	s13	s22	Language use in SC/TC	-	-
s5	s14	s23	Family and friends	-	-
s6	s15	s24	-	The Station The Clochard	Applying for housing Stage direction (not in s3)
s7	s16	s25	Discrimination Cultural differences	-	Self-confr. s6 play scene
s8	s17	s26	Going on holiday to SC	-	Route direction (not in s8) Route description (not in s8)
s9	s18	s27	-	The Car Modern Times	The Remigration office Route description (only in s9)

For referring to the different 27 sessions two notation conventions are used. First the numbers 1 to 27, e.g. session 1, session 2, session 10, session 27. In the second notation convention the cycle number is given followed by a dot and the session number within the cycle, e.g. session 1.2, session 1.2, session 2.1, session 3.9.

Table 3.6: Number of words used by the informants and their native interlocutors

		Informant	Native speakers	Total
Core group:	Mahmut	61,768	45,657	107,425
	Ergün	64,628	55,177	119,805
	Mohamed	56,386	48,966	105,352
	Fatima	31,952	44,644	76,596
Shadow group:	Osman	57,495	51,629	109,124
	Abdullah	32,648	52,371	85,019
	Hassan	61,312	47,796	109,108
	Husseyn	65,983	49,960	115,943
Total number		432,172	396,200	828,372

The sessions were audio-recorded, every third session was also recorded on video-tape. For each language activity a computerized transcript was made, which offers detailed and annotated information about what was said during that activity. The data collection resulted in an extensive computer-stored data bank (see Feldweg 1991). The total number of words that are used by each of the core and shadow informants and their native interlocutors in the Netherlands is given in Table 3.6. This table shows that the total number of words by the informants and their native speakers is fairly constant. However, first of all Table 3.6 shows that the total number of words (i.e. 828,372) is quite high for a data base of spoken language data. If we compare it to a widely used data base of native spoken Dutch language data, that used in De Jong (1979) for counting word frequencies in native spoken Dutch, we find that that only contains 120,000.

CHAPTER 4

CROSS-LINGUISTIC PERSPECTIVE ON PRONOUNS

This chapter starts with a brief overview of the historical treatments of pronominal reference. Next, the pronoun systems of Dutch, Turkish, and Moroccan Arabic are discussed. On the basis of this comparison of the source and target language systems of the Turkish and Moroccan informants, a set of predictions is formulated about the informants' acquisition of Dutch.

4.1   HOW DO PRONOUNS REFER?

In a historical account of different perspectives on pronominal reference, Bosch (1983) shows how this problem has been dealt with. He discusses terms, notions, and misconceptions in a number of traditional and modern treatments of pronouns and anaphora. The following perspectives on pronouns are distinguished by Bosch (1983:1-31):

Classical accounts of pronouns
    The foundations of traditional grammar in the Western world can be found in the works of classical grammarians like Dionysius Thrax and Apollonius Dyskolus. They generally used three criteria in their classification of the "parts of speech" (cf. Bosch 1983:3): (1) whether the form is subject to case inflection, (2) the relationship to other, already established parts of speech, and (3) the function of the form. On the basis of these criteria, Dionysius in his *Técnè Grammatikè* (100 BC) distinguished the class of "antōnymía" (translated into Latin as "pro-nomen"). This class consists of possessive and personal pronouns, which are used instead of the noun and which are indicative of specific personal reference. A second and related class, the "árthra", comprises definite articles, relative pronouns and demonstrative pronouns. These forms do not have case inflections and are placed before and after nouns. Dionysius addressed the substitutional nature of pronouns (cf. Bosch 1983:4). About two hundred years later, Apollonius wrote the first comprehensive treatment of pronouns (*Perì Antōnymías*). In answer to the question how pronouns refer, Apollonius, who

strongly relied on Dionysius, proposed a deictic and an anaphoric mode of pronominal reference: "deixis is a reference to objects that are not known or not yet introduced into discourse; anaphora is a reference to objects that have already previously figured in discourse or are generally known" (Bosch 1983:7).

Bühler's Zweifeldertheorie

The deixis-anaphora distinction was rediscovered by the Indo-European scholars in the second half of the 19th century and the beginning of the 20th century, and influenced in particular Bühler's work (1934). In his *Organon Model of Communication* Bühler introduced what he calls a "pointing" field within which the referents of a linguistic sign may be located. The pointing field is made up of physical/imagined objects or states of affairs. The linguistic sign can be divided into pointing words and denoting words. Denoting words (such as nouns) have a constant, situation independent relationship to the referent. In contrast, pointing words select their referents relative to the situation from the pointing field. The class of pointing words can be used for two ways of pointing: "objectual" pointing which concerns reference to objects or states of affairs in the external world, e.g. *This I would like to offer you*, and "syntactic" pointing which concerns elements of the linguistic context, e.g. *This worries me: the deterioration of the ozone layer*. Bosch (1983:11) remarks that Bühler is wrong in claiming that the two ways of pointing are similar to the classical deixis-anaphora distinction. In fact, Apollonius distinguished reference to given vs. new information within the linguistic discourse, whereas Bühler dealt with reference within the linguistic discourse vs. reference to the external world.

Pronouns as substitutes

Within Bloomfieldian structuralism (1935), pronouns are conceived as substitutes: forms which replace other elements in the linguistic discourse (in line with the classical account of Dionysius). A pronoun is defined by its domain of substitution (i.e. the class of linguistic forms which a pronoun can replace), and its substitution type (i.e. the semantic meaning of the domain of substitution). Thus the pronoun *I* is defined as follows: "the substitute *I* replaces any singular substantive expression, provided that this substantive expression denotes the speaker of the utterance in which the substitute is used" (Bloomfield 1935:247). Within structuralism, the focus was on the anaphoric function of pronouns, i.e. on syntagmatic substitution. The same focus is found in a second influential linguistic school in the 20th century: generative grammar.

Constraints on pronominal reference

Chomsky (1957) introduced the concept of generative grammar. In early theories of generative grammar, called TGG, the structuralist account of pronouns as substitutes is stated in a transformation rule of pronominalization: a full-NP in deep structure is converted into a pronoun in surface structure. The transformation rule is directed towards anaphoric relations with an explicit linguistic antecedent located within the same sentence as the pronoun (e.g. Lees & Klima 1963). In recent theories of generative grammar, in the *Government/Binding* model (GB), the idea of transformations is abandoned (Chomsky 1981). Instead, the focus is on constraints on pronominalization. A number of binding principles restrict the possibilities of co-reference between an antecedent and a pronoun. A distinction is made between anaphors, pronominals and referring expressions (r-expressions). The latter refer to something in the world, outside the sentence, e.g. *John hurts*. In contrast, anaphors always have their antecedent within the same sentence, or in GB-formulation: anaphors must be bound within their governing category, e.g. *John hurts himself*. Finally, pronominals do not have the antecedent within the same sentence: they must be free outside their governing category, e.g. *John hurts him*. Generative grammar theories deal with structural properties of pronouns.

Non-structural approaches to pronominal reference
   In contrast to the generative perspective, a number of studies focus on discourse properties of pronouns (e.g. Bosch 1983, Givón 1983, Cornish 1986, Fox 1987). There the idea is that pronouns cannot be understood merely through their struc-tural, linguistic properties, within the restricted context of one sentence. The central notion in these studies is "discourse anaphora". The main function of discourse anaphora is to contribute to the establishment and maintenance of the addressee's model of a proceeding discourse (cf. Cornish 1986:133-141).

The preceding historical account of perspectives on pronouns shows that in general anaphoricity is considered to be the primary function of pronouns. The deictic func-tion of pronouns is typically marginalized. Lyons (1977:637) defines the notion of "deixis" as follows:

> "the location and identification of persons, objects, events, processes and activities being talked about, or referred to, in relation to the spatio-temporal context created and sustained by the act of utterance and the participation in it, typically, of a single speaker and at least one addressee".

A number of good arguments for a more prominent place of the deictic use of pro-nouns in the study of language can be derived from Lyons (1977:636-724) and Mühlhäusler & Harré (1990:47-86):
- Certain aspects of deixis can only be explained on the assumption that they devel-oped for communication in face-to-face interaction, an example being the gram-matical category of person which encodes the (non-)participant roles in the con-versation.
- In many languages the difference between deictic and anaphoric use of pronouns is not grammaticalized. In contrast, different modes of deixis exhibit a consistent lexically or morphologically based encoding across languages.
- Anaphorically used pronouns contain at least some deictic information, whereas deictically used pronouns do not necessarily need a linguistic antecedent.

- Deictic aspects of pronouns may have a situation creating effect, thus, e.g. a conversation can shift to informality, through the use of informal address forms.

In this chapter the focus is on the deictic use of pronouns. Rather than with pronouns as syntagmatic substitutes, it deals with paradigmatic choices of pronoun use. Paradigmatic choice refers to the selection of an item from a set of items. The items constitute a meaningful unit because they can be used in the same deictic context. Selecting one item rather than another generates differences in meaning. In the next section a paradigmatic account of the Dutch pronoun system is presented, on the basis of which a number of predictions about processes of language acquisition are specified.

4.2 THE DUTCH PRONOUN SYSTEM

In many languages the pronoun system constitutes a delimited and fixed set of referential devices, which are essentially the same for all speakers of a particular language. The existence of a system of pronouns implies that the best way to define a pronoun is to characterize its reciprocal relation to the other items in the system. An extensive collection of descriptions of pronominal systems in a variety of languages is given in Wiesemann (1986). Other typological studies are: Forchheimer (1953), Ingram (1978), Thun (1985), and Anderson & Keenan (1985). Table 4.1 presents the linguistic devices which constitute the system of personal and possessive pronouns in spoken Dutch.

Table 4.1: Dutch personal and possessive pronouns

Role	Number	Status	Gender	Subject Full	Subject Red.	Object Full	Object Red.	Possessive Full	Possessive Red.
1	Sg.			ik(ke)	'k	mij	me	mijn	m'n
	Pl.			wij	we	ons		on(s/ze)	
2	Sg.	Inform.		jij	je	jou	je	jouw	je
		Formal		u		u		uw	
	Pl.	Inform.		jullie		jullie		jullie	
3	Sg.		Msc.	hij	ie	hem	'm	zijn	z'n
			Fem.	zij	ze	haar	(d)'r, ze	haar	d'r
			Neut.	het	't	het	't	zijn	z'n
	Pl.			zij	ze	hun	ze	hun	d'r

The overview in Table 4.1. is based on the standard grammar for spoken Dutch by Geerts et al. (1984). They also give a detailed account of regional and social variants. In the present study these variants are discussed only where and when they are relevant for the interpretation of the pronouns used by our informants.

The Dutch pronoun system comprises a set of subject forms, a set of object forms, and a set of possessive forms. From a grammatical point of view subject and object forms are used independently, i.e. as separate constituents. In contrast, the possessive pronouns given in Table 4.1 are used attributively in NPs. Independently used possessive pronouns, e.g. *mijn boek en het zijne* ('my book and his'), are rare in spoken Dutch (see De Jong 1979:138) and even more rare in L2 varieties of Dutch; they are not included in the present study. In contrast to subject and object pronouns, possessive pronouns are relational devices. They necessarily express a possessive relation between two (classes of) individuals or things, i.e. between the possessor(s) and the possessed entity(-ies).

In this study the distinction between the sets of subject, object and possessive forms (i.e. the ones given in Table 4.1) will be regarded as belonging to the area of "case". Note that this is related, although not identical, to what is commonly done in grammatical descriptions of Dutch (see Geerts et al. 1984:162-177,197-214). Although the sets of subject, object, and possessive forms constitute a fairly coherent pronoun system, no appropriate cover term is available in traditional grammatical theory. Rather than inventing a new and even more confusing term, the cover term "case" is used. In fact, a similar use of the term "case" can be found in the standard English grammar of Quirk & Greenbaum (1973:101).

In addition to case distinctions, the following deictic information is lexicalized in the Dutch pronoun system:

Role: Reference to the speaker(s), the addressee(s), or to person(s) who are neither speaker(s) nor addressee(s).

Number: Reference to one person (singular) or more than one person (plural).

Status: Formal or informal reference (only for 2nd role).

Gender: Reference to male or female person(s) (only for 3rd role singular).

As can be derived from Table 4.1, there is a highly systematic distinction between full/emphatic forms and reduced/non-emphatic forms. The full-reduced distinction has implications for perceptual saliency, i.e. the degree to which a pronoun attracts attention in the speech stream due to its prosodic prominence (i.e. pronunciation and stress). Reduced pronouns are always unstressed. Full pronouns are normally stressed, although the stress is not always equally strong (cf. Geerts et al. 1984:173).

The pronominal system as a closed class is in keeping with the idea of a paradigm representing a set of related linguistic encoding devices. Paradigm formation is taken up in several studies. Recently, Pinker (1984:166-208) gave a detailed account of how paradigm formation might work as a driving force in the acquisition of inflection. A paradigm is conceived as a matrix representation consisting of a number of dimensions, levels and cells. The matrix for the Dutch pronoun system could be represented as follows:

- Three paradigms: sets of 1st role, 2nd role, and 3rd role pronouns.
- The dimension case with three levels: subject, object, and possessive.
- The dimension number with two levels: singular and plural.
- The dimension status with two levels: formal and informal.
- The dimension gender with three levels: masculine, feminine, and neuter.
- Cells are the conjunctions of levels and contain the lexical entries; hereby a systematic subdivision emerges between full and reduced forms.

There are several alternatives to this operationalization of the pronoun system. The main reason for taking role as the basis for distinguishing three paradigms is that there is a fundamental difference between 1st, 2nd, and 3rd role reference (see Chapter 1). The information lexicalized in the Dutch pronoun system is different for each of the three paradigms: number is lexicalized in the paradigms for 1st, 2nd and 3rd role reference; status, however, is lexicalized only in the 2nd role paradigm, and gender is lexicalized only in the 3rd role paradigm and only for singular reference. These differences between the three paradigms exhibit general principles of pronominal reference, such as for example that sets of pronouns for reference to others (i.e. 2nd/3rd role) reveal a greater number of distinctions than pronouns referring to self (i.e. 1st role), or that the referents of 1st/2nd role pronouns can be derived from the communicative cast itself, whereas the referents of 3rd role pronouns most commonly need a more detailed identification.

By way of illustration, the paradigm for the set of full pronouns for 1st role reference is given in Table 4.2.

Table 4.2: Paradigm representation for 1st role full pronouns in Dutch

NUMBER   CASE

	Subject	Object	Possessive
Singular	*ik*	*mij*	*mijn*
Plural	*wij*	*ons*	*on(s/ze)*

The paradigm in Table 4.2 has two dimensions: number (with singular and plural levels) and case (with subject, object, and possessive levels). The frequency of use for the forms of the Dutch pronoun system can be derived from two different kinds of data bases: (1) a project-internal corpus, and (2) a project-external corpus of native spoken Dutch. The project-internal corpus derives from the ESF data base: the language input by the native speakers in the same activities in which the four core informants of the present study participated (see Chapter 3).

Table 4.3: Frequency of personal and possessive pronouns in native speaker Dutch

1st role			ESF data base (194,444 word forms)					De Jong's data base (120,000 word forms)		
			Erg.	Mah.	Moh.	Fat.	Total		Total	English
Subject:	Sg:	ik	797	725	820	658	3,000	ik	4,117	I
	Pl:	wij	34	27	63	45	169	wij	145	we
		we	130	116	80	105	431	we	382	we
Object:	Sg:	mij	41	42	54	32	169	mij	156	me
		me	18	5	11	7	41	me	197	me
	Pl:	ons	8	14	19	11	52	ons	51	us
Possess:	Sg:	mijn	13	25	29	20	87	mijn	152	my
		m'n	11	2	2	2	17	m'n	18	my
	Pl:	onze	2	2	1	-	5	onze	28	us
								ons	12	us

2nd role			Erg.	Mah.	Moh.	Fat.	Total		Total	English
Subject:	Sg:	jij	540	390	443	316	1,689	jij	177	you
		je	2,282	1,488	1,852	1,303	6,925	je	1,511	you
		u	296	271	185	368	1,120	u	108	you
	Pl:	jullie	89	33	64	38	224	jullie	25	you
Object:	Sg:	je	20	19	23	9	71	je	83	you
		jou	67	60	72	63	262	jou	22	you
		u	12	6	11	15	44	u	10	you
	Pl:	jullie	11	10	5	2	28	jullie	4	you
Possess:	Sg:	jouw	156	155	84	82	477	jouw	15	your
		je	218	183	198	60	659	je	132	your
		uw	52	23	31	40	146	uw	4	your
	Pl:	jullie	7	2	6	-	15	jullie	1	your

3rd role			Erg.	Mah.	Moh.	Fat.	Total		Total	English
Subject:	Ms:	hij	237	153	154	201	745	hij/ie	840	he
		ie	162	113	178	187	640	-	-	he
	Fe:	zij	38	19	25	20	102	zij	54	she
		ze	57	51	42	97	247	ze	399	she
	Pl:	zij	15	11	23	16	65	zij	21	they
		ze	189	106	155	143	593	ze	1,004	they
		hun	-	-	-	-	-	hun	2	them
Object:	Ms:	hem	17	10	21	12	60	hem/'m	120	him
		'm	17	14	10	6	47	-	-	him
	Fe:	haar	7	4	13	13	37	haar/d'r	42	her
		d'r	-	-	5	-	5	-	-	her
	Pl:	ze	-	-	-	-	-	ze	73	them
		hun	2	-	5	3	10	hun	17	them
		hen	1	2	1	1	5	-	-	them
Possess:	Ms:	zijn	28	9	19	16	72	zijn/z'n	12	his
		z'n	12	7	9	7	35	-	-	his
	Fe:	haar	9	2	6	7	24	haar/d'r	56	her
		d'r	2	1	2	-	5	-	-	her
	Pl:	hun	3	3	4	1	11	hun	79	their

The project-external corpus derives from the spoken language data of the *Werkgroep Frequentie Onderzoek in het Nederlands* (De Jong 1979), which includes 120,000 word forms (tokens) of adult native speakers of Dutch. Within De Jong's corpus, the following variables were matched: sex, age, educational background of the interlocutors, and type of interaction. A number of frequency counts and a detailed tagging (i.e. assigning tags such as noun, verb or pronoun) for the latter corpus are reported by De Jong (1979). In this report, some relevant information about pronominal reference is unfortunately lost because of rather arbitrary procedures in "normalizing" the data. Thus, e.g. a number of reduced forms were combined with their corresponding full forms; *zijn/z'n* ('his'), *hem/'m* ('him'). Moreover, some information was not tagged in this corpus, such as whether the homonym *zij* encoded singular ('she') or plural ('they') reference. I have tried to derive as much relevant information as possible through an additional analysis of the original data. This analysis has been combined with the analysis by De Jong (1979). The results are presented in Table 4.3.

A much discussed determinant of language acquisition is frequency of forms in the input learners are confronted with and in varieties of the target language. It is a reasonable conjecture that, other things being equal, the most frequently recurring forms are acquired before infrequent forms. On the basis of the frequency data in native varieties of Dutch a number of predictions can be formulated. Apart from frequency, the informational complexity of forms within the pronoun system has to be taken into consideration. Thus *we*, for example, is more complex than *I* in that *we* refers to the speaker and some other person(s), whereas *I* refers to the speaker only.
Below the different dimensions and levels within the three paradigms will be discussed in detail with a view to language acquisition processes. Successively, emphasis, role, number, status, gender, and case will be dealt with.

4.2.1 EMPHASIS

The analytical task of language learners consists in segmenting the available speech stream into meaningful units (cf. Klein 1986:63-78). In spoken native Dutch the full forms are phonetically more prominent than the reduced forms. Whenever prosodic prominence (e.g. heavy stress) is given to a pronoun, the full variant is required: a circumstance which adds to the perceptual saliency of the set of full forms. The influence one would expect this to have on the segmentation of the speech stream and thereby on the order of acquisition is that:

P1   Full forms are acquired before reduced forms

Interestingly enough, this prediction contrasts with what one would expect on the basis of the frequency of forms in native varieties of Dutch. With respect to the reduced-full distinction the frequency of use in De Jong's corpus is only partly useful because for a number of dimensions full forms and reduced forms have been combined. However, in the ESF data base this information is available. As can be derived from Table 4.3 it is obvious that reduced pronouns occur considerably more frequently in spoken native Dutch than their corresponding full forms.

4.2.2 ROLE

1st role pronouns and 2nd role pronouns have a basic reference point. This so-called "origo" (cf. Bühler 1934) includes the spatio-temporal context of the speaker. As a result, 1st/2nd role pronouns should always be understood from the perspective of the speaker. A shift in the communicative cast implies a shift of the origo, as a consequence of which 1st/2nd role pronouns get other referents. In contrast, 3rd role pronouns are relatively stable. They have a fixed reference point which is only slightly affected by changes in the communicative cast.

Because of the relatively high frequency of 1st role pronouns compared to 2nd role pronouns (see Table 4.3) the following prediction is formulated:

P2   1st role reference is acquired before 2nd role reference

A characteristic feature of adult language learners is that, in contrast to children acquiring their first language, from the very start of their acquisition career they by and large already possess the cognitive prerequisites for the linguistic acquisition task. Thus, cognitive maturation can be expected to play a significantly smaller role in adult language acquisition than in child language acquisition. A case in point is the particular perspective shift required to grasp the meaning of the lexical entries in the 1st role paradigm vs. those in the 2nd role paradigm. While there is ample evidence that this cognitive prerequisite plays an important role in the development of an initial pronoun system in children's first language acquisition (see Clark 1978 and Loveland 1984 for further references), there is little reason to assume that the same determinant should play a significant role in adult language acquisition. On the basis of this, the following prediction can be formulated:

P3   There will be no 1st/2nd role pronoun reversal

4.2.3 NUMBER

For 1st role reference the singular forms commonly refer to the speaker and exclude the addressee. In contrast, the 1st role plural forms can either include or exclude the addressee. The difference in perceptual saliency between the full form *wij* ('we') and the reduced form *we* ('we') is distinctive in the encoding of number. In some contexts the reduced pronoun *we* ('we') can be used for singular reference as well, e.g. *Kom, we gaan* ('Come, we go' - 'I've got to be off').

For 2nd role reference the plural inclusive/exclusive distinction found with 1st role reference does not apply. The full singular forms *jij* ('you') and *jou(w)* ('you(r)') refer to one person. The full plural form *jullie* ('you(r)') refers to more than one person. In contrast, the reduced informal form *je* ('you(r)') and the formal form *u(w)* ('you(r)') refer to one or more persons.

Compared with 1st/2nd role reference the encoding of the plural in 3rd role reference is relatively clear: plural reference means reference to more than one person. A remarkable homonym can be found with the form *zij* ('she/they'), which can be used for both singular reference to a woman, e.g. *zij loopt*, ('she walks') and plural sex-neutral reference, e.g. *zij lopen* ('they walk'). Storms (1978) assumes that the homonymy of *zij* ('she/they') is related to the increasing use of the object form *hun* ('them') in subject function, e.g. *hun lopen* ('them walk'). This generalized use of *hun* ('them') was first noticed by Vor der Hake (1911) and has been discussed regularly since then (e.g. Karsten 1939, Kooiman 1967,1969, and in particular Van Hout 1989 for further references). It is clear that in contemporary informal spoken Dutch the plural subject form *zij* ('they') is replaced more and more often by the object form *hun* ('them'). A comparable shift from object function to subject function took place in earlier periods with the form *u* ('you') for 2nd role reference (see Section 4.2.4 below).

Within the number dimension the plural level emerges as informationally more complex than the singular level in that plural pronouns most commonly refer to more than one entity and singular pronouns to only one. In addition it can be noted that in spoken Dutch singular forms are used much more frequently than the plural forms. For the number dimension the following prediction is made:

P4   *Singular forms are acquired before plural forms*

4.2.4 STATUS

Brown & Gilman (1960) did pioneering work on 2nd role pronominal reference as address terms. They introduced the distinction between T(u)-forms (i.e. familiar pronouns) and V(ous)-forms (i.e. polite pronouns). These categories are defined through differences in "power" and "solidarity". The pronoun use of interlocutors is determined by their social and personal relationship (which in turn is determined by, for example, socio-economic rank, age or degree of intimacy) or the relationship between the interlocutor(s) and the communicative setting (the setting of a board meeting vs. a weekly game of billiards, for example). Given these constraints, there may be a symmetrical or an asymmetrical use of T/V forms: each of the interlocutors may use the same set of pronouns, or a different one, depending on the type of relationship the interlocutors have. For example, in those cases where the relationship is dominated by age differences the younger one(s) might address the older one(s) using V-forms, while the latter would use T-forms. Brown & Gilman based their ideas on observations of four Western European languages: English, French, German and Italian. Their work has been developed and generalized by Head (1978), who covers 100 languages, and in particular by Braun (1988).

The set of 2nd role pronouns in spoken Dutch has been investigated extensively (see Paardekooper 1969 and Van den Toorn 1977 for an overview). Historically, the way in which status is manifested in the Dutch pronoun system is strongly subject to an evolutionary process. Much attention has been paid to the origin and etymology of 2nd role pronouns. The following evolutionary phases are distinguished (derived from Van den Toorn 1977):

Table 4.4: Historical development of T/V-forms in Dutch

Phase	T-forms Sg.	Pl.	V-forms Sg.	Pl.	Time table (global)
I	du	ghi	du	ghi	Old-Germanic
II	du	ghi	ghi	ghi	until 1600
III	jij	gij	gij	gij	17th century
IV	jij	jullie	gij	gij	17th century
V	jij	jullie	gij	u, gij	around 1800
VI	jij	jullie	u	u	contemporary

This evolutionary account should be interpreted with some caution, particularly where the time table is concerned. However, sufficient evidence is reported in the literature that these phases can be distinguished. In the historical development of the set of 2nd role pronouns the differentiation in the number dimension preceded that in the status dimension, whereby the plural form *jullie* ('you') arose as a T-form. Even more interesting is the development of the V-form *u* ('you'): in phase V this form is used in object/possessive function, in phase VI it is also used in subject function. A detailed historical account of this phenomenon can be found in Paardekooper (1987, 1988). The form *gij* ('you') can still be found in spoken Southern Dutch, including Flemish varieties of Dutch spoken in Belgium. However, also in these varieties the form *gij* ('you') is losing ground to the V-form *u* ('you') and the T-form *jij* ('you') (cf. Deprez & Geerts 1976,1977 and Klootwijk et al. 1986).

The encoding of status in spoken Dutch is still changing. The general trend is towards an increasing use of the traditional T-forms alongside a decrease in the use of the traditional V-forms. The decrease in the use of the traditional V-forms *u* ('you') and *uw* ('your') is coupled with a differentiation within the set of traditional T-forms (see Van den Toorn 1977, Daan 1978, Geerts et al. 1984:164-167, and Vermaas 1990), so that the set of 2nd role pronouns in spoken standard Dutch could be ordered according to a relative status scale:

Table 4.5: Status scale for 2nd role pronominal reference in Dutch

LOW STATUS (T-form)	jij/jou(w)	je	jullie	u(w)	HIGH STATUS (V-forms)

Hereby, differences in degree of status imply differences in equality, rather than in formality or politeness. The differentiation of the traditional T-forms includes: (1) the use of the plural T-form *jullie* ('you(r)') in V-function, and (2) the use of the reduced form *je* ('you(r)'), which can be used to neutralize the T-V distinction, cf.:

(1)   Meneer, weet u de molenstraat?   Sir, do you know the way to millstreet?
(2)   Opa, kom je morgen?   Grandpa, will you come tomorrow?
(3)   Peter, kun je dit repareren?   Peter, can you repair this?

In spoken varieties of Dutch the frequency with which T-forms are used exceeds that of the V-forms (see Table 4.3). With respect to the status dimension, the following prediction is made:

P5   T-forms are acquired before V-forms

It should be kept in mind that with respect to this prediction some intervening factors are at work in the present study. Firstly, there is an activity effect in that the data of the ESF project were often collected in rather informal situations. Secondly, there is a familiarity effect in that learners and target language interlocutors were well acquainted. As a result of this the interlocutors were more likely to use T-forms than V-forms.

4.2.5   GENDER

A description of gender in Dutch can be found in Geerts et al. (1984:39-46), Deutsch & Wijnen (1985), and Verhoeven (1990). The classification into male, female, and inanimate entities is called natural gender. In addition, there is a related, although opaque classification of nominal devices according to grammatical gender. In the latter classification a distinction is made between (1) "de-words", which can have masculine or feminine gender, e.g. *de ezel* ('the donkey') and (2) "het-words", e.g. *het paard* ('the horse') which have neuter gender. In Dutch the number of "de-word" types exceeds the number of "het-word" types (cf. Extra 1978). With respect to "de-words" there is a difference in pronominal reference between regional varieties, which is accepted as a variation within standard spoken Dutch (cf. Geerts et al. 1984:51). An example is the Dutch word *tafel* ('table'), which is referred to by means of a masculine pronoun in the Northern part of the Netherlands and by means of a feminine pronoun in the Southern part.

For 1st role plural reference the choice between the forms *ons* ('our') and *onze* ('our') depends on the grammatical gender of the noun to which they are used attributively: *ons* ('our') is used before singular (neuter) "het-words", e.g. *het paard* ('the horse') and *ons paard* ('our horse'); in all other cases the form *onze* ('our') is used, e.g. *de hond* ('the dog'), *onze hond* ('our dog'), *onze honden* ('our dogs'), but also *onze paarden* ('our horses').

For 3rd role singular reference, masculine, feminine, and neuter information is lexicalized. Within the sets of the masculine, feminine and neuter pronouns a further distinction can be made between reduced and full forms. In general, the reduced forms can refer both to personal animates and to impersonal (in)animates, whereas full forms only refer to personal animates (or personified entities). However, there are two exceptions. The first exception applies to the use of the male full subject pronoun *hij* ('he') which refers to impersonal (in)animates as well. Compare sequences (4) and (5).

(4) Waar heb ik mijn auto geparkeerd?   Where did I park my car?
     O ja, hij staat daar.   Oh yes, he is there.

(5) Waar is die pan?   Where is that pan?
     O ja, *zij-ze staat op de vensterbank.   Oh yes, she is on the windowsill.

The second exception applies to the female singular forms *'r* ('her') and *d'r* ('her') which only refer to personal animates. Compare sequences (6) and (7).

(6) Waar is lia?   Where is lia?
     Heb je ze-d'r ergens gezien?   Did you see her anywhere?

(7) Waar is die pan?   Where is that pan?
     Heb je ze-*d'r ergens gezien?   Did you see her anywhere?

In the 3rd role paradigm in Dutch, masculine forms are more basic than feminine forms, because they can be used in a wider range of situations or contexts. For example, generic reference to any person of a kind that could either be male or female is made by means of a masculine form rather than a feminine form, e.g. *de mens, hij zal ten gronde gaan aan zijn eigen kennis* ('man, he will be destroyed by his own knowledge') rather than *de mens, zij...* ('man, she...'). The large range of masculine pronouns is also reflected in their frequency of use. Table 4.3 clearly shows that in native spoken Dutch masculine forms occur much more frequently than feminine forms. The following prediction is formulated with respect to the acquisition of the gender encoding pronouns:

P6   Masculine forms are acquired before feminine forms

4.2.6 CASE

Subject and object pronouns are non-relational terms, i.e. they denote one entity, whereas possessive pronouns are relational terms, i.e. they denote a possessive relation between entities. Furthermore, possessive forms generally contain more information than subject or object forms in that they preserve the information of person and number encoded by the subject or object forms and, in addition, contain information about the possessive relation. This, all other things being equal, makes the possessive level more complex than the subject or object levels.

In addition to this, subject forms rather than object forms are promoted by the interaction between pronominalization, grammatical subject/object, and given/new information. Thus, the subject NP is often used to maintain reference to a topic (e.g. a person, an object, a concept), while the VP is used to convey new and focussed information. As a result, the following predictions can be formulated with respect to the order of acquisition:

P7   *Subject forms are acquired before object forms*
P8   *Subject forms are acquired before possessive forms*
P9   *Forms in object function are acquired before forms in possessive function*

Table 4.3 shows that subject pronouns are used much more frequently by native speakers of Dutch than object and possessive pronouns. This underlines the validity of predictions 7 and 8. A rather diffuse picture emerges for the relative frequency of the pronouns in object function vs. those in possessive function. There are differences between 1st role and 2nd role pronouns, between the informants, and between the internal and external corpus. As a result, frequency of use does not underline prediction 9.

4.2.7 DEMONSTRATIVES

In many languages there is a close relationship between the sets of personal and possessive pronouns and the set of demonstrative pronouns. Table 4.6 shows the demonstrative pronouns in spoken Dutch (adapted from Kirsner 1979, see also Geerts et al. 1984:215-229).

Table 4.6: Demonstrative pronouns in Dutch

Number	Gender	Spatial distance: Proximate	Distal	English equivalent	
Sg.	"de-woord"	dit	dat	this	that
	"het-woord"	deze	die	this	that
Pl.		deze	die	these	those

The demonstrative pronouns in Dutch constitute a two-term system. The basic set distinction applies to form variants indicating "near to speaker" and those indicating "far from speaker" (cf. Anderson & Keenan 1985). In spoken Dutch the proximate demonstratives are *dit* ('this') and *deze* ('this/these'), whereas the distal demonstratives are *dat* ('that') and *die* ('that/those'). Demonstrative pronouns can be used independently as well as attributively. The semantic information that is lexicalized through the demonstrative pronouns is number and gender. The demonstratives *dit* ('this') and *dat* ('that') encode singular "het-woord" gender, e.g. *dit paard* ('this horse'); the demonstratives *deze* ('this/these') and *die* ('that/those') are used for singular "de-woord" gender, e.g. *deze ezel* ('this donkey') and for plural reference, e.g. *deze ezels* ('these donkeys') but also *deze paarden* ('these horses').

4.3   THE SOURCE LANGUAGES

In this section properties of the source languages, i.e. Turkish and Moroccan Arabic, of the informants are examined as determinants of the structure of the acquisition of the Dutch pronoun system. In the Turkish and the Moroccan Arabic pronoun systems there are enclitics (suffixes) and free lexical forms. This distinction is related but not similar to the reduced/full distinction in the Dutch pronoun system.

4.3.1 THE TURKISH PRONOUN SYSTEM

A detailed description of colloquial Turkish can be found in Mardin (1961:24-28), Lewis (1967:67-78) and Underhill (1976:32). The basic set of free lexical forms in the Turkish pronoun system is given in Table 4.7. This overview shows that the following dimensions and levels are distinguished (note that there is no gender dimension):
- The case dimension with six levels.
- The number dimension with two levels: singular and plural.
- The status dimension with two levels: formal and informal for 2nd role reference singular.

Table 4.7: Turkish pronoun system

Role	Number	Status	Case Nominative	Genitive	Dative	Accusative	Locative	Ablative
1	Sg.		ben	benim	bana	beni	bende	benden
	Pl.		biz	bizim	bize	bizi	bizde	bizden
2	Sg.	Inform.	sen	senin	sana	seni	sende	senden
		Formal						
	Pl.		siz	sizin	size	sizi	sizde	sizden
3	Sg.		o	onun	ona	onu	onda	ondan
	Pl.		onlar	onların	onlara	onları	onlarda	onlardan

Case

Turkish pronouns are declined in six cases which also apply to nominal devices. The declension for the Turkish noun *valiz* ('suitcase') is given in Table 4.8.

Table 4.8: Case marking in Turkish

Case	Suffix	Examples	English equivalent
Nominative	-∅	valiz	(the) suitcase
Genitive	-(n)In	valiz-in	of (the) suitcase
Dative	-(y)E	valiz-e	in (the) suitcase
Accusative	-(y)I	valiz-i	the suitcase
Locative	-DE	valiz-de	in (the) suitcase
Ablative	-DEn	valiz-den	out of (the) suitcase

In this table the conventional writing of archiphonemes in capitals is applied, i.e. I equals {ı, i, u, ü} and E equals {e, a} in accordance with rules of vowel harmony,

D equals {d, t} in accordance with rules of consonant assimilation. A comparison of the pronoun system given in Table 4.7 with the case marking endings in Table 4.8 reveals some irregularities for the declension with 1st/2nd role reference. However, as a whole, the system of case declension is fairly regular.

Number
   As Table 4.7 shows there is analogous pluralization in 1st and 2nd roles. The element *-z* is probably an old dual (cf. Forchheimer 1953:54). For 3rd role plural the suffix *-lEr* can be used.

Status
   With singular 2nd role reference in Turkish, status is marked through a set of T-forms and V-forms. Hereby status conflates with the dimension number in that the V-form *siz* ('you') can be used for singular as well as plural reference. Disambiguation is possible through the plural suffix *-lEr*, i.e. *siz-ler*.

In addition to free lexical pronouns, Turkish also has different sets of bound pronouns (see Table 4.9). Personal suffixes are attached to the tense marker of the verb. Possessive suffixes are attached to the noun. The possessive suffix is obligatory in standard language use, but in colloquial speech it is often left out with 1st and 2nd role reference.

Table 4.9: Bound pronouns in Turkish

Role	Personal suffixes		Possessive suffixes	
	Sg.	Pl.	Sg.	Pl.
1	-(y)Im	-(y)Iz	-(I)m	-(I)mIz
2	-sIn	-sInIz	-(I)n	-(I)nIz
3	-∅	-∅/-lEr	-(s)I	-(s)I/lErI

Demonstratives
   Demonstrative pronouns in Turkish (see Table 4.10) constitute a three-term system (cf. Lewis 1967:71). The forms *şu* ('this/that') and *bu* ('this') are declined for case in the same way as the form *o* ('that'). Demonstratives can be used independently as well as attributively. Differences in meaning between these forms relate to the relative distance from the speaker/addressee. A moot point is the meaning of the form *şu* ('this/that'). Lyons (1977), for example, argues that Turkish demonstrative pronouns constitute a person-oriented system in which *şu* ('this/that') means "identifiable to addressee". However, this is disputed by Bastuji (1976), who argues for a distance-oriented system in which *şu* ('this/that') is a middle term between proximate and distal. An account of alternative interpretations of the Turkish demonstrative pronoun system can be found in Anderson & Keenan (1985).

Table 4.10: Demonstrative pronouns in Turkish

Form	Function	English equivalent
bu	close to the speaker	this
şu	a little further away	this/that
o	remote from the speaker/addressee	that (also, he/she/it)

4.3.2 THE MOROCCAN ARABIC PRONOUN SYSTEM

The free forms and the enclitics of the Moroccan Arabic pronoun system are given in Table 4.11 (derived from Harrell 1962:134-145 and Otten 1983:877-881). The following dimensions and levels are distinguished:
- The number dimension with two levels: singular and plural.
- The gender dimension with two levels: masculine and feminine, both within the 2nd role and the 3rd role paradigms.

Table 4.11: Moroccan Arabic pronoun system

Role	Number	Gender	Free forms	Enclitics
1	Sg.		ana	-i, -ya, -y, -ni
	Pl.		ḥna	-na
2	Sg.	Msc.	nta	-ek, -k
		Fem.	nti(-ya)	
	Pl.		ntuma	-kom
3	Sg.	Msc.	huwa	-u, -h, -eh
		Fem.	hiya	-ha
	Pl.		huma	-hom

Case

The Moroccan Arabic pronoun system is rather restricted with respect to case marking. Compared with the simple and limited set of free pronouns, the enclitics exhibit a greater variety in form and a complex relation exists between the enclitics and the stems to which they are attached. Stems might be nouns, e.g. *weld* ('son') and *weld-i* ('my son'), verbs, e.g. *šaf* ('he saw)' and *šaf-ni* ('he saw me'), prepositions, e.g. *mᶜa* ('with') and *mᶜa-ha* ('with her'), and a few other particles, e.g. *ᶜemmeṛ* ('never') and *ᶜemmeṛ-ni* ('I never') (cf. Harrell 1962:135).

Number

In Classical Arabic number has a third level: common dual. This occurs both within the 2nd role paradigm, i.e. *antum-ā* and *-kum-ā,* and the 3rd role paradigm, i.e. *hum-ā* and *-hum-ā.* As can be seen in Table 4.11 common dual is not present in the Moroccan Arabic pronoun system. Note, however, the similarity between the forms for dual number in Classical Arabic and the forms for plural number in Moroccan Arabic. Dual number can still be found with some Moroccan Arabic nouns, e.g. *yum* ('day'), *yumayn* ('two days'), and *iyyam* ('more than two days').

Gender

Compared to the Dutch pronoun system and even more so compared to the Turkish pronoun system, the gender dimension is encoded extensively in the Moroccan Arabic pronoun system: for both 2nd role reference and 3rd role reference singular. Within the 2nd role paradigm there is in some regional varieties of Moroccan Arabic, even an additional level of common gender with the form *ntina.* This form is used for both masculine and feminine reference.

Demonstratives

In Moroccan Arabic the form *had* used in combination with the definite article functions as a demonstrative article in adnominal position, e.g. *had le-ktab* ('this/that book'). In addition, there is a set of "near" and "far" demonstrative pronouns which are used independently (see Table 4.12). Note that these forms are inflected for number and gender (cf. Harrell 1962:143).

Table 4.12: Demonstrative pronouns in Moroccan Arabic

Number	Gender	Spatial distance Proximate	Distal	English equivalents	
Sg.	Msc.	had-a	had-ak	this one	that one
	Fem.	had-i	had-ik	this one	that one
Pl.		had-u	had-uk	these ones	those ones

On the basis of the preceding typological description of the Turkish and the Moroccan Arabic pronoun system a set of predictions can be made with respect to the acquisition of pronominal reference in Dutch. It is a well-known assumption that similarities between a source system and a target system will facilitate the acquisition of the target system, while differences will make the acquisition task harder. Thus, the following predictions are made:

P10　*The case dimension will be easier for Turkish learners than for Moroccan learners of Dutch*

P11　*The status dimension will be easier for Turkish learners than for Moroccan learners of Dutch*

P12　*The gender dimension will be easier for Moroccan learners than for Turkish learners of Dutch*

4.4   PROSPECTIVE

In this chapter a list of predictions was presented on the basis of a typological, cross-linguistic perspective on Dutch, Turkish and Moroccan Arabic pronoun systems.

Detailed predictions were derived from the frequency, informational complexity, and the perceptual saliency of forms in the pronoun system of Dutch as the target language of the informants in the present study.

Global predictions were derived from the degree in which specific dimensions (i.e. case, status, and gender) are lexicalized in the pronoun systems of Turkish and Moroccan Arabic as the source languages of the informants.

The predictions reveal that competing principles are at work in the language acquisition process, such as: judging by differences in perceptual saliency, one would expect that full forms are acquired before reduced forms (cf. prediction 1); however, on the basis of frequency of use, one would expect the reverse order of acquisition. On the basis of frequency of use, one would expect that masculine forms are acquired before feminine forms (cf. prediction 6); however, because of the striking differences between Moroccan Arabic and Turkish in the encoding of gender, one would expect that the masculine-feminine distinction in the Dutch pronoun system is much easier for Moroccan than for Turkish learners of Dutch (cf. prediction 12). Competing principles are excellent candidates for evaluating the relative importance of various types of determining factors.

In Chapters 5 and 6 the predictions specified in this chapter will be tested through a form-function analysis of the pronouns used by the core and shadow informants. As can be derived from the description of pronoun systems, there is an essential difference between, the 1st/2nd role paradigms which encode reference to speaker(s)/addressee(s), and the 3rd role paradigm which encodes reference to person(s) who are neither speaker(s) nor addressee(s). Chapter 5 goes into the paradigms for 1st/2nd role reference. The 3rd role paradigm is discussed in Chapter 6.

FIRST AND SECOND ROLE PRONOMINAL REFERENCE

This chapter examines the acquisition of pronouns within the 1st role and 2nd role paradigms. First, the research questions are spelled out. After this, a number of predictions are made about the way in which the learner proceeds in accomplishing the acquisition task. Secondly, the method of analysis is specified. Thirdly, a detailed pronoun profile for each of the core informants, and a global account of the pronoun use by the shadow informants is presented. Next the predictions are tested on the basis of data provided by the core and shadow informants. Finally, the analytical findings are abstracted into a number of conclusions.

5.1 RESEARCH QUESTIONS AND PREDICTIONS

For Dutch, the learner's task in acquiring the 1st role and 2nd role paradigms consists at least of discovering the pertinent forms on the distinctions of emphasis, role, status, number and case. Language learners will not start with all the relevant forms and functions at the same time. The intriguing question is which forms and functions they will begin with and why. In this respect the basic research questions can be specified as follows (cf. Chapter 1):

I Which set of forms is used in early learner varieties and what are the referential functions of these forms?
II How is the initial set expanded over time in subsequent stages of language acquisition?
III How can learner preferences be explained?

In the preceding chapter a number of factors were examined which might determine the acquisition of the Dutch pronoun system by Turkish and Moroccan adult learners. The following predictions are relevant for the 1st role and 2nd role paradigms:

Emphasis:	P1	Full forms are acquired before reduced forms
Role:	P2	1st role reference is acquired before 2nd role reference
	P3	There will be no 1st/2nd role pronoun reversal
Number:	P4	Singular forms are acquired before plural forms
Status:	P5	T-forms are acquired before V-forms
	P11	The status dimension will be easier for Turkish learners than for Moroccan learners of Dutch
Case:	P7	Subject forms are acquired before object forms
	P8	Subject forms are acquired before possessive forms
	P9	Forms in object function are acquired before forms in possessive function
	P10	The case dimension will be easier for Turkish learners than for Moroccan learners of Dutch

These predictions address two aspects of the acquisition process of pronominal reference in Dutch: (1) the temporal order of acquisition, e.g. the subject form *ik* ('I') is acquired before the possessive form *mijn* ('my'), and (2) the generalized use, e.g. the subject form *ik* ('I') is used both in subject function (*ik loop* 'I walk') and in possessive function (*ik boek* 'I book' meaning 'my book'). These predictions will be tested through a form-function analysis. This implies that the function in which a form is used by these informants will have to be established. The hypothesized function may coincide with, but also differ from the standard function in spoken Dutch.

5.2   METHOD

5.2.1 INFORMANTS AND LANGUAGE ACTIVITIES

This chapter focusses on the four core informants: Ergün, Mahmut, Mohamed, and Fatima. For each of them a pronoun profile was made. In order to get as complete a picture as possible of their L2 acquisition process the pronoun profiles were based on an extended data base. All the relevant interactional data that were collected for the core informants were taken into account. Empirical cross-learner evidence is provided by a data scanning for the four shadow informants: the Turks Osman and Abdullah, and the Moroccans Husseyn and Hassan. A detailed account of the informants has been given in Chapter 3.

5.2.2 PROCEDURE IN THE ANALYSIS

The procedure in setting up a pronoun profile for each of the core informants can be summarized as follows:

(1)　For all the pronominal forms a concordance of the utterances of the informant in the transcript is made by a concordance program (OCP). In alphabetical order the concordance list gives the pronouns used by each learner, together with both the verbal context (concordance) and the frequency of each pronoun.

(2)　The list of pronouns in the concordance list is "cleaned up". Excluded, for example, are other-repetitions which function as repair requests and in which the occurring pronoun is not intended by the learner to be referential. An example is given in sequence (1).

(1) N:	Heb je 'n huis?		Have you got a house?
	MAH:	Heb je?	Have you?
	(Mahmut, session 1.6)		

(3)　For each pronoun the form-function relation is established. This means that for each pronoun the following aspects are taken into account in the analysis:

- The hypothesized learner meaning; the referential intention with which the learner uses a pronoun. As a result each form-function relation can be operationalized with respect to the pronominal distinctions involved in terms of standardlike use of a pronoun (i.e. normatively according to the use of the target language by native speakers) vs. generalized use of a pronoun (i.e. a different use compared to native use).
- The context of distribution; whether or not the use of a pronoun is restricted to specific context(s), e.g. only in combination with specific words.
- The consistency of use; generalized use of a pronoun (e.g. 'he' for male as well as female referents) alongside the standardlike form (e.g. 'she').
- The productivity of use; to distinguish between sporadic use of a pronoun (which are sometimes just slips of the tongue) and systematic use of a pronoun.

(4)　Special attention is paid to self-editing phenomena, e.g. *that is him/ his book* and metalinguistic comments, e.g. *the word "they" means "more people"*.

(5)　Confusion arises when pronouns are used in combination with the preposition *van* ('of'), e.g. *boek van hem* ('book of him'). With respect to the object/ possessive distinction the following decision is taken:

- Excluded from the object function are possessive NPs in which the pronoun refers to the possessor(s), i.e. possessive NPs with an internal pronoun. The possessive function covers the pronominal forms that refer to the possessor(s) in a possessive relation. This implies that also those pronouns which occur together with the preposition *van* ('of') in the same nominal phrase are detected as being used in possessive function. In addition, it should be pointed out that also the way learners use a preposition may differ from standardlike use. In those cases again the hypothesized learner meaning is decisive. Table 5.1 shows some examples.

Table 5.1: Examples of analytical decisions in form-function analysis*

Representation	Examples	English	Equivalents
Object function:			
mij	hij blijft bij mij	me	he stays with me
mij	hij houdt van mij	me	he loves me
mij	die tolk van mij vertellen	me	that interpreter of me say
Possessive function:			
mijn X	dat is mijn pen	my X	that is my pen
mijn X	ik kreeg een boek van mijn vriend	my X	I got a book from my friend
X van mijn Y	de pen van mijn vriend is rood	X of my Y	the pen of my friend is red
van mij	de witte pen is van mij	of me	the white pen is of me
X van mij	die pen van mij is waardeloos	X of me	that pen of mine is worthless

* X and Y represent (pro-)nominals

5.3   THE LEARNER VARIETIES

In this section, first for each of the core informants an overview is presented of the form-function relationships found in their L2 varieties of Dutch. Most tables are self-evident and exhibit the acquisition of the pronouns within the 1st and 2nd role paradigms. Important and typical instances as well as peculiar and deviant ones are illustrated through sequences derived from the relevant sessions with the informants. Secondly, a global overview is presented of the pronominal forms found in the Dutch varieties of the shadow informants.

5.3.1   MAHMUT

1st role reference

The pronominal form-function relationships occurring in the 27 sessions which took place with Mahmut are given in Table 5.2.

1st role singular

In subject function Mahmut frequently uses the forms *ik* ('I') and *ikke* ('I'). Especially in the early sessions the form *ik* ('I') can be found relatively often in formulaic constructions (i.e unanalysed wholes) such as *weet ik* ('I know' meaning "to know") and *weet ik niet* ('I do not know' meaning "not to know"). Some instances are given in sequence (2).

Table 5.2: Pronominal 1st role reference by Mahmut

CYCLE 1	s1	s2	s3	s4	s5	s6	s7	s8	s9	Total	English
Subject:											
Sg: ik	22	8	29	49	51	20	75	112	49	415	I
ikke	-	-	1	1	4	2	4	10	6	28	I
Object:											
Sg: mij	-	-	-	-	-	1	1	-	1	3	me
mijn (=mij)	-	-	-	-	-	-	-	2	-	2	my (=me)
Possess:											
Sg: mijn X	-	-	-	11	65	12	22	34	9	153	my X
mij X (=mijn)	-	-	-	-	-	1	-	-	2	3	me X (=my)
van mijn X	-	1	-	-	-	-	1	-	-	2	of my X
van mij X	-	-	-	-	-	-	-	-	1	1	of me X
ik X (=mijn)	-	-	2	6	7	-	5	-	-	20	I X (=my)
ikke X (=mijn)	-	-	-	1	-	-	-	-	-	1	I X (=my)
je X (=mijn)	-	-	1	-	-	-	-	-	-	1	you X (=my)

CYCLE 2	s10	s11	s12	s13	s14	s15	s16	s17	s18	Total	English
Subject:											
Sg: ik	67	30	55	46	106	81	58	88	45	576	I
ikke	-	3	2	34	10	19	21	55	6	150	I
Pl: wij	-	-	-	-	-	-	1	1	-	2	we
Object:											
Sg: mij	2	-	1	4	22	5	2	6	4	46	me
mijn (=mij)	-	-	-	-	-	1	-	-	-	1	my (=me)
ik (=mij)	2	-	-	-	-	-	-	-	-	2	I (=me)
Possess:											
Sg: mijn X	14	1	3	5	32	18	8	26	2	109	my X
van mijn X	-	-	-	-	-	-	-	-	3	3	of my X
mij X (=mijn)	-	-	-	2	-	-	1	1	-	4	me X (=my)
van mij	-	-	-	-	-	-	-	-	1	1	of me
ikke X (=mijn)	-	-	-	-	1	-	-	-	-	1	I X (=my)

CYCLE 3	s19	s20	s21	s22	s23	s24	s25	s26	s27	Total	English
Subject:											
Sg: ik	75	75	37	165	33	68	125	195	58	831	I
ikke	4	1	11	8	3	16	10	10	3	66	I
Pl: wij	-	-	-	-	-	-	-	2	2	4	we
Object:											
Sg: mij	3	2	1	17	-	3	22	8	5	61	me
mijn (=mij)	-	-	-	-	-	1	-	-	-	1	my (=me)
ik (=mij)	-	-	-	-	-	-	-	2	2	I (=me)
Pl: ons	-	-	-	-	-	-	1	-	2	3	our
Possess:											
Sg: mijn X	9	6	4	17	20	20	4	12	10	102	my X
mij X (=mijn)	-	-	-	1	-	-	-	1	-	2	me X (=my)
van mijn (=mij)	-	1	-	-	-	-	-	-	-	1	of my (=me)
van mijn X	-	-	-	-	-	-	1	-	-	1	of my X
van mij	-	-	-	-	1	-	-	-	-	1	of me
ik X (=mijn)	-	2	-	2	1	1	-	4	1	11	I X (=my)
ikke X (=mijn)	-	-	-	-	-	-	-	2	-	2	I X (=my)

(2) N: Maar als een nederlander heel snel   But if a dutchman talks to you
            praat tegen jou he.   very fast right.
     MAH: Ja.   Yes.
     N: Je kunt hem niet verstaan.   You cannot understand him.
     MAH: Ja.   Yes.
     N: Wat doe jij dan?   What do you do then?
     MAH: Ja snel praten he^   Yes talk fast right^
            ik weet ik niet. Die andere he.   I know I not. That other one right.
     N: Maar zeg je dan uh ja "Ik begrijp 't   But do you say er yes "I don't understand.
            niet. Kan je 't nog een keer zeggen?"   Can you say it again?"
     MAH: Ja nog 'n keer. Ja nog een keer uh praten^   Yes again. Yes again er talk^
            nog een keer snel. Niet rustig. Jij weet again fast. Not slowly. You know
            ik niet. Ik niet verstaan he. Andere mensen I not. I not understand right. Other
            weet ik niet verstaan ik.   people know I not understand I.
            Ja goed/ uh snel praten^ ik weet niet.   Yes good/ er fast talk^ I know not.
     (session 8)

In early sessions *ik* ('I') often occurs in isolation as a request to identify or disambig-
uate the referent of the pronoun used by the native interlocutor in the immediately
preceding turn. Sequences (3) and (4) contain some examples of this so-called "ik-
request".

(3) N: Wat voor werk doet zij?   What kind of work does she do?
     MAH: +   +
     N: Wat moet zij doen?   What does she have to do?
     MAH: Ik?   I?
     N: Nee jouw vrouw.   No your wife.
     MAH: Vrouw?   Wife?
     (session 1)

(4) N: Waar wil je ergens wonen?   Where would you like to live?
     MAH: Ik?   I?
     N: Ja + waar?   Yes + where?
     MAH: Waar?   Where?
     (session 6)

In the course of the succeeding sessions this "ik-request" as well as the use of the full
subject pronoun in formulaic utterances decreases.

In object function the object pronoun *mij* ('mij') is used standardlike for the first
time in session 6. Over time the use of this form increases. The subject pronoun *ik*
('I') and the possessive pronoun *mijn* ('my') are generalized occasionally in object
function:

(5) MAH: Ik heb brief uh sturen.   I have letter er send.
     N: Ja.   Yes.
     MAH: Energiebedrijf ik brief sturen   Power company I letter send
            "Ja jij uh de/ vijf maanden de/   "Yes you er the/ five months the/
            deze meter gas weggooi".   this meter gas throw away".
     N: Ja.   Yes.
     MAH: "En jij hier zo betalen".   "And you here thus pay".

N: Ja.   Yes.
MAH: "Deze betalen".   "This pay".
(session 10)

(6) MAH: Ja die + mijn dochter he.   Yes that + my daughter eh.
     N: Ja.   Yes.
     MAH: Hier mijn naast komen/ mij komen.   Here my beside come/ me come.
     (session 15)

(7) MAH: Die meneer ge/ gezien die meisje.   That gentleman se/ seen that girl.
     N: Ja.   Yes.
     MAH: "Jij mij gezien gezien" zegt. "Ken ik"   "You me seen seen" says. "I know"
            zegt. Ja meisje even denk't.   says. Yes girl for a moment think'it.
            "Ja" zegt. En dan "Kom hier zitten" zegt.   "Yes" says. And then "Come sit here" says.
     (session 27)

In possessive function Mahmut uses the possessive pronoun *mijn* ('my') for the first
time in session 2. We sporadically observe in all three cycles a generalized use of the
object pronoun *mij* ('me') and the subject pronouns *ik* ('I') and *ikke* ('I'). With
respect to the latter there is only one instance in cycle 2, while there are many in
cycles 1 and 3. Examples of generalized use of object and subject pronouns in possessive function are given in sequences (8)-(11).

(8) MAH: Die ergün vader he   That ergün father right
     N: Ja.   Yes.
     MAH: auto en mij auto ongeluk maken.   car and me car accident make.
     (session 16)

(9) MAH: Ikke hier niet nodig   I not needed here
            mij uh vrachtwagenrijbewijs he.   me er lorry driving licence eh.
     (session 17)

(10) MAH: Ja zoveel overwerk maken.   Yes make so much overtime.
     N: Kreeg je wel geld voor?   Did you get money for it?
     MAH: Ja.   Yes.
     N: Ja.   Yes.
     MAH: En ik contract aflopen.   And I contract end.
     (session 22)

(11) MAH: Ja ik auto groot he.   Yes I car big right.
     (session 23)

Some instances can be found in which standardlike use of the possessive pronoun
mijn ('my') occurs alongside generalized use of the subject pronoun *ik* ('I'):

(12) N: En uh heb jij ook 'n naam als klein   And er have you also a name as a little
            broertje?   brother?
     MAH: Mijn broer?   My brother?
     N: Jouw naam?   Your name?
     MAH: Ik naam mahmut.   I name mahmut.
     (session 5)

(13) MAH: Ik niet tillen he. Mijn schoonbroer   I not lift right. My brother-in-law takes.
           meenemen. Ik schoonbroer tillen. Ik   I brother-in-law lift. I
           die/ die kopen.   that/ that buy.
     N: Ja ja.   Yes yes.
     MAH: Alles tas ingooien. Schoonbroer   Throw everything into bag. Brother-in-law
           tillen met wagen he.   lift with car right.
     (session 20)

There is one instance of pronoun reversal. As can be seen in sequence (14) Mahmut repeats the interlocutor, but then corrects the pronoun reversal *je* ('your') into the non-standardlike 1st role subject pronoun *ik* ('I').

(14) N: Ja waar moet die naar toe?   Yes where must that go?
     MAH: Naam?   Name?
     N: Ja.   Yes.
     MAH: Mama.   Mommy.
     N: Naar je moeder [uh]   To your mother [er]
     MAH: [nee] je moeder/   [no] your mother/
           ik moeder.   I mother.
     N: Ja.   Yes.
     (session 3)

1st role plural

With Mahmut, instances of 1st role plural reference occur very infrequently and relatively late (see Table 5.2). In subject function *wij* ('we') first appears in session 16 (see sequence 15). In object function *ons* ('us') does not appear until session 25 (see sequence 16). Plural reference in possessive function is not used by Mahmut for 1st role reference.

(15) N: Vuurwerk.   Fireworks.
     MAH: Nee.   No.
     N: Nee.   No.
     MAH: Jij wel?   Did you?
     N: Ik? Nee.   I? No.
     MAH: Wij wel jij niet. Ik/ jij nederlandse mensen.   We did you didn't. I/ you dutch people.
     (session 16)

(16) MAH: Ja ja iedereen minder. Niet zo minder he   Yes yes everybody less. Not so less eh
           helemaal. Ja bij ons die vaste   completely. Yes with us that permanent
           dienst he vaste dienst contract.   position eh permanent position contract.
     N: Ja.   Yes.
     MAH: Die vast werk^ beetje/ beetje meer.   That permanent job^ little/ little more.
     (session 25)

2nd role reference

The pronominal form-function relationships for 2nd role reference in the 27 sessions with Mahmut are given in Table 5.3.

Table 5.3: Pronominal 2nd role reference by Mahmut

CYCLE 1	s1	s2	s3	s4	s5	s6	s7	s8	s9	Total	English
Subject:											
Sg: jij	-	-	6	-	1	3	6	31	8	55	you
Object:											
Sg: jij (=jou)	-	-	-	-	-	1	-	-	-	1	you
Possess:											
Sg: jij X (=jouw)	-	-	-	-	-	1	4	-	-	5	you X (=your)

CYCLE 2	s10	s11	s12	s13	s14	s15	s16	s17	s18	Total	English
Subject:											
Sg: jij	27	-	17	15	25	17	21	29	21	172	you
je	-	-	-	-	1	-	-	1	1	3	you
Pl: jullie	-	1	-	1	5	-	-	1	1	9	you
Object:											
Sg: jij (=jou)	3	-	-	1	3	-	-	-	-	7	you
Possess:											
Sg: jouw X	-	-	-	-	-	-	-	2	-	2	your X
jij X (=jouw)	4	-	-	4	4	-	2	5	-	19	you X (=your)

CYCLE 3	s19	s20	s21	s22	s23	s24	s25	s26	s27	Total	English
Subject:											
Sg: jij	6	16	11	35	18	17	24	53	24	204	you
je	-	-	1	-	-	1	2	-	-	4	you
u	-	-	1	-	-	-	-	-	-	1	you
Pl: jullie	1	-	-	8	-	1	1	3	-	14	you
Object:											
Sg: jou	-	-	-	-	-	-	2	1	-	3	you
jij (=jou)	-	-	-	3	1	-	-	-	-	4	you
Possess:											
Sg: jouw X	-	-	-	-	-	-	-	1	-	1	your X
X van jou	-	-	-	-	-	1	-	-	-	1	X of you
jij X (=jouw)	-	-	-	2	1	1	1	-	-	5	you X (=your)

2nd role singular

From session 3 onwards Mahmut uses the subject pronoun *jij* ('you') in subject function. From session 14 onwards the reduced form *je* ('you') occurs as well. However, initially this form can only be noticed in formulaic speech (see sequences 17 and 18).

(17) MAH: Weet je *battaniye*?   Do you know *blanket*?
        (session 14)

(18) N: U mag daar gaan zitten meneer.   You may take a seat there sir.
     MAH: Ja dankjewel uh mevrouw jansen.   Yes thank you er mrs. jansen.
     (session 17)

Only one occurrence of the V-form *u* ('you') can be found. This form is used in the opening sequence of a job interview (see sequence 19).

(19) MAH: Ja dag. Cantürk.   Yes hello. Cantürk.
     N: Jansen.   Jansen.
     MAH: Ik/ hebt u personeel nodig?   I/ do you need personnel?
     (session 21)

The context in which the V-form *u* ('you') occurs is very similar to the context of sequence (20) from a session which takes place one month later. However, in this session Mahmut uses the reduced T-form *je* ('you'):

(20) MAH: Ik daar vragen "Heb je personeel nodig/   I there ask "Do you need personnel/
            die jullie/ jullie personeel nodig?".   that you/ you need personnel?".
     (session 22)

During all three cycles Mahmut generalizes the subject pronoun *jij* ('you') in object function. Sequences (21) and (22) contain some examples.

(21) MAH: Zij mij zeggen "Ik/ jij mij helpen^   She say to me "I/ you help me^
            ik/ ik ook/ ik jij ook helpen".   I/ I too/ I you help too".
     N: Ik jou helpen ja.   I you help yes.
     (session 14)

(22) MAH: Snipperdag. Jij niet opmaken^   Day off. You not spend^
            misschien fabriek jij duizend/   maybe factory you thousand/
            duizend gulden geven jij/ jij geven.   give you/ thousand guilders you give.
     N: Aan jou ja.   To you yes.
     (session 22)

Note that in these sequences Mahmut is corrected by the native speaker with the pronoun *jou* ('you'). Mahmut uses this form standardlike in object function only at the end of the third cycle (see sequences 23 and 24).

(23) MAH: Ja chef gezien misschien van jou boos.   Yes boss seen maybe of you angry.
     (session 25)

(24) MAH: "Jij twaalfduizend geven ik jou geven". "You twelve thousand give I you give".
     (session 25)   < =if you give me twelve thousand guilders
                                                      I'll give you the car>

In possessive function Mahmut initially generalizes the subject pronoun *jij* ('you'), as sequences (25)-(27) illustrate.

(25) MAH: Ja peter he hm "Jij vader thuis.   Yes peter eh um "You father home.
            Jij familie veel familie".   You family many family".
     (session 7)

(26) MAH: Jij vader katholiek?   You father catholic?
     (session 10)

(27) N: Dan koop je die van mij.   Then you buy that of me.
      MAH: Ja klein jij auto.   Yes small you car.
      (session 13)

In session 17 the possessive pronoun *jouw* ('you') is used standardlike in possessive
function. However, there is also still the generalized use of the subject pronoun *jij*
('you') in possessive function (see sequence 28).

(28) MAH: Ja mijn dochter he en uh broer zoon   Yes my daughter er and brother son
              mag wel uh trouwen. Jouw dochter en   can er marry. Your daughter and
              broer uh zoon he.   brother er son right.
      N: Ja.   Yes.
      MAH: Mag wel trouwen he [of niet]?   Can marry er [or not]?
      N: [Nee]   [No]
      MAH: Nee?   No?
      N: In turkije wel?   In turkey they can?
      MAH: Ja wel. Hoef niet?   Yes they can. Not necessary?
      N: Nee in nederland niet.   No in the netherlands not.
      MAH: Ja jij dochter he.   Yes you daughter right.
      N: Ja.   Yes.
      MAH: Jij dochter en uh jij broer zoon.   You daughter and er you brother son.
      (session 17)

2nd role plural

As can be seen in Table 5.3 above, plural references are used for the first time in
subject function by Mahmut in session 11. Some occurrences are given in sequences
(29) and (30).

(29) N: Is dat rijk?   Is that rich?
      MAH: Rijk?   Rich?
      N: Ja die jullie veel werk he?   Yes that you work much right?
      (session 13)

(30) N: Dan ben je wel kapitalist dus.   So then you are capitalist?
      MAH: Wie?   Who?
      N: Jij.   You.
      MAH: Nee ik niet kapitalist.   No I not capitalist.
      N: Nee?   No?
      MAH: Nee. Wij/ wij niet kapitalist jullie wel.   No. We/ we not capitalist you are.
      N: Wie ik?   Who I?
      (session 26)

In particular in early sessions instances can be found where the singular full form *jij*
('you') is followed by a plural nominal specification (see sequences 31 and 32).

(31) MAH: Jij + hollandse mensen + jij he. Ik   You + dutch people + you right. I
              vragen deze "Wat is dat?". Weet ik   ask this "What is that?". I do
              niet. Turks *kitap*. Hollands boek.   not know. Turkish *book*. Dutch book.
      (session 8)

(32) N: Moet ik turks leren?   Do I have to learn turkish?
     MAH: Ja jij he hollandse mensen niks.   Yes you eh dutch people nothing.
              Jij eentje man he.   You one man right.
     N: Hm.   Um.
     MAH: Turkije vakantie.   Turkey holidays.
     (session 8)

5.3.2 ERGÜN

1st role reference

Table 5.4 lists the pronominal 1st role references that could be found with Ergün.

Table 5.4: Pronominal 1st role reference by Ergün (cycles 1 and 2)

CYCLE 1		s1	s2	s3	s4	s5	s6	s7	s8	s9	Total	English
Subject:												
Sg:	ik	11	16	59	97	51	49	74	272	80	709	I
	ikke	-	1	9	5	4	3	5	19	6	52	I
Pl:	wij	-	-	1	-	-	-	-	-	-	1	we
Object:												
Sg:	mij	-	-	2	-	-	-	-	2	-	4	me
Possess:												
Sg:	mijn X	-	1	-	-	-	1	6	39	3	50	my X
	van mijn X	-	-	1	-	4	-	-	1	-	6	of my X
	jouw X (=mijn)	-	-	-	-	-	1	-	-	-	1	your X (=my)
Pl:	ons X	-	-	-	-	-	-	-	2	-	2	our X

CYCLE 2		s10	s11	s12	s13	s14	s15	s16	s17	s18	Total	English
Subject:												
Sg:	ik	78	77	81	252	215	74	232	273	171	1453	I
	ikke	3	5	-	3	1	3	3	2	-	20	I
Pl:	wij	-	-	-	-	-	-	-	2	-	2	we
Object:												
Sg:	mij	-	-	1	4	12	-	4	6	7	34	me
	mijn (=mij)	-	-	-	-	-	-	1	-	1	2	my (=me)
Pl:	ons	-	1	-	-	-	-	-	-	4	5	us
Possess:												
Sg:	mijn X	3	8	4	25	36	4	25	11	9	125	my X
	X van mijn (=mij)	-	-	-	-	1	-	-	-	-	1	X of my (=me)
	X van mij	-	-	-	-	1	-	1	-	-	2	X of me
	jouw X (=mijn)	-	-	-	-	-	-	-	-	1	1	your X (=my)
Pl:	ons X	1	-	-	-	-	1	-	-	-	2	our X
	onze X	-	-	1	-	3	-	3	1	-	8	our X
	van ons X	-	-	-	-	-	-	-	3	-	3	of us X
	van onze X	-	-	-	-	-	-	-	8	-	8	of us X
	van ons	-	-	-	-	-	-	-	-	1	1	of us
	van onze	-	-	-	-	-	-	-	4	-	4	of us
	X onze	-	1	-	1	-	-	-	-	-	2	X us

Table 5.4 (cont.): Pronominal 1st role reference by Ergün (cycle 3)

CYCLE 3	s19	s20	s21	s22	s23	s24	s25	s26	s27	Total	English
Subject:											
Sg: ik	343	280	117	190	118	114	188	307	108	1765	I
ikke	1	5	1	2	1	1	2	2	-	15	I
Pl: wij	-	3	1	14	3	4	30	38	6	99	we
Object:											
Sg: mij	22	4	-	8	4	2	13	14	5	72	me
mijn (=mij)	-	3	-	-	1	-	-	5	-	9	my (=me)
Pl: ons	1	4	-	-	-	-	2	1	3	11	us
wij (=ons)	-	1	-	-	-	-	-	-	-	1	we (=us)
Possess:											
Sg: mijn X	18	11	1	7	14	5	32	15	2	105	my X
van mijn X	3	10	2	28	4	5	4	1	12	69	of my X
van mijn (=mij)	1	4	1	2	-	2	-	-	1	11	of my (=me)
X van mij X	-	-	1	-	-	-	-	-	-	1	X of me (=my)
Pl: van ons X	5	7	-	3	-	1	-	1	-	17	of us X
van onze X	-	3	-	-	-	1	-	-	-	4	of us X
X van ons	1	-	-	-	-	-	-	-	-	1	X of us
X van ons X	-	-	-	-	-	-	-	1	-	1	X of us X

1st role singular

In subject function Ergün frequently uses the subject pronouns *ik* ('I') and *ikke* ('I') in all 27 sessions. As with Mahmut it often concerns formulaic utterances such as *ik weet ik niet* ('I know I not'). Ergün also regularly uses *ik* ('I') as a request for reference identification (see sequences 33 and 34).

(33) N: Ben je wel 'ns ziek?   Are you ever ill?
ERG: Ja.   Yes.
N: Weet je wat ziek is?   Do you know what ill is?
ERG: Ikke?   I?
N: Ja.   Yes.
ERG: Ik niet ziek.   I not ill.
(session 3)

(34) N: Je gaat niet met vakantie?   You are not going on vacation?
ERG: Wie? Ikke?   Who? I?
(session 22)

In object function the object pronoun *mij* ('me') is first used in session 3. However, only in cycle 2 is this form regularly used. Several times the form *mijn* ('my') is generalized in object function. Typical instances of this generalized use are given in sequences (35) and (36). The meaning of *mijn* ('my') is something like "to me".

(35) N: Als jij straks in 'n huis woont in   If you later on you live in a house in
nederland zou je dan verzekering   the netherlands, would you then take
nemen?   insurance?
ERG: Jawel.   Yes.
N: Voor 't huis?   For the house?

ERG:	Ja tuurlijk.	Yes of course.
N:	Waarom?	Why?
ERG:	Als mijn een dief komt denk ik he.	If my a thief comes I think right.
N:	Ja.	Yes.
ERG:	Dat klopt he?	That is right eh?
N:	Ja.	Yes.
ERG:	Als ik verzekeren^ dan ik moet geld verdienen.	If I insure^ then I must money make.

(session 16)

(36) N:	Als jij garage heeft.	If you have garage.
ERG:	Jawel.	Yes.
N:	Hoeveel mensen moeten daar komen?	How many people should come there?
ERG:	Als mijn tien man komt he.	If my ten man come right.
N:	Ja.	Yes.
ERG:	Als ik goed auto maken he.	If I make car good right.
<..>		
ERG:	Dan als/ alles mensen hier komen. Bij mijn garage komen.	Then if/ all people come here. Come to my garage.

(session 18)

One might speculate that the generalized use of the possessive pronoun *mijn* ('my') is an amalgamation of (1) a pronoun as object of preposition, e.g. *bij mij* ('with me'), and (2) an adnominal possessive pronoun, e.g. *mijn garage* ('my garage').

In possessive function Ergün in all cycles mostly uses the possessive pronoun *mijn* ('my'). It appears that this form in later sessions is regularly used together with the preposition *van* ('of'). Compare the typical use of *mijn* ('my') in sequences (37)-(40).

(37) ERG:	Mijn moeder ook niet werken.	My mother also not work.

(session 8)

(38) ERG:	Die mijn vriend zeggen mij.	That my friend say me.

(session 12)

(39) ERG:	Ja van mijn vriend zeggen.	Yes of my friend say.

(session 21)

(40) ERG:	Ik heb van mijn vrouw fabriek gewerk.	I have of my wife factory worked. < = my wife worked in a factory>

(session 27)

The use of *mijn* ('my') in a construction that will henceforth be referred to as "*van*-Pro-N" can in particular be found in cycle 3. One instance can be found in which Ergün generalizes the 2nd role pronoun *jouw* ('you') for 1st role reference. As can be seen in sequence (41) it concerns a repetition of the native interlocutor.

(41) N:	Maar wat zegt jouw vader dan?	But what does your father say then?
ERG:	Jouw vader niks drinken alcohol.	Your father nothing drink alcohol.

(session 18)

Finally a very peculiar circumscription can be noticed in session 21 with *zelf van mij baas* ('own of me boss') instead of standard *mijn eigen baas* ('my own boss').

1st role plural

In subject function plural references sporadically occur in cycles 1 and 2 with the standardlike use of the subject pronoun *wij* ('we'). Only in cycle 3 this form seems to have taken a steady place in the pronoun system. When almost identical sequences derived from different stages are compared it appears that in a number of instances in cycle 3 the plural pronoun *wij* ('we') is used where in cycles 1 and 2 the singular pronoun *ik* ('I') is used. Compare sequences (42) and (43) which are taken from the housing office play scene in sessions 6 and 24 respectively. The housing official is explaining to Ergün how long Ergün and his wife have to wait before they will be eligible for housing accommodation.

(42)	N:	Half jaartje.	Half a year.
	ERG:	Half jaar?	Half a year?
	N:	Ja.	Yes.
	ERG:	Ik wachten?	I wait?
	(session 6)		

(43)	N:	Maar dan moet je minstens een jaar wachten.	But then you will have to wait at least a year.
	ERG:	Drie jaar wachten?	Wait for three years?
	N:	< knikt >	< nods >
	ERG:	Dat kan. Ja wij moeten wachten.	That is possible. Yes we must wait.
	(session 24)		

In object function the form *ons* ('us') is occasionally used in a standardlike fashion from session 11 onwards. The subject pronoun *wij* ('we') is generalized and repaired once in object function:

(44)	ERG:	Hij is nou weg he.	He is gone now away right.
	N:	Ja.	Yes.
	ERG:	Hij moet zeggen tegen/ tegen wij/ ons.	He must say to/ to we/ us.
	N:	Tegen ons ja.	To us yes.
	ERG:	Dan moet "*Allaha ısmarladık*".	Then must "*Bye*".
	(session 20)		

In possessive function the pronoun *ons* ('our') is first tried out and used in session 8:

(45)	ERG:	Mijn/ mijn/ ons familie he heel groot.	My/ my/ our family eh very big.
	(session 8)		

It appears that *onze* ('us/our') is occasionally used in combination with the demonstrative pronoun *die* ('that') in pre- and post-position. Some examples are given in sequences (46) and (47).

(46)	ERG:	En dan uh vliegtuig.	And then er airplane.
	N:	Hm.	Um.
	ERG:	Turkije.	Turkey.
	N:	Ja.	Yes.
	ERG:	En dan ikke die onze terugkomen he.	And then I that our come back right.
		Die auto weet ik niet naam.	That car I do not know name.
	(session 11)		

(47)	N:	Je bent verhuisd.	You have moved.
	ERG:	Ja ik + heb/ die onze pension.	Yes I + have/ that our boarding house.
	N:	Ja.	Yes.
	ERG:	Die daar ook die turkse mensen	That there also those turkish people all
		allemaal blijven he.	stay right.
	(session 14)		

With respect to the use of the plural forms *ons* ('us/our') and *onze* ('us/our') the same development can be observed as was found earlier for singular reference. From session 17 onwards these forms are only used in "*van*-Pro-N" constructions. Sequences (48) and (49) give some examples.

(48)	ERG:	"*Was ist da los?*" Van onze fabriek alle	"*What is going on*" Of our factory all
		nederlandse jong he "*Was ist da los?*".	dutch boy eh "*What is going on?*".
	N:	Oja?	Really?
	ERG:	Ja alle turkse jong ook "*Was ist da	Yes all turkish boy also "*What is
		los?*".	going on?*".
	(session 17)		

(49)	ERG:	Rode eerste divisie. Witte eerste	Red first division. White first
		divisie. Ik weet ik niet. Maar	division. I do not know I. But
		van ons elftal vierde. <..>	of our team fourth. <..>
		Nou ik heb/ ik ben ziekenhuis geweest.	Now I have/ I have hospital been.
		Vier twee verloren. Als/ als ik/ als	Four two lost. If/ If I/ If
		van ons elftal wint	of our team wins
	N:	Ja.	Yes.
	ERG:	dan goed vierde, misschien tweede.	then good fourth, maybe second.
	(session 19)		

Finally, for 1st role reference a number of instances can be observed in which a singular form is repaired into a plural form:

(50)	ERG:	Zij is elke/ elke avond ik wij/ wij	She is every/ every evening I we/ we
		hebben vasten he.	have fast right.
	N:	Ja.	Yes.
	ERG:	Dan tien uur ik/ ik/ wij hebben eten.	Then ten o'clock I/ I/ we have eat.
	(session 22)		

(51)	ERG:	Ik heb die ankara dan mijn familie/	I have that ankara then my family/
		ons familie.	our family.
	(session 8)		

(52) ERG: Hij zegt "Ja uh rachid he".   He says "Yes er rachid eh".
     N: Ja.   Yes.
     ERG: "Die marokkaanse mensen nou feest".   "Those moroccan people now celebrate".
     N: Ja.   Yes.
     ERG: "Jullie niet?".   "You not?".
            "Nee jullie/ ik niet of bij ons niet".   "No you/ I don't or with us don't."
     (session 11)

Self-corrections in the other direction, that is from plural to singular, cannot be observed with Ergün.

2nd role reference

The form-function relationships of the pronouns which Ergün used for 2nd role reference are given in Table 5.5.

Table 5.5: Pronominal 2nd role reference by Ergün

CYCLE 1	s1	s2	s3	s4	s5	s6	s7	s8	s9	Total	English
Subject:											
Sg: u	-	-	-	3	-	-	-	6	-	9	you
je	-	-	-	1	-	-	2	2	-	5	you
jij	1	-	4	7	3	3	6	11	2	37	you
Pl: jullie	-	-	1	1	-	-	1	-	-	3	you
Object:											
Sg: jou	-	-	-	-	-	1	-	-	-	1	you
jij (=jou)	-	-	-	-	-	-	-	-	1	1	you
Possess:											
Sg: jouw X	-	-	-	-	-	-	1	-	-	1	your X
CYCLE 2	s10	s11	s12	s13	s14	s15	s16	s17	s18	Total	English
Subject:											
Sg: u	1	2	1	-	1	-	-	-	-	5	you
je	3	-	4	4	-	-	3	21	10	45	you
jij	2	-	6	2	5	1	6	31	17	70	you
Pl: jullie	1	2	1	-	1	-	-	-	-	5	you
Object:											
Sg: jou	-	-	-	1	3	1	-	7	1	13	you
Possess:											
Sg: jouw X	-	-	-	-	-	2	1	-	-	3	your X
CYCLE 3	s19	s20	s21	s22	s23	s24	s25	s26	s27	Total	English
Subject:											
Sg: u	-	-	-	-	5	-	-	1	4	10	you
je	-	5	2	1	-	-	8	36	16	68	you
jij	19	26	24	3	2	-	9	48	11	142	you
Pl: jullie	-	2	-	-	-	-	-	1	-	3	you
Object:											
Sg: jou	2	2	2	6	-	2	1	11	1	27	you
jij (=jou)	-	-	-	-	-	-	-	1	-	1	you
Possess:											
Sg: X van jou	-	-	-	-	-	-	-	-	1	1	X of you

2nd role singular

In subject function Ergün most commonly uses the subject pronoun *jij* ('you'). In contrast to Mahmut, Ergün also frequently uses the reduced subject pronoun *je* ('you') and the V-form *u* ('you'). In early sessions the reduced form *je* ('you') is most commonly used in formulaic expressions such as *weet je* ('you know'), *weet je wel* ('you know'), or *dankjewel* ('thank you'). In later sessions a more productive use of the reduced form can be noted. In early sessions Ergün prefers the full pronoun *jij* ('you'). Sequence (53) shows how a symptom of uncertainty on the part of Ergün after the use of the reduced form by the native speaker results in a reformulation with the full form. Also the native speaker adjusts to Ergün's preference for full forms.

(53)	N:	Hoe oud ben je?	How old are you?
	ERG:	Hoe oud ben jij?	How old are you?
	N:	Ben jij?	Are you?
	ERG:	Uh zeventien.	Er seventeen.
	(session 1)		

The V-form *u* ('you') is exclusively used in formulaic expressions such as *wat zegt u?* ('what do you say?'), *weet u wel* ('you know'), *Weet u ook niet* ('don't you know either') and *Wat blieft u?* ('pardon?'). The encoding of status through the V-form *u* ('you') is seldom taken up by Ergün (see sequence 54) and often leads to misunderstandings (see sequence 55).

(54)	ERG:	Goeiedag.	Hello.
	N:	Dag.	Hello.
	ERG:	Ik ben ergün.	I am ergün.
	N:	Josee jansen, gaat u zitten.	Josee jansen, take a seat.
	ERG:	Die heb je werk?	That do you have work?
	(session 12)		

(55)	N:	Ja heeft u al 's eerder uh ingepakt?	Yes have you done any packing before?
	ERG:	Welk?	What?
	N:	Heeft u al eens eerder dit soort werk gedaan?	Have you done this kind of work before?
	ERG:	Ja.	Yes.
	N:	Heeft u al 's gewerkt?	Have you worked before?
	ERG:	Ja.	Yes.
	N:	Ja hier in nederland?	Yes here in the netherlands?
	ERG:	Ja.	Yes.
	N:	Als wat?	As what?
	ERG:	Wat?	What?
	N:	Wat voor werk?	What kind of work?
	ERG:	Wat voor werk?	What kind of work?
	N:	Ja.	Yes.
	ERG:	Uh pro/ wacht even \ [ja]	Er/ pro/ wait a minute \ [yes]
	N:	\nee u [ja]	\no you [yes]
	N:	heeft gewerkt?	has worked?
	ERG:	+	+

N:	In nederland	In the netherlands.
ERG:	U geeft werk?	You give work?
N:	Ja.	Yes.
ERG:	Uh.	Er.
N:	Is dit de eerste/ het eerste werk?	Is this the first/ the first job?
ERG:	Ja eerste werk.	Yes first job.
	(session 3)	

In object function the form *jou* ('you') is first used in session 6. An example is given in sequence (56).

(56)	ERG:	Hij komt trouwen ge/ zien.	He comes to marry se/ seen.
	N:	Oja?	Really?
	ERG:	Ik zeggen/ voor jou zeggen.	I say/ for you say.
	N:	Ja dat heb je verteld ja?	Yes I you told that right?
		(session 13)	

Ergün twice generalizes the subject pronoun *jij* ('you') in object function (see sequence 57). This is much less than with Mahmut.

(57)	ERG:	Wie zegt dat jij?	Who says that you?
		(session 26)	

In possessive function only a few instances of singular reference can be observed with Ergün. The forms *jouw* ('your') and *jou* ('you') are used standardlike. There are no generalizations.

2nd role plural

As can be seen in Table 5.5 plural references only occur in subject function. The plural form *jullie* ('you') is used regularly from session 3 onwards. A number of instances can be noted in which the singular subject pronoun *jij* ('you') is repaired into the plural pronoun *jullie* ('you'):

(58)	ERG:	En dan een maand. Hoeveel kosten/ betaal jij/ jullie?	And then one month. How much cost/ you pay/ you?
		(session 3)	

(59)	ERG:	Dan veelste probleem jongen. Echt. "Jij moet/ jullie moeten met/ met mij komen" zegt politie.	Than much too problem boy. Really. "You must/ you must come with/ with me come" says police officer.
		(session 26)	

5.3.3 MOHAMED

1st role reference

The pronominal form-functions for 1st role reference occurring in the 27 sessions which took place with Mohamed are given in Table 5.6.

1st role singular

In subject function Mohamed frequently uses the subject pronouns *ik* ('I') and *ikke* ('I'). As was observed with Mahmut and Ergün, these forms are frequent particularly in early sessions in formulaic expressions, e.g. *ik weet ik niet* ('I don't know I') and *snap ik niet* ('I don't understand'). Moreover, *ik* ('I') and *ikke* ('I') are often used as repair requests.

In object function the object pronoun *mij* ('me') is used already in session 2. Two instances can be found in which Mohamed generalizes the possessive pronoun *mijn* ('my') in object function (see sequences 60 and 61).

Table 5.6: Pronominal 1st role reference by Mohamed (cycles 1 and 2)

CYCLE 1	s1	s2	s3	s4	s5	s6	s7	s8	s9	Total	English
Subject:											
Sg: ik	48	20	160	163	29	73	26	73	49	641	I
ikke	6	-	3	6	1	-	-	-	-	16	I
Pl: wij	-	4	-	4	5	-	-	2	6	21	we
Object:											
Sg: mij	-	4	4	8	7	3	2	1	16	45	me
mijn (= mij)	-	-	-	-	-	-	-	-	1	1	my (= me)
Pl: ons	1	2	-	-	-	-	-	1	-	4	us
Possess:											
Sg: mijn X	2	1	8	1	4	2	3	1	1	23	my X
X van mijn Y	7	-	-	-	-	-	-	-	-	7	X of my Y
van mijn X	-	-	1	-	-	-	-	-	-	1	of my X
mij X (= mijn)	2	-	3	-	1	7	5	5	5	28	me X (= my)
van mij	-	-	-	-	1	-	-	-	1	2	of me
X van mij	-	-	-	-	2	-	-	-	-	2	X of me
jouw X (= mijn)	-	-	-	-	-	1	-	-	-	1	your (= my)
Pl: ons X	-	-	-	-	2	-	-	-	-	2	our X
X van ons	-	-	-	-	-	1	-	-	-	1	X of us
CYCLE 2	s10	s11	s12	s13	s14	s15	s16	s17	s18	Total	English
Subject:											
Sg: ik	80	99	111	141	135	104	174	197	79	1120	I
ikke	3	-	-	8	-	-	2	1	-	14	I
Pl: wij	5	6	3	12	20	3	49	26	1	125	we
Object											
Sg: mij	3	3	2	5	8	1	12	15	5	54	me
Pl: ons	1	-	-	4	3	-	7	1	-	16	us
wij (= ons)	-	-	-	4	1	-	-	-	-	5	we (= us)
Possess:											
Sg: mijn X	20	2	2	6	2	-	1	20	-	53	my X
m'n X	-	-	-	1	-	-	-	1	-	2	my X
X van mijn Y	1	-	-	-	-	-	-	-	-	1	X of my Y
mij X (= mijn)	2	7	4	-	9	20	10	3	11	66	me X (= my)
van mij	-	-	-	-	-	-	1	1	1	3	of me
X van mij	-	-	-	-	-	-	1	-	-	1	X of me
X van mij Y	-	3	-	-	-	-	-	-	-	3	X of me Y
Pl: onze X	-	-	1	-	-	-	-	-	-	1	our X
X van ons	-	2	-	-	-	-	-	-	-	2	X of us

Table 5.6 (cont.): Pronominal 1st role reference by Mohamed (cycle 3)

CYCLE 3	s19	s20	s21	s22	s23	s24	s25	s26	s27	Total	English
Subject:											
Sg: ik	80	129	52	149	176	58	154	106	61	965	I
ikke	-	-	-	1	-	-	-	-	-	1	I
Pl: wij	18	3	-	21	9	2	33	26	2	114	we
Object:											
Sg: mij	18	3	1	7	15	3	12	10	8	77	me
mijn (=mij)	-	1	-	-	-	-	-	-	-	1	my (=me)
Pl: ons	1	4	-	3	3	-	12	6	1	30	us
Poss:											
Sg: mijn X	-	-	-	1	2	-	2	2	-	7	my X
mij X (=mijn)	11	2	1	6	26	3	21	16	6	92	me X (=my)
X van mij	1	1	-	2	1	-	1	1	4	11	X of me
Pl: ons X	-	-	-	5	2	-	1	9	1	18	our X
van ons X	-	-	-	-	1	-	-	-	-	1	of our X
X van ons	-	-	-	-	-	-	-	-	1	1	X of us

(60) MOH: Nee die moet uh bij mijn blijven.   No that must er stay with my.
     (session 9)

(61) MOH: Moet saudia arabia geef mijn 'n uh benzine.   Must saudia arabia give my a er petrol.
     (session 20)

In possessive function Mohamed uses the possessive pronoun *mijn* ('my') right from the start. Also, two instances of the reduced possessive pronoun *m'n* ('my') can be observed in cycle 2 (see sequence 62).

(62) MOH: Ja moet ik m'n eten maken.   Yes must make I my food.
     (session 13)

The object pronoun *mij* ('me') is frequently generalized in possessive function, in particular in adnominal position. This form also occurs in combination with the preposition *van* ('of') in a "N-*van*-Pro" construction:

(63) MOH: Deze foto ook in spanje in sebastian.   This photo also in spain in sebastian.
     N: Ja.   Yes.
     MOH: Ik met uh vriend van mij. Portugal.   I with er friend of mine. Portugal.
     (session 23)

One instance of pronoun reversal can be found in which the 2nd role form *jouw* ('your') is generalized for 1st role reference:

(64) MOH: Zeshonderd is uh duur uh voor mij.   Six hundred is er expensive er for me.
     Ik uh te/ ik krijgt zes met uh jouw   I er te/ I gets six with er your
     moeske uh zeventienhondervijftig.   girl er seventeen hundred and fifty
     N: Ja.   Yes.
     MOH: Huis + zeshonderd.   House + six hundred.
     (session 6)

1st role plural

In contrast to Ergün and Mahmut, Mohamed from a very early stage onwards regularly uses plural pronouns with 1st role reference (see Table 5.6).

In subject function the subject pronoun *wij* ('we') is used from session 2 onwards. The first appearance of this form is accompanied by a shift to Moroccan Arabic as can be seen in sequence (65).

(65) MOH:	Half dag uh + *ḥna mši-na*. Wij gaan naar een garage	Half a day er + *we went*. We go to a garage
N:	Ja.	yes
MOH:	van uh renault.	of er renault.
(session 2)		

In object function the form *ons* ('us') is used for the first time in session 1. However, it is not until cycle 2 that this form occurs regularly. Mohamed also generalizes the subject pronoun *wij* ('we') in object function. In session 13 this generalized use is always preceded by the preposition *bij* ('with/at'). Some examples are given in sequences (66) and (67).

(66) MOH:	Daar alleen maar met een 'n mens dood. Wij doen die mens in stof.	There only with one a man dead. We put that man in cloth.
N:	Ja.	Yes.
MOH:	Stof.	Cloth.
N:	Ja.	Yes.
MOH:	Dan in de grond he.	Then in the ground right.
N:	Ja.	Yes.
MOH:	Hier moet in doos van hout he. En dan moet uh ja.	Here must in box of wood right. And then must er well.
N:	In wat in?	In what in?
MOH:	In dozen van hout.	In boxes of wood.
N:	Ja dozen van hout ja.	Yes boxes of wood right.
MOH:	Bij wij niet he. Hier met kleren/ moet met kleren.	Not with we eh. Here with clothes/ must with clothes.
N:	Ja.	Yes.
MOH:	Bij wij niet.	Not with we.
N:	Nee.	No.
MOH:	Bij moslim is niet.	With muslim is not.
(session 13)		

(67) MOH:	Ja kan jullie nou doen 'n feest alleen maar voor wij twee en mij oom.	Yes you can now do a party alone but for we two and me uncle.
(session 14)		

In possessive function the pronouns *ons* ('our/us') and *onze* ('our') are used occasionally in cycles 1 and 2. In cycle 1 a more frequent and regular use can be noticed.

2nd role reference

The form-function relationships of the pronouns which Mohamed has used for 2nd role reference are given in Table 5.7.

Table 5.7: Pronominal 2nd role reference by Mohamed

CYCLE 1	s1	s2	s3	s4	s5	s6	s7	s8	s9	Total	English
Subject:											
Sg: je	-	-	-	-	-	-	-	1	1	2	you
jij	2	2	23	13	1	31	7	18	16	113	you
Pl: jullie	-	-	9	1	-	4	-	-	2	16	you
Object:											
Sg: jou	-	-	-	-	-	6	-	-	-	6	you
Pl: jullie	-	-	1	1	-	2	-	-	-	4	you
Possess:											
Sg: jouw X	-	-	-	-	-	1	2	-	-	3	your X
Pl: jouw X (=jullie)	-	-	-	1	-	-	-	-	-	1	your X

CYCLE 2	s10	s11	s12	s13	s14	s15	s16	s17	s18	Total	English
Subject:											
Sg: je	3	6	1	3	3	1	9	10	1	37	you
jij	9	33	13	52	25	2	18	80	15	247	you
Pl: jullie	-	5	1	1	2	-	4	-	1	14	you
Object:											
Sg: jou	-	3	3	2	-	2	3	7	2	22	you
Pl: jullie	1	5	4	3	-	3	3	-	2	21	you
Possess:											
Sg: jouw X	-	-	-	-	2	-	-	1	1	4	your X
van jou	-	-	-	-	-	-	-	2	-	2	of you
je X	-	-	-	-	-	-	1	2	-	3	your X
jij X (=jouw)	-	3	-	-	-	-	-	-	-	3	you X

CYCLE 3	s19	s20	s21	s22	s23	s24	s25	s26	s27	Total	English
Subject:											
Sg: je	3	15	1	8	5	1	16	17	1	67	you
jij	17	53	39	23	9	5	21	36	19	222	you
Pl: jullie	-	4	-	-	1	1	4	17	3	30	you
Object:											
Sg: jou	2	5	3	3	3	1	4	7	1	29	you
Pl: jullie	-	-	2	4	1	1	5	3	-	16	you
Possess:											
Sg: jouw X	1	4	6	1	-	-	3	3	-	18	your X
X van jou	-	-	-	-	-	-	-	-	1	1	X of you
je X	-	2	-	-	-	-	-	-	-	2	your X
Pl: jullie X	-	-	-	-	-	-	-	1	1	2	your X
jouw X (=jullie)	-	-	-	-	-	-	-	1	-	1	your X

2nd role singular

In subject function the full subject pronoun *jij* ('you') is used from session 1 onwards. Mohamed first uses the reduced form *je* ('you'), in session 8, and afterwards keeps on using it frequently. However, the form often occurs in formulaic expressions like *snap je* ('do you understand') and *weet je* ('do you know'). The same observation for the use of *je* ('you') was made earlier for Ergün. Note that, in contrast to Ergün, Mohamed never uses the V-form *u* ('you'), not even in formulaic expressions.

In object function the pronoun *jou* ('you') appears in session 6; it is, however, not used regularly until cycles 2 and 3.

In possessive function the pronoun *jouw* ('your') also appears for the first time in session 6. Mohamed also generalizes the subject pronoun *jij* ('you') in possessive function. This use can be observed in session 11 (see sequence 68).

(68)	MOH:	Als jij man auto kopen of uh + + als jij man jarig he.	If you husband buys car or er + + if you man has birthday right.
	N:	Ja ja.	Yes yes.
	MOH:	En dan wij zeggen [proficiat]	And then we say [congratulations]
	N:	[proficiat] ja.	[congratulations] yes.
	MOH:	Ja als jij man auto kopen he	Yes if you husband buy car right
	N:	Ja.	Yes.
	MOH:	kan ook.	also possible.
	(session 11)		

From session 14 onwards the pronoun *jouw* ('your') is regularly used in possessive function. Occasionally, Mohamed uses the reduced form *je* ('your'):

(69)	MOH:	Ja die/ die vrienden familie niet als je ouders he.	Yes those/ those friends family not like your parents right.
	N:	Ja ja.	Yes yes.
	MOH:	Je ouders kan voor jou zorgen.	Your parents can take care of you.
	(session 17)		

2nd role plural

For 2nd role plural reference Mohamed uses the pronoun *jullie* ('you') standard-like in subject and object function as early as the first cycle. It is not until the end of the third cycle that this form is used in possessive function. Mohamed's generalization of the singular pronoun *jouw* ('you') for plural reference is striking. The pertinent instances are given in sequences (70) and (71).

(70)	MOH:	Ik uh + in de feest jouw feest deze kerst uh kerst uh + allemaal die bar en disco dicht.	I er + in the party your party these x-mas er x-mas er + all those bar and disco closed.
	(session 4)		

(71)	MOH:	Ja jullie mogen bij jouw ouder/ jullie ouders alles doen ja.	Yes you allowed at your parent/ your parents do everything right.
	(session 26)		

Finally, there are a number of self-repairs which almost exclusively come down to correcting the singular form into plural:

(72)	MOH:	Als jij/ jullie niet wilt uh + + geef een huis^ snapt?	If you/ you not want er + + give a house^ you understand?
	N:	Hm hm.	Uh-huh.
	MOH:	Dan + dan ik/ ik kom uh woont bij jullie.	Then + then I/ I come er lives with you.
	(session 6)		

5.3.4 FATIMA

1st role reference

The pronominal form-functions for 1st role reference occurring in the 27 sessions which took place with Fatima are given in Table 5.8.

1st role singular

In subject function the subject pronouns *ik* ('I') and *ikke* ('I') are used as early as the first sessions. Compared to Mahmut and Ergün, Fatima far less frequently uses these forms in formulaic expressions and as repair requests.

In object function the object pronoun *mij* ('me') is used from session 5 onwards. An example is given in sequence (73).

(73)	N:	'n flat.	A flat.
	FAT:	Ja.	Yes.
	N:	Voor zeshonderd gulden + daar kan ik misschien over drie maanden aankomen.	Voor six hundred guilders + I may be able to get that (for you) in three months.
	FAT:	Zestien guld?	Sixteen guild?
	N:	Voor zeshonderd gulden.	For six hundred guilders.
	FAT:	Nee + veel voor mij.	No + a lot for me.
	(session 7)		

There are a number of instances in which Fatima generalizes the subject pronoun *ik* ('I') in object function (see sequences 74 and 75 for some examples).

(74)	FAT:	Afspraak ik makkelijk.	Appointment I easy.
	(session 7)		

(75)	FAT:	Haar man	Her husband
	N:	Ja.	Yes.
	FAT:	doen voor ik + broer zus alles.	do for I + brother sister everything.
	N:	Oja.	Really.
	FAT:	Mij vader niet doen.	Me father do not.
	(session 16)		

In possessive function Fatima most commonly uses the possessive pronoun *mijn* ('my'). The object pronoun *mij* ('me') is regularly generalized in possessive function (see sequences 76 and 77).

(76)	FAT:	Mij man woon die breda.	Me husband lives that breda.
	(session 6)		

(77)	FAT:	Maar moeilijk voor uh mij zoon.	But difficult for er me son.
	(session 24)		

Fatima sometimes uses the pronouns *ik* ('I') and *mijn* ('my') together for expressing possession. Some examples are given in sequences (78) and (79).

Table 5.8: Pronominal 1st role reference by Fatima

CYCLE 1	s1	s2	s3	s4	s5	s6	s7	s8	s9	Total	English
Subject:											
Sg: ik	12	6	79	13	23	35	49	42	26	285	I
ikke	-	2	-	-	-	-	-	-	-	2	I
Pl: jullie (=wij)	1	-	-	-	-	-	2	-	-	3	you (=we)
Object:											
Sg: mij	-	-	-	-	1	4	3	-	1	9	me
ik (=mij)	-	-	1	-	-	-	1	-	-	2	I (=me)
Possess:											
Sg: mijn X	-	3	-	1	18	5	1	17	10	55	my X
ik mijn X	2	-	4	-	2	-	-	1	1	10	I my X
X van mijn X	-	-	-	-	5	-	-	-	-	5	X of my X
mij X (=mijn)	-	-	6	-	-	2	5	2	5	20	me X (=my)
ik mij X	-	-	1	-	-	-	-	1	-	2	I me X
X mij	-	-	1	-	-	-	-	-	-	1	X me
van mijn (=mij)	-	-	-	-	1	-	-	-	-	1	of my
jouw X (=mijn X)	-	-	-	-	-	1	1	-	1	3	your X (=my)

CYCLE 2	s10	s11	s12	s13	s14	s15	s16	s17	s18	Total	English
Subject:											
Sg: ik	8	15	33	59	23	48	33	68	43	330	I
ikke	1	1	1	2	-	-	-	4	-	9	I
Pl: wij	2	2	1	-	-	-	-	1	-	6	we
Object:											
Sg: mij	1	-	1	3	2	7	7	6	6	33	me
ik (=mij)	-	-	-	-	-	1	1	-	-	2	I (=me)
Possess:											
Sg: mijn X	2	-	6	27	6	3	6	2	2	54	my X
X van mijn X	-	-	-	3	-	-	1	-	-	4	X of my X
mij X (=mijn)	-	-	2	-	-	-	5	2	-	9	me X (=my)
X van mij X	-	-	-	-	-	-	1	-	-	1	X of me X
jouw X (=mijn)	-	-	1	3	2	-	-	1	-	7	your X (=my)

CYCLE 3	s19	s20	s21	s22	s23	s24	s25	s26	s27	Total	English
Subject:											
Sg: ik	31	61	27	77	17	41	46	59	36	395	I
ikke	9	1	-	1	-	-	-	-	-	11	I
Pl: wij	-	-	-	-	-	4	2	-	1	7	we
Object:											
Sg: mij	1	2	1	-	4	6	2	10	3	29	me
Pl: ons	1	-	-	-	-	-	-	1	2	4	us
Possess:											
Sg: mijn X	7	8	-	3	3	16	3	2	3	45	my X
mij X (=mijn)	-	8	4	1	-	1	-	-	1	15	me X (=my)
X van mij X	-	1	-	-	-	-	-	-	-	1	X of me X

(78) FAT: Ik mijn vriend   I my friend
      N: Ja.   Yes.
      FAT: hier werken.   work here.
      (session 3)

(79) FAT: Die altijd ziek. Niet goed.   That always ill. Not good.
               Ik mijn vader ook uh veel *cigare*.   I my father also er much *cigars*.
      (session 5)

Such adjacent pairs are only found in cycle 1. Moreover, the forms *ik* ('I') and *mijn* ('my') are used adjacently to *man* ('husband'), *vader* ('father'), *vriend* ('friend'), and *broer* ('brother'), which are all kinship/friendship terms. It is a reasonable conjecture that these pairs concern "unanalysed wholes" (formulaic expressions).

Fatima also generalizes the 2nd role pronoun *jouw* ('your') for 1st role possessive reference. The occurrences are mostly the result of immediate repeats of a preceding N-utterance (see sequence 80).

(80) FAT: Mijn familie niet goed.   My family not good.
      N: Jouw familie niet?   Your family not?
      FAT: Ja jouw familie niet.   Yes your family not.
      (session 7)

However, also non-repeated occurrences of pronoun reversal with *jouw* ('your') can be noted (see sequence 81).

(81) N: Ze werken niet in marokko?   They do not work in morocco?
      FAT: Nee moet ik hier uh jouw man hier   No do I have to here er your husband
               ander twee uh kinder hier. Twee niet   here other two er kids here. Two not
               goed.   good.
      (session 9)

The generalized use of *jouw* ('your') for 1st role reference can only be observed in cycles 1 and 2.

1st role plural

For plural references in subject function Fatima uses the subject pronoun *wij* ('we') in cycles 2 and 3. This standardlike use is preceded in cycle 1 by a generalized use of the 2nd role plural pronoun *jullie* ('you'):

(82) FAT: Jullie [ruzie maak]   You [fight]
      N: [ja in Marokko] ja + wij.   [yes in Morocco] yes + we.
      FAT: Jij uh veel geld. Ik kan niet.   You er a lot of money. I cannot.
               Ik moet naar politie.   I must go to police.
      <.>
      FAT: Jij geld met uh politie of uh die/   You money with er police or er that/
               jullie zeg met uh *qaḍi*.   you call it er *judge*.
      N: Rechter/ ['n rechter]   Judge [a pidge]
      FAT: [*wakil d-ula*] ja.   [*counsel for the prosecution*] yes.
      (session 7)

In object function the pronoun *ons* ('us') can be observed in cycle 3. This form is always used after the preposition *bij* ('at'):

(83) N: Maar dit doen wij als je weggaat.   But this is what we do when you leave.
              <gebaart>   <gestures>
      FAT: Nee bij ons zo. <gebaart>   No with us like this. <gestures>
      (session 26)

2nd role reference

The form-function relationships of the pronouns which Fatima used for 2nd role reference are given in Table 5.9.

Table 5.9: Pronominal 2nd role reference by Fatima

CYCLE 1	s1	s2	s3	s4	s5	s6	s7	s8	s9	Total	English
Subject:											
Sg: jij	3	-	7	1	5	3	27	12	-	58	you
Pl: jullie	-	-	-	-	2	-	1	-	-	3	you
Object:											
Sg: jij (=jou)	-	-	-	-	-	-	1	-	-	1	you
jou	-	-	-	-	-	-	3	-	-	3	you
Pl: jullie	-	-	-	-	-	-	-	2	-	2	you
CYCLE 2	s10	s11	s12	s13	s14	s15	s16	s17	s18	Total	English
Subject:											
Sg: jij	3	4	6	4	2	5	9	12	5	50	you
je	-	-	-	-	-	-	-	1	-	1	you
Pl: jullie	1	-	1	1	-	-	-	-	1	4	you
Object:											
Sg: jou	1	-	-	-	-	2	-	1	-	4	you
jij (=jou)	-	-	-	-	-	-	-	1	1	2	you
Possess:											
Sg: jouw X	-	-	-	-	1	-	-	1	-	2	your X
CYCLE 3	s19	s20	s21	s22	s23	s24	s25	s26	s27	Total	English
Subject:											
Sg: jij	2	5	5	7	5	4	1	19	-	48	you
Pl: jullie	2	-	4	2	-	-	1	1	2	12	you
Object:											
Sg: jou	1	-	-	-	-	1	-	-	1	3	you
jij (=jou)	-	-	-	-	-	1	-	-	-	1	you
Pl: jullie	-	-	-	-	-	-	-	-	2	2	you
Possess:											
Sg: jouw X	-	2	2	-	2	1	-	1	-	8	your X

2nd role singular

In subject function the full pronoun *jij* ('you') is used regularly from session 1 onwards. In session 13 the reduced pronoun *je* ('you') occurs in the formulaic expression *dankjewel* ('thank you').

In object function the standardlike use of the object pronoun *jou* ('you') can be observed regularly (see sequence 84).

(84) FAT: Jij zien die huis misschien goed   You see that house maybe good
           voor jou of niet.   for you or not.
      (session 7)

However, Fatima also generalizes the subject pronoun *jij* ('you') in object function (see sequence 85).

(85) FAT: Zeg van charlo "Ik uh + heeft uh   Say about charlo "I er + has er
           goeie praat voor jij".   good talk for you".
      (session 18)

In possessive function the possessive pronoun *jouw* ('your') is used regularly from session 14 onwards. Sequence (86) gives an example of this standardlike use.

(86) FAT: Mij broer ook heeft 'n dochter.   Me brother also has a daughter.
     N: Ja.   Yes.
     FAT: Jouw haar/ zelf jouw haar.   Your hair/ same your hair.
      (session 20)

2nd role plural

For plural reference Fatima uses the pronoun *jullie* ('you') in subject function regularly from session 5 onwards (see sequence 87). A few times this form is also used in object function (see sequence 88).

(87) FAT: Jullie heeft uh bus?   You have er bus?
      (session 12)

(88) FAT: Niet allemaal mensen ook naar met uh   Not all people also to with er church
           kerk uh bij jullie niet vijf dag met kerk. er with you not five day with church.
      (session 8)

5.3.5   THE SHADOW INFORMANTS

The observations for the core informants discussed in the preceding sections will be checked against empirical data derived from the shadow informants. Table 5.10 gives a simple frequency list of the pronominal forms used by the shadow informants. Some information on pronoun use by the shadow informants cannot immediately be derived from the empirical data presented in this table. Thus for example, it cannot be decided whether *jullie* ('you') is used in subject, object or possessive function. In addition, it is important to note that part of the information is not reliable, such as, for example, the possessive pronoun *jouw* ('your') which was sometimes incorrectly transcribed as the object pronoun *jou* ('you'). In practical terms, it was much too time-consuming to check the pronoun use by the shadow informants on unreliabilities in the same way as was done for the core informants. Bearing in mind the traps, however, these empirical data still provide interesting cross-learner evidence.

Table 5.10: Overview 1st/2nd role pronouns used by the shadow informants

	Osman (57,495)	Abdullah (32,648)	Hassan (61,312)	Husseyn (65,983)	Total	English
ik	2,031	388	378	2,371	5,168	I
ikke	97	24	12	51	184	I
wij	192	88	118	15	413	we
we	7	1	20	69	97	we
mij	99	77	524	521	1,221	me
ons	56	16	72	15	159	us/our
onze	23	19	-	2	44	us/our
mijn	318	122	144	122	706	my
m'n	-	2	2	-	4	my
jij	529	212	328	412	1,481	you
je	119	84	422	289	914	you(r)
u	10	31	4	27	72	you
jullie	63	80	22	57	222	you(r)
jou	66	16	59	34	175	you
jouw	37	2	98	85	222	your
uw	-	1	-	-	1	your
Total	3,647	1,163	2,203	4,070	11,083	

5.4 RESULTS

In Section 5.1 a number of predictions were formulated which will be tested on the basis of the pronominal preferences of the core and shadow informants. For one aspect of pronoun use a remarkable difference between native varieties and learner varieties of Dutch seems to emerge: emphasis. The following prediction was formulated:

P1   Full forms are acquired before reduced forms

This prediction derives from the systematic division of full-reduced pairs within the Dutch pronoun system (see Table 4.1 in Chapter 4). Within each pair the reduced member is used more frequently in spoken native Dutch than the full member. The use of pronouns in our learner varieties clearly confirms prediction 1. In the pronoun profiles of the four core informants discussed in Section 5.3 an overwhelming dominance of full forms can be observed in all cycles. Occasionally, however, reduced forms can be found. Especially in the early sessions these forms are used in formulaic expressions. In the L2-Dutch varieties of our shadow informants (see Table 5.10) full forms are also generally more frequent than reduced forms. In fact, the only reduced forms that can be found are *we* ('we'), *je* ('you'), and infrequently *m'n* ('my').

From the pronoun profiles of the core informants presented in the previous sections it is possible to make a more or less accurate judgement about the time at which a specific pronoun is acquired by each of the informants. As a whole this reveals that from the moment a pronoun is used standardlike, it has also been acquired. In other words: the orders of acquisition can be derived from the moment of the first standardlike and non-formulaic appearance of a pronoun. These occurrences have also been selected for the shadow informants: for each pronoun a form-function analysis was carried out until the first moment of standardlike appearance was found. The acquisition orders of pronouns within the 1st and 2nd role paradigms are given in Tables 5.11 and 5.12 respectively.

Table 5.11: Order of acquisition 1st role pronouns (standardlike use)

	Turkish Mahmut	Ergün	Osman	Abdullah	Moroccan Mohamed	Fatima	Hassan	Husseyn
CYCLE 1								
s1	ik	ik	ik	ik	ik	ik	ik	ik
	-	-	-	mijn	mijn	-	mijn	wij
	-	-	-	-	ons (o)	-	mij	we
s2	-	mijn	-	-	mij	mijn	-	mijn
	-	-	-	-	wij	-	-	-
s3	-	mij	mijn	mij	-	-	-	mij
	-	wij	-	-	-	-	-	-
s4	mijn	-	-	wij	-	-	m'n	-
s5	-	-	mij	-	ons (p)	mij	-	-
s6	mij	-	ons (p)	-	-	-	ons (o)	-
s7	-	-	wij	-	-	-	wij	-
s8	-	ons (p)	-	m'n	-	-	-	-
s9	-	-	we	-	-	-	-	ons (o)
CYCLE 2								
s10	-	-	-	onze (p)	-	wij	ons (p)	onze (p)
	-	-	-	-	-	-	we	ons (p)
s11	-	ons (o)	-	we	-	-	-	-
	-	-	-	ons (o+p)	-	-	-	-
s12	-	onze (p)	-	-	onze (p)	-	-	-
s13	-	-	onze (p)	-	m'n	-	-	-
s14	-	-	-	-	-	-	-	-
s15	-	-	ons (o)	-	-	-	-	-
s16	wij	-	-	-	-	-	-	-
s17	-	-	-	-	-	-	-	-
s18	-	-	-	-	-	-	-	-
CYCLE 3								
s19	-	-	-	-	-	ons (o)	-	-
s20	-	-	-	-	-	-	-	-
s21	-	-	-	-	-	-	-	-
s22	-	-	-	-	-	-	-	-
s23	-	-	-	-	-	-	-	-
s24	-	-	-	-	-	-	-	-
s25	ons (o)	-	-	-	-	-	-	-
s26	-	-	-	-	-	-	-	-
s27	-	-	-	-	-	-	-	-

(s = subject; o = object; p = possessive)

Table 5.12: Order of acquisition 2nd role pronouns (standardlike use)

	Turkish Mahmut	Ergün	Osman	Abdullah	Moroccan Mohamed	Fatima	Hassan	Husseyn
CYCLE 1								
s1	-	jij	u	jij	jij	jij	jij	-
	-	-	-	u	-	-	-	-
s2	-	-	jij	je (o)	-	-	jou	jij
	-	-	-	-	-	-	-	jou
	-	-	-	-	-	-	-	je (s)
s3	jij	jullie (s)	jou	-	jullie (s+o)	-	je (s)	jullie (s)
	-	-	-	-	-	-	-	u (s)
s4	-	je (s)	jullie (s)	-	-	-	jouw	-
	-	u (s)	-	-	-	-	-	-
s5	-	-	jullie (o)	je (s)	-	jullie (s)	-	-
s6	-	jou	-	-	jou	-	-	jouw
	-	-	-	-	jouw	-	-	-
s7	-	jouw	jouw	jou	-	jou	-	-
s8	-	-	-	jullie (s)	je (s)	jullie (o)	jullie (s)	-
s9	-	-	-	-	-	-	-	-
CYCLE 2								
s10	-	-	jullie (p)	jouw	-	-	-	-
s11	jullie (s)	-	je (s)	-	-	-	u (o)	-
s12	-	-	-	-	-	-	u (s)	-
	-	-	-	-	-	-	jullie (o)	-
s13	-	-	-	jullie (o)	-	je (o)	-	-
s14	je (s)	-	-	-	-	jouw	-	jullie (o)
s15	-	-	-	uw	-	-	-	-
s16	-	-	-	je (p)	je (p)	-	-	-
s17	jouw	-	-	-	-	je (s)	-	-
s18	-	-	-	-	-	-	-	-
CYCLE 3								
s19	-	-	-	-	-	-	-	-
s20	-	-	-	-	-	-	-	-
s21	u (s)	-	-	jullie (p)	-	-	-	je (p)
s22	-	-	-	-	-	-	-	-
s23	-	-	-	-	-	-	-	-
s24	-	-	-	-	-	-	-	-
s25	jou	-	-	-	-	-	-	-
s26	-	-	-	-	jullie (p)	-	-	-
s27	-	-	-	-	-	-	-	-

(s = subject; o = object; p = possessive)

In the next subsections our earlier predictions will be tested against the available data base. Hereby only the full forms are considered. There are good reasons for not taking reduced forms into account in testing the remaining predictions. Firstly, they are remarkably infrequent. With the shadow informants a number of occurrences can be found. However, one should be more careful in interpreting their data. Secondly, the reduced forms appear to occur in formulaic expressions.

The predictions will be tested for the standardlike use of pronouns on the basis of the order of acquisition that emerges as presented in Tables 5.11 and 5.12. Next, where relevant, the generalized use of the pronouns will be taken into account.

5.4.1 ROLE

P2   1st role reference is acquired before 2nd role reference

The results of testing this prediction on the basis of the first standardlike use of the pronouns are given in Table 5.13. The following conventions are used: "+ +" indicates that the prediction is confirmed, "– –" that it is contradicted (in fact the reverse tendency may occur), "+–" indicates that the corresponding 1st and 2nd role pronouns are acquired simultaneously, and "··" indicates lack of evidence (i.e. no instances can be found).

Table 5.13: Testing the order of acquisition of 1st role vs. 2nd role pronouns

P2	1st role	before	2nd role	Turkish				Moroccan			
				Mah.	Erg.	Osm.	Abd.	Moh.	Fat.	Has.	Hus.
	ik	before	jij	+ +	··	+ +	··	··	··	··	+ +
	mij	before	jou	+ +	+ +	– –	+ +	+ +	+ +	+ +	– –
	mijn	before	jouw	+ +	+ +	+ +	+ +	+ +	+ +	+ +	+ +
	wij	before	jullie (s)	– –	+ –	– –	+ +	+ +	– –	+ +	+ +
	ons (o)	before	jullie (o)	+ +	+ +	– –	+ +	– –	– –	+ +	+ +
	ons/ze (p)	before	jullie (p)	··	+ +	+ +	+ +	+ +	··	+ +	+ +

The order of acquisition of some corresponding 1st/2nd role pronouns does not confirm prediction 2. As a whole, however, 1st role pronouns are acquired before 2nd role pronouns.

With respect to generalized use of 1st/2nd role pronouns in their speech role function, the following prediction was formulated:

P3   There will be no instances of pronoun reversal

One would not expect to find instances of pronoun reversal in the language acquisition processes of adults, because they are mature learners with an L1-based awareness that 1st role and 2nd role pronouns have a basic reference point, i.e. that they have to be understood and used relatively to the point of view of the speaker. The instances of pronoun reversal found in the L2-Dutch varieties of our core informants are given in Table 5.14. 1st/2nd role pronoun reversal was indeed almost non-existent: with three out of four informants it occurred only once. Most instances of pronoun reversal can be observed with Fatima. Interestingly, it always concerned the generalized use of 2nd role pronouns. Generalizations in which a 1st role pronoun is used for 2nd role reference did not occur.

Table 5.14: Generalizations for role (1st/2nd role)

Form	Function	Generalization	Mahmut c1 c2 c3			Ergün c1 c2 c3			Mohamed c1 c2 c3			Fatima c1 c2 c3			Total
je X	mijn X	2nd > 1st	1*	-	-	-	-	-	-	-	-	-	-	-	1
jouw X	mijn X	2nd > 1st	-	-	-	1*	-	-	1	-	-	3*	7	-	12
jullie	wij	2nd > 1st	-	-	-	-	-	-	-	-	-	3	-	-	3

* = other-repetition

Five out of sixteen pronoun reversals occurred as repetitions of the utterance used by the native interlocutor (i.e. other-repetition). Those instances, i.e. *jouw* ('your') and *jullie* ('you') in which the pronoun reversal was not a native speaker repetition will be discussed below.

Jouw

An interesting phenomenon emerges for the Moroccan informants, if the analysis is extended with the learner varieties of the four shadow informants. Table 5.15 gives the form-function relationships for the possessive pronoun *jouw* ('your'), which occurred in the L2-Dutch varieties of both the core and shadow informants.

Table 5.15: Use of "jouw" by core and shadow informants

Form	Function	Generalization	Turkish Mah.	Erg.	Osm.	Abd.	Moroccan Moh.	Fat.	Has.	Hus.	Total
jouw X	jouw X	-	3	4	37	4	25	10	47	74	204
	mijn X	2nd > 1st	-	1	-	-	1	10	-	-	12
	zijn X	2nd > 3rd	-	-	-	1	1	5	40	11	58
	haar X	2nd > 3rd	-	-	-	-	-	3	6	-	9

The Moroccan informants use the possessive pronoun *jouw* ('your') more frequently than the Turkish informants. The Moroccans Mohamed and Fatima generalize the 2nd role pronoun *jouw* ('your') for 1st role reference. All Moroccans, in particular Hassan and Husseyn, generalize this form for 3rd role reference. Some examples of the two Moroccan shadow informants are given in sequences (89)-(91).

(89) HAS: Hij wil boos met jouw vader. Hij komt naar   He wants angry with your father. He comes
              thuis van jouw/ jouw vriend.   to home of your/ your friend.
      (session 3)   < = he is angry with his father and goes
                                                                            to his friend's house >

(90) HAS: *Meqbara*.   *Graveyard*.
      N: Oja?   Really?
      HAS: *Et* dan in de + in de begraaf*place*.   *And* then in the + in the burial*place*.
      N: Ja.   Yes.
      HAS: Gaan naar daar. Die moet de uh/ die man +   Go to there. That must the er/ that man +
              moet jouw hoofd + kijken naar uh mekka.   must your head + look to er mekka.
      (session 5)

(91) HUS: Die man hij moet uh/ jouw tas pakken.   That man he must er/ take your bag.
      (session 15)

The form *jouw* ('your') mostly occurs in possessive constructions which encode kinship relations. It is unlikely that these constructions are unanalysed wholes. Firstly, *jouw* ('your') is used productively in combination with different kinship terms and occasionally in combination with other entities, as sequences (90) and (91) above illustrate. Besides, generalizations of *jouw* ('your') coincide with standardlike use of the corresponding 1st/3rd role pronouns, e.g.

(92) FAT: Kinza zeg voor mij "Jouw moeder?"   Kinza says for me "Your mother?"
            Ik zeg "Jouw moeder hier".   I say "Your mother here".
      N: Ja.   Yes.
      FAT: Ja "Mij uh moeder nou uh negen jaar   Yes "Me er mother now er nine years
            van nederland".   of the netherlands".
      N: Oh zo.   Ah like that.
      (session 17)

The phenomenon of pronoun reversal disappears over time, the last instances for Mohamed and Hassan occurring in session 12 and for Fatima and Husseyn in sessions 17 and 21 respectively.

Jullie
      As can be derived from Table 5.15 above, apart from the speech role generalization of *jouw* ('your'), one Moroccan informant (Fatima) also generalizes the plural form *jullie*. Table 5.16 gives the form-function relationships for *jullie* as used by Fatima per cycle.

Table 5.16: Use of "jullie" by Fatima

Form	Function	Generalization	c1	c2	c3	Total
jullie	jullie (s)	-	3	4	12	19
	jullie (o)	-	3	-	2	5
	jullie (p)	-	1	-	-	1
jullie	wij	2nd > 1st	3	-	-	3
	zij	2nd > 3rd	-	4	5	9

Fatima generalizes *jullie* in subject function: she does so in early sessions for encoding 1st role reference (instead of *wij* 'we'), and in later sessions for 3rd role reference (instead of *zij* 'they'). Compare sequences (93) and (94).

(93) FAT: Jullie [ruzie maak]   You [fight]
      N: [ja in marokko] ja + wij.   [yes in morocco] yes + we.
      FAT: Jij uh veel geld. Ik kan niet.   You er much money. I cannot.
            Ik moet naar politie.   I must go to police.
      (session 7)

(94) N: Ben jij mee geweest 't schaap ophalen?   Did you go along as well to get the sheep?
      FAT: Ja. <..> Wij naar met/ jullie met uh.   Yes. <..> We to with/ you with er.
      N: Wij ja.   We yes.
      FAT: Wij   We
      N: Ja.   Yes.
      FAT: naar met uh.   to with er.
      N: *ḥna*.   *We*.
      FAT: Ik niet.   Not I.
      N: Jij niet?   You didn't?
      FAT: Nee + jullie kemal vader van turia.   No + you kemal father of turia.
      N: *Huma*?   *They*?
      FAT: *Huma*.   *They*.
      N: Zij.   They.
      FAT: Zij.   They.
      N: Niet jullie + jullie *ntuma*.   Not you + you *you*.
      FAT: + Ja + + zij naar *l'abattoir*.   + Yes + + they to *the slaughterhouse*.
      (session 11)

5.4.2 NUMBER

P4   Singular forms are acquired before plural forms

Prediction 4 is clearly confirmed: with all informants the singular form is acquired before the plural form (see Table 5.17).

Table 5.17: Testing the order of acquisition on the number dimension (1st/2nd role)

| | | | Turkish | | | | Moroccan | | | |
P4 *Singular*	*before*	*Plural*	Mah.	Erg.	Osm.	Abd.	Moh.	Fat.	Has.	Hus.
ik	before	wij	+ +	+ +	+ +	+ +	+ +	+ +	+ +	··
mij	before	ons (o)	+ +	+ +	+ +	+ +	− −	+ +	+ +	+ +
mijn	before	ons/ze (p)	+ +	+ +	+ +	+ +	+ +	+ +	+ +	+ +
jij	before	jullie (s)	+ +	+ +	+ +	+ +	+ +	+ +	+ +	+ +
jou	before	jullie (o)	+ +	+ +	+ +	+ +	− −	+ +	+ +	+ +
jouw	before	jullie (p)	+ +	+ +	+ +	+ +	+ +	+ +	+ +	+ +

The only disconfirmations can be found with Mohamed's use of *mij-ons* ('me-us') and *jou-jullie* ('you'). Mohamed is also the only informant who makes a generalized use of a singular form for plural reference (see Table 5.18).

Table 5.18: Generalizations for number (1st/2nd role)

Form	Function	Generalization	Mahmut	Ergün	Mohamed	Fatima	Total
jouw X	jullie X	Sg. > Pl.	-	-	2	-	2

5.4.3 STATUS

P5   T-forms are acquired before V-forms
P11   The status dimension will be easier for Turkish learners than for Moroccan learners of Dutch

In the learner varieties of the four core informants there are very few instances of the V-form *u* ('you'). Moreover, it turns out that these instances almost always occur in formulaic expressions like *wat zegt u?* ('pardon'), *weet u wel?* ('you know'), *wat blieft u?* ('pardon?'), and *dankuwel* ('thank you'). In these unanalysed wholes the informants are probably not aware of the formal status features of the form *u* ('you') in productive language use. In the learner varieties of the four shadow informants (see Table 5.10) the V-form *u* ('you') does not occur frequently either. The absence of V-forms in the learner varieties might be explained by a familiarity effect: the informants and their native interlocutors are well acquainted. However, it is unlikely that familiarity is the only explanatory factor. In a number of activity types such as play scenes like *Applying for a Job* and *Applying for Housing* the native speakers explicitly defined a formal situation through the use of V-forms. However the encoding of status through these forms is simply not noticed by the informants and often leads to misunderstandings (see Ergün's pronoun profile for some examples).

Next to the V-form *u* ('you') the reduced pronoun *je* ('you') can also be used as a V-form. However, as was pointed out above, reduced forms can rarely be found in the learner varieties of the core and shadow informants.

With a view to the infrequent use of *je* ('you') and *u* ('you'), and a familiarity effect, one should be careful with testing the status predictions. Nevertheless, the data in Table 5.12 suggest that prediction 5 is confirmed, whereas there is no evidence in favour of prediction 11.

5.4.4 CASE

P7   Subject forms are acquired before object forms
P8   Subject forms are acquired before possessive forms
P9   Forms in object function are acquired before forms in possessive function
P10   The case dimension will be easier for Turkish learners than for Moroccan learners of Dutch

The results given in Table 5.19 show that predictions 7 and 8 are clearly confirmed: subject pronouns are acquired before object and possessive pronouns.

With respect to prediction 9 a less coherent picture emerges. Within the 1st role paradigm the prediction is confirmed only for the Moroccan informants' acquisition of the form *ons* ('us/our'), which is first acquired in object function and then in possessive function. In contrast, within the 2nd role paradigm prediction 9 is confirmed with the exception of Mahmut's *jou-jouw* ('you-your').

Table 5.19: Testing the order of acquisition on the case dimension (1st/2nd role)

			Turkish				Moroccan			
			Mah.	Erg.	Osm.	Abd.	Moh.	Fat.	Has.	Hus.
P7	Subject	before	Object							
	ik	before	mij							
			++	++	++	++	++	++	..	++
	wij	before	ons (o)							
			++	++	++	++	--	++	--	++
	jij	before	jou							
			++	++	++	++	++	++	++	+-
	jullie (s)	before	jullie (o)							
			++	++	++	++	+-	++	++	++
P8	Subject	before	Possessive							
	ik	before	mijn							
			++	++	++	..	..	++	..	++
	wij	before	ons/ze (p)							
			++	++	--	++	++	++	++	++
	jij	before	jouw							
			++	++	++	++	++	++	++	++
	jullie (s)	before	jullie (p)							
			++	++	++	++	++	++	++	++
P9	Object	before	Possessive							
	mij	before	mijn							
			--	--	--	--	--	--	..	--
	ons (o)	before	ons/ze (p)							
			++	--	--	--	++	++	++	++
	jou	before	jouw							
			--	++	++	++	+-	++	++	++
	jullie (o)	before	jullie (p)							
			..	..	++	++	++	++	++	++

Table 5.20: Generalizations for case (1st/2nd role)

Form	Function	Generalization	Mahmut c1 c2 c3	Ergün c1 c2 c3	Mohamed c1 c2 c3	Fatima c1 c2 c3	Total
ik	mij	S > O	- 2 2	- - -	- - -	2 2 -	8
	mijn	S > P	21 1 13	- - -	- - -	- - -	35
wij	ons	S > O	- - -	- - 1	- 5 -	- - -	6
mij	mijn	O > P	3 4 2	- - -	28 71 92	21 9 15	245
mijn	mij	P > O	2 1 1	- 3 22	1 - 1	1 - -	32
jij	jou	S > O	1 7 4	1 - 1	- - -	1 2 1	18
	jouw	S > P	5 19 5	- - -	- 3 -	- - -	32

The instances of 1st/2nd role reference in which the case function differs from stan-dardlike use are given in Table 5.20. The dominance of subject pronouns is also reflected in the generalized use of these forms in the 1st and 2nd role paradigms.

Within the 1st role paradigm the subject pronouns *ik* ('I') and *wij* ('we') are gene-ralized in object and possessive function, while the reverse, i.e. generalized use of object and possessive pronouns in subject function, does not occur. It appears that Fatima and in particular Mahmut generalize the singular subject pronoun *ik* ('I'), whereas Mohamed and Ergün generalize the plural subject pronoun *wij* ('we'). Also the object pronoun *mij* ('me') and the possessive pronoun *mijn* ('mijn') are gene-ralized. Especially the Moroccan informants frequently generalize the object pronoun *mij* ('me') in possessive function.

Within the 2nd role paradigm again only for the subject pronoun *jij* ('you'), a generalized use in object and possessive function *jouw* ('your') can be noted.

Across the board the differences between the informants do not point at a clear source language-related determinant. In this respect no evidence can be found which would confirm prediction 10 holding that the case dimension is easier for the Turkish informants than for the Moroccan informants.

5.5 CONCLUSIONS

On the basis of the analyses presented for both the core and shadow informants, it is now possible to take into account the research questions specified in Section 5.1.

I   *Which set of forms is used in early learner varieties and what are the referential functions of these forms?*

As a whole the 1st and 2nd role paradigms consist of a rather close set of forms, in which there is an overall-dominance of full forms over reduced forms. The 1st role and 2nd role paradigms with the full forms, as used by our informants, are given in Tables 5.21 and 5.22.

Table 5.21: Paradigm representation for 1st role full pronouns in Dutch

NUMBER	CASE		
	Subject	Object	Possessive
Singular	*ik*	*mij*	*mijn*
Plural	*wij*	*ons*	*on(s/ze)*

Table 5.22: Paradigm representation for 2nd role full pronouns in Dutch

NUMBER	CASE		
	Subject	Object	Possessive
Singular	*jij*	*jou*	*jouw*
Plural	*jullie*	*jullie*	*jullie*

Occasionally a conflation between the 1st role and 2nd role paradigms can be observed. However, generalizations in which a 1st role pronoun is used for 2nd role reference do not occur. In all instances 2nd role pronouns are used for 1st role reference. This use can be observed in particular with Fatima. It appears, somewhat unexpectedly, that the Moroccan core/shadow informants remarkably frequently use the 2nd role singular pronoun *jouw* ('your') for 3rd role reference.

On the number dimension of both 1st role and 2nd role paradigms an overall-dominance of singular forms over plural forms can be observed.

On the status dimension within the 2nd role paradigm the infrequent use of V-forms, both the reduced form *je* ('you(r)') and the full form *u* ('you(r)'), is worth noting.

On the case dimension of both paradigms an overall-dominance of subject forms over object and possessive forms is observed. Subject forms are also generalized in non-subject function, while the reverse, i.e. generalized use of object/possessive pronouns in subject function, cannot be observed.

II   How is the initial set expanded over time in subsequent stages of language acquisition?

The following general principles could be observed in the acquisition processes of the core and shadow informants:
- 1st role forms are acquired before 2nd role forms.
- Subject forms are acquired before object/possessive forms.
- Singular forms are acquired before plural forms.

These general principles can be specified further through the order of acquisition of forms/functions within both the 1st role and 2nd role paradigms. However for a start, this order of acquisition should be based on the learner varieties of the core informants because only for them a detailed pronoun profile is available. This implies that for the core informants it is possible to investigate whether there is a relationship between the moment a pronoun is used standardlike and the types of generalizations within the pronoun system.

For the core informants a clear distinction emerges between Mahmut and Fatima on the one hand, and Ergün and Mohamed on the other.

Mahmut and Fatima
    The acquisition order observed for Mahmut and Fatima within the 1st role and 2nd role paradigms reveals striking similarities (see Table 5.23).

They start with the basic pronouns *ik* ('I') and *jij* ('you') and regularly generalize these subject pronouns in non-subject function, even after the moment at which the standard object/possessive forms can be observed. It is worth noting that Fatima in the first cycle regularly uses the possessive construction "*ik-mijn*-N" ('I-my-N').

Table 5.23: Order of acquisition for Mahmut and Fatima (1st/2nd role)

Mahmut			Fatima		
	1st role	2nd role		1st role	2nd role
s1	ik	-	s1	ik	jij
s3	-	jij		-	-
s4	mijn	-	s2	mijn	-
s6	mij	-	s5	mij	jullie (s)
s11	-	jullie (s)		-	-
	-	-	s7	-	jou
	-	-	s8	-	jullie (o)
s16	wij	-	s10	wij	-
s17	-	jouw	s14	-	jouw
s25	ons (o)	jou	s19	ons (o)	-

(s = subject; o = object; p = possessive)

After acquisition of the basic subject pronouns a differentiation on the case dimension can be observed. Within the 1st role paradigm this means that subsequently object and possessive forms are acquired. In contrast, within the 2nd role paradigm the case differentiation is only reflected in the generalized use of the subject pronouns in non-subject function.

Next, a differentiation on the number dimension can be observed. Within the 2nd role paradigm Mahmut and Fatima both acquire the plural subject form *jullie* ('you'). However, after this a remarkable difference between the two informants can be observed within the 1st role paradigm. Mahmut completes the number differentiation by acquiring the plural form *wij* ('we'). In contrast, Fatima skips this form and starts working on the case dimension within the 2nd role paradigm, i.e. *jou* ('you') and *jullie* ('you') in object function. Interestingly, it is exactly during this phase that she generalizes the 2nd role forms *jullie* ('you') and *jouw* ('your') for 1st role reference. The latter conclusion can be derived from a comparison of Tables 5.8 and 5.9.

Finally, Fatima also acquires the plural form *wij* ('we'). Mahmut and Fatima come together with the differentiation on the case dimension: first within the 2nd role paradigm, i.e. *jouw* ('your'), next on the 1st role paradigm, i.e. *ons* ('us'). In this phase Fatima acquires the plural subject form *wij* ('we'). Remarkably enough, she no longer generalizes the 2nd role pronouns *jullie* ('you') for 1st role reference, but for 3rd role reference.

Ergün and Mohamed

As can be derived from Table 5.24 the acquisition orders within the 1st role and 2nd role paradigms observed for Ergün and Mohamed are rather similar. It is difficult, however, to establish any phases on the basis of these observations. Already after the first three sessions a fairly complete set of pronouns emerged. Nevertheless, in later sessions (i.e. in cycle 3) quite an unexpected difference between Ergün and Mohamed emerges within the 1st role paradigm. In possessive function Ergün increasingly uses "*van*-Pro-N" constructions, whereas Mohamed sticks to "N-*van*-Pro" constructions. This difference cannot be observed within the 2nd role paradigm.

Table 5.24: Order of acquisition for Ergün and Mohamed (1st/2nd role)

Ergün			Mohamed		
	1st role	2nd role		1st role	2nd role
s1	ik	jij	s1	ik	jij
s2	mijn	-	s1	mijn	-
-	-	-	s1	ons (o)	-
s3	mij	-	s2	mij	-
s3	wij	-	s2	wij	-
s3	-	jullie (s)	s3	-	jullie (s+o)
-	-	-	s5	ons (p)	-
s6	-	jou	s6	-	jou
s7	-	jouw	s6	-	jouw
s8	ons (p)	-	-	-	-
s11	ons (o)	-	-	-	-
-	-	-	s26	-	jullie (p)

(s = subject; o = object; p = possessive)

The order of acquisition observed for the core informants can be checked by the observations made for the shadow informants (see Tables 5.11 and 5.12). With respect to the first standardlike and non-formulaic use of forms within the 1st role paradigm striking similarities between the informants become apparent. The observed order is summarized in Table 5.25:

Table 5.25: Order of acquisition 1st role forms

EARLY	ik	-->	mijn	-->	mij	-->	wij	-->	on(s/ze)	LATE

In the acquisition processes of the core/shadow informants only minor deviations from this order can be observed (see Table 5.11). The order of acquisition reflects that in the process of acquiring the relevant entries within the 1st role paradigm, the access route taken by the informants is the case dimension. They first fill in the singular level in the order: subject, possessive, object. Next, the plural level is filled in. Interestingly, differences between the Turkish and Moroccan informants emerge when they start working on the homonym part of the 1st role paradigm, i.e. *ons* ('us/our'). Here, the Turkish informants follow the same order as for the singular level, i.e. subject, possessive, object, while the Moroccan informants follow the order of subject, object, possessive.

With respect to the 2nd role paradigm a less coherent picture emerges. The observed order of acquisition is summarized in Table 5.26.

Table 5.26: Order of acquisition 2nd role forms

EARLY	jij	-->	jullie	-->	jou(w)	LATE
		\-->	jou(w)	-->	jullie	

All informants acquire the subject form *jij* ('you') relatively early. With respect to the next form that is acquired a difference emerges between the informants: for some Turkish/Moroccan informants the order *jullie-jou(w)* ('you(r)') can be observed, whereas for others the reverse order appears. In fact, the order of acquisition reveals that within the 2nd role paradigm both access routes, case and number, are taken by the informants. However, the difference between the informants do not point at source language-related determinants.

III   How can learner preferences be explained?

The following potential determinants of pronoun acquisition are considered: frequency, perceptual saliency, source language conventions, and paradigm formation.

The conclusion is that the frequency of full forms in the input corresponds with the dominance and early acquisition of both subject forms and singular forms.

However, there is clear evidence that the perceptual saliency of forms overrules the frequency effect. Although reduced forms occur frequently in native spoken Dutch and in the input the informants are confronted with, these forms can rarely be observed in our L2-Dutch learner varieties. The distribution of reduced and full pronouns in our learner varieties reveals that what appears frequently in the target language does not necessarily appear early in the language acquisition processes, if competitive principles are at work.

On the basis of a typological comparison of the Dutch, Turkish and Moroccan Arabic pronoun systems areas for L1 transfer were stipulated: the case and status dimensions in Dutch were expected to be easier for L2 learners with Turkish as their source language, than for those with Moroccan Arabic as their source language. With respect to the status dimension no difference between the two groups can be observed: V-forms are almost absent in the learner varieties of Dutch. With respect to the case dimension only minor differences emerge: in the 1st role paradigm the Turkish informants use the form *ons* first in possessive function ('our'), whereas the Moroccan informants first use this form in object function ('us').

Nevertheless, a clear difference between the Turkish and Moroccan informants can be found in the use of the 2nd role pronoun *jouw* ('your') in possessive function. In particular the Moroccans generalize this form for 1st role and 3rd role reference. It is difficult to find a single conclusive explanation. The Moroccans may be more inclined to see the form which refers to the possessor and the form which refers to the possessed entity as one unit. In the initial stages *jouw* ('your') is part of an unanalysed whole in some types of possessive relationships, in particular where kinship is involved, e.g. *jouw moeder* ('your mother') and *jouw man* ('your husband/man'). In the course of the interaction it is usually clear who the possessor is, also in the case of pronoun reversal. The interactional context itself even promotes the use of 2nd role pronoun reversal by providing the opportunity of repeating the inter-locutor. This might explain why pronoun reversal of 1st role pronouns was never observed.

All in all, striking similarities and striking differences between the acquisition processes of individual informants are found. In particular the paradigm account of the similarities between Mahmut and Fatima showed how a number of at first sight rather unexpected generalizations found a reasonable place in their acquisition.

CHAPTER 6

THIRD ROLE PRONOMINAL REFERENCE

In this chapter the focus is on the acquisition of pronominal forms and functions within the 3rd role paradigm. First, the research questions are presented. The idea of paradigm formation as a driving force is developed further. After this, an account of the method is given, followed by a discussion of the pronoun profiles of the four core informants. Cross-learner evidence is again provided by pronominal preferences of the shadow informants.

In the final section the findings of Chapters 5 and 6 will be related to available studies on three processes of language development: (1) adult language acquisition, (2) child language acquisition, and (3) pidgin and creole languages.

6.1 RESEARCH QUESTIONS AND PREDICTIONS

As with the 1st role and 2nd role paradigms, the following research questions can be specified for the 3rd role paradigm:

I   Which set of forms is used in early learner varieties and what are the referential functions of these forms?
II   How is this initial set expanded over time in subsequent stages of language acquisition?
III   How can learner preferences be explained?

The paradigm representation for the set of full 3rd role pronouns is given in Table 6.1. The learner's task in the acquisition of the 3rd role paradigm consists in discovering forms in three dimensions: number (with singular and plural levels), gender (with masculine and feminine levels), and case (with subject, object, and possessive levels).

Table 6.1: Paradigm representation for 3rd role full pronouns in Dutch

NUMBER	GENDER	CASE		
		Subject	Object	Possessive
Singular	Masculine	hij	hem	zijn
	Feminine	zij	haar	haar
Plural		zij	hun	hun

On the basis of the description of the Dutch, Turkish, and Moroccan Arabic pronoun systems presented in Chapter 4, the following predictions will be tested in this chapter:

Emphasis: P1 Full forms are acquired before reduced forms

Number: P4 Singular forms are acquired before plural forms

Gender: P6 Masculine forms are acquired before feminine forms
P12 The gender dimension will be easier for Moroccan learners than for Turkish learners of Dutch

Case: P7 Subject forms are acquired before object forms
P8 Subject forms are acquired before possessive forms
P9 Forms in object function are acquired before forms in possessive function
P10 The case dimension will be easier for Turkish learners than for Moroccan learners of Dutch

These predictions address: (1) the order in which specific forms will appear in the acquisition process, e.g. the form *hij* ('he') will be used in an earlier stage than the form *zij* ('she'), and (2) the direction of expected generalizations, e.g. the form *hij* ('he') will be used for reference to men as well as women.

In particular, the case and gender differences between the Turkish and Moroccan Arabic pronoun systems (cf. predictions 10 and 12), may be a decisive factor in the acquisition processes of the Dutch pronoun system. In this respect the assumption is that a so-called uni-functionality principle operates within the learner's paradigm of the Dutch pronoun system. The uni-functionality principle states that "one function is encoded through only one form". This principle is well-known under various names and formulations (e.g. Pinker 1984, Slobin 1985, Andersen 1984). Within a model of paradigm formation the uni-functionality principle implies that a cell contains only one entry.

Armed with the uni-functionality principle, potential effects of the source language can be tackled. If the Turkish and Moroccan informants construct a new paradigm for the Dutch pronoun system according to known paradigms in their first language, a number of pronouns will not fit: in their source systems different dimensions and levels are distinguished compared to the Dutch target system. Table 6.2 shows the Dutch pronouns for 3rd role reference in a Turkish-based paradigm.

Table 6.2: Dutch 3rd role pronouns in a Turkish-based paradigm
    ([ ] = blocked)

NUMBER	CASE		
	Subject	Object	Possessive
Singular	*hij* *[zij]*	*hem* *[haar]*	*zijn* *[haar]*
Plural	*zij*	*hun*	*hun*

This Turkish-based paradigm for the Dutch pronoun system shows that the Turkish informants will run into problems in the dimension of gender, where they do not expect two levels. According to the uni-functionality principle only one entry is allowed in a cell. Within a Turkish-based paradigm, a conflict will arise on the singular level of the dimension of number between the masculine and feminine forms for each of the three case levels: i.e. *hij* ('he') vs. *zij* ('she'), *hem* ('him') vs. *haar* ('her'), and *zijn* ('his') vs. *haar* ('her'). It is a reasonable conjecture that the most frequently used form will win the competitive struggle within a cell and will therefore be generalized. Frequency of use of the 3rd role pronouns was calculated in Chapter 4. The result of these calculations clearly shows that in native spoken Dutch masculine pronouns are used much more frequently than their corresponding feminine equivalents. As a result, the feminine forms are blocked in the Turkish-based paradigm of the Dutch pronoun system. This might be a factor that makes the acquisition task harder for the Turkish informants. Interestingly, the blocking of the feminine forms results in a rather transparent paradigm. Multi-functionality with homonym forms *zij* ('she' or 'they') and *haar* ('her') is covered.

The Moroccan Arabic-based paradigm for the Dutch pronoun system reveals some interesting differences compared to the Turkish-based paradigm (see Tables 6.2 and 6.3).

The informants who start from a Moroccan Arabic-based paradigm are confronted with a competitive struggle between the object pronouns and the possessive pronouns. On the masculine level the struggle is won by the more frequently used object pronoun *hem* ('him'). On the feminine and plural levels there is no competition due to the homonyms *haar* ('her') and *hun* ('their') respectively.

Compared to the Turkish-based paradigm, homonyms in the Moroccan Arabic-based paradigm will have a different effect on the initial expectations of the Moroccan informants. The form *haar* ('her') confirms their expectations that the encoding of object and possessive cases is joined in Dutch. They are, however, puzzled by the form *zij* which can encode singular feminine reference ('she') as well as plural reference ('they').

Table 6.3: Dutch 3rd role pronouns in a Moroccan Arabic-based paradigm
([ ] = blocked)

NUMBER	GENDER	CASE		
		Subject	Non-subject	
Singular	Masculine	*hij*	*hem*	*[zijn]*
	Feminine	*zij*	*haar*	*haar*
Plural		*zij*	*hun*	*hun*

For illustrating purposes let us now imagine how L2 learners might use their L1-based paradigms in the acquisition process. Suppose the utterance to tackle is *zij springt op haar fiets en roept hem* ('she jumps on her bicycle and calls him'). The L2 learner could subsequently use three procedures (see also Pinker 1984:166-208):

Procedure 1:   Choose a relevant feature from among the features contained in the inferred sentence meaning and create an equation expressing the value of that feature. This procedure implies that Turkish learners will be more likely to choose case equations (e.g. *hem* = "object", *zij* = "subject"), whereas Moroccan learners will be more likely to choose gender equations (e.g. *hem* = "masculine", *zij* = "feminine").

Procedure 2:   Enter the word in a paradigm on the dimension defined by the equation. Allow only a single entry to fill the relevant cell. This procedure implies, for example, that with the equation *hem* = "object" the feminine form *haar* ('her') is blocked in the Turkish-based paradigm and, that with the equation *hem* = "masculine" the possessive pronoun *zijn* ('his') is blocked in the Moroccan Arabic-based paradigm.

Procedure 3:   Create a new dimension or level within the paradigm, if the new hypothesized equation involves a new feature. This procedure implies that the Turkish learners will create the dimension of gender, while the Moroccan learners will split the dimension of case into three levels.

These procedures constitute, of course, a hypothetical route which might be followed by the Turkish/Moroccan adults in acquiring Dutch as the target language. Below the actual route observed for the core informants will be investigated.

6.2 METHOD

In the investigations the same data base (i.e. informants and language activities) has been used as in the previous chapter. Also, the same analytical procedure has been followed (see Section 5.2).

6.3 THE LEARNER VARIETIES

6.3.1 MAHMUT

3rd role reference
The pronominal 3rd role references used by Mahmut in each of the 27 sessions are given in Table 6.4.

3rd role singular
In subject function, pronouns are used by Mahmut in session 3 for the first time, i.e. *hij* ('he'). Next, in session 4 Mahmut generalizes the female form *zij* ('she') for reference to a man, i.e. in talking about his brother-in-law (see sequence 1).

(1)	MAH:	Ik schoonvader zoon.	I father-in-law son.
	N:	Ja.	Yes.
	MAH:	Die uh zeven jaar.	That one er seven years old.
	N:	Ja.	Yes.
	MAH:	School. Die mahmut.	School. That mahmut.
	N:	Ja.	Yes.
	MAH:	Hollands praten. Ja. Die/ zij is hollands.	Speak dutch. Yes. That/ she is dutch.
	(session 4)		

From session 6 onwards the masculine subject form *hij* ('he') has found a firm place in the pronoun system as a form in subject function for reference to a man. Pronouns in subject function by which Mahmut refers to a woman are relatively infrequent. The first reference to a woman by means of *zij* ('she') occurs in session 8. However, also the masculine form *hij* ('he') is still used for feminine reference. An example of this is given in sequence (2). Mahmut uses this form to refer to his daughter.

(2)	MAH:	Hij "Niet mooi" zeggen. "Niet mooi" zeg. "Niet mooi" zeggen hij.	He say "Not nice". "Not nice" say. "Not nice" he say.
	(session 13)		

Table 6.4: Pronominal 3rd role reference by Mahmut

CYCLE 1	s1	s2	s3	s4	s5	s6	s7	s8	s9	Total	English
Subject:											
Sg: hij	-	-	5	-	-	11	3	-	8	27	he
zij	-	-	-	-	-	-	-	1	-	1	she
zij (=hij)	-	-	-	1	-	-	-	-	-	1	she (=he)
Pl: zij	-	-	-	1	-	-	8	-	-	9	they
hunnie	-	-	-	-	-	-	-	1	-	1	they
Object:											
Sg: hij (=hem)	-	-	-	-	-	-	1	-	-	1	he (=him)
zij (=hem)	-	-	-	-	-	-	1	-	-	1	she (=him)

CYCLE 2	s10	s11	s12	s13	s14	s15	s16	s17	s18	Total	English
Subject:											
Sg: hij	2	1	12	6	13	29	5	2	64	134	he
hij (=zij)	-	-	-	8	-	-	-	-	-	8	he (=she)
zij	-	-	-	1	2	-	-	-	-	3	she
Pl: zij	-	-	-	1	2	-	-	-	-	3	they
hij (=zij)	-	-	-	-	-	-	-	-	1	1	he (=they)
Object:											
Sg: hij (=hem)	-	-	-	-	1	1	-	-	-	2	he (=him)
Pl: zij (=hun)	-	-	-	-	2	-	-	-	-	2	they (=them)
Possess:											
Sg: zijn X	-	-	2	-	-	-	-	-	-	2	his X
hij X (=zijn)	-	-	-	-	-	-	-	-	1	1	he X (=his)

CYCLE 3	s19	s20	s21	s22	s23	s24	s25	s26	s27	Total	English
Subject:											
Sg: hij	3	4	17	24	1	83	13	8	85	238	he
zij	-	-	-	-	-	-	-	3	6	9	she
Possess:											
Sg: haar X	-	-	-	-	-	-	-	-	1	1	her X
hij X (=zijn)	-	-	-	-	-	3	-	-	-	3	he X (=his)

In object function Mahmut uses a subject pronoun four times. This is relatively infrequent. Sequence (3) contains an example.

(3)	MAH:	En dan hij verkeerd he. Tas halen/	And then he wrong right. Get bag/
		eerste moet tas halen. <..>. En dan	first must get bag. <..>. And then
		vrouw roepen hij. En dan wachten.	woman call he. And then wait.
	(session 15)		

In session 12 Mahmut makes a standardlike use of the possessive form *zijn* ('his') in possessive function for a man as possessor. However, as can be seen in sequence (4), it concerns a repetition in a non-understanding sequence and the form is probably not yet acquired.

(4)	N:	En hoe vindt ie/ vindt zijn vriend	And how does he/ does his friend
		dat?	like that?
	MAH:	Zijn vriend?	His friend?
	N:	Zijn vriend.	His friend.

MAH:	Zijn?	His?	
N:	Ja.	Yes.	
MAH:	+	+	
N:	Jongen met dat gele t-shirt.	Boy with that yellow t-shirt.	
	(session 12)		

Occasionally (in sessions 18 and 24) Mahmut generalizes the subject form *hij* ('he') in possessive function (see sequences 5 and 6).

(5)   MAH: Hij politie praten he.   He talks to police right.
        N: Ja.   Yes.
        MAH: Hij auto weg.   He car gone.
        (session 18)

(6)   MAH: Hij trein komt aan he.   He train arrives right.
        N: Ja.   Yes.
        MAH: Hij vrouw/ ook vrouw moeder vader.   He woman/ also woman mother father.
        (session 24)

As sequence (7) shows, the feminine pronoun *haar* ('her') is used standardlike in session 27.

(7)   MAH: Vrouw ook inzetten   Woman also put in
        N: Hmhm.   Uh-huh.
        MAH: inzitten. En haar buurman gezien   sit in. And her neighbour saw
                 "Kijk/ kom maar kijkus".   "Look/ come and look".
        (session 27)

3rd role plural

In subject function the pronoun *zij* ('they') first occurs in session 4. The singular form *hij* ('he') is used once (in session 18) for expressing plural reference. However, this is an unclear instance, the interpretation being dependent on the learner meaning of the word *samen* ('together'):

(8)   MAH: Ja meisje eten klaar maken.   Yes girl fix food.
        N: Ja.   Yes.
        MAH: Hij komen. Hij eten doen. En dan +   He come. He do food. And then +
                 hij baas he. Groot huis. Hij samen   he boss right. Big house. He sit together
                 zitten he.   right.
        (session 18)

In Southern Dutch dialects the plural form *hunnie* ('them/they') is used for subject reference. Mahmut uses this form too, remarkably, in the same sequence in which he uses the homonym form *zij* ('she' or 'they') as the singular form:

(9)   MAH: Ikke ja uh disco en meisje halen   I yes er disco and go get girl right
                 he samen praten + goed. Ja ik niet café.   talk together + good. Yes I not cafe.
        N: Hmhm, 'n nederlands meisje?   Uh-huh, a dutch girl?

MAH:	Ja nederlands meisje. Turkse mensen	Yes dutch girl. Turkish people
N:	niet. Ik turkish zij turkish he	not. I turkish they turkish right
N:	Hmhm.	Uh-huh.
MAH:	Hunnie hollandse mensen [(x)] praten.	They dutch people [(x)] talk.
N:	[Hun]	[They<them>]
(session 8)		

For plural reference in object function the subject pronoun *zij* ('they') is generalized twice. An example is given in sequence (10).

| (10) MAH: | Ik altijd zij helpen he. | I always help they right. |
| (session 14) | | |

6.3.2 ERGÜN

3rd role reference
The form-function relationships of the pronouns used by Ergün for 3rd role reference are given in Table 6.5.

3rd role singular
Compared with Mahmut, Ergün uses 3rd role pronouns more frequently. In subject function the form *hij* ('he') first appears in session 3. The feminine subject form *zij* ('she') is used regularly from cycle 2 onwards. Also after he has used *hij* ('he') and *zij* ('she') standardlike, Ergün keeps generalizing the pronoun *hij* ('he') to refer to female persons. Ergün keeps struggling with the referential meanings here, as is evidenced in many self-corrections. Some examples are given in sequences (11-14).

(11) N:	Dat meisje stond op. Toen ben ik weggegaan.	That girl stood up. Then I went away.
ERG:	Ja.	Yes.
N:	Net als 't meisje.	Just like the girl.
ERG:	Die hij/ zij die meisje weg he.	That he/ she that girl go away right.
(session 12)		

| (12) ERG: | Ik heb/ ik heb drie zus. Ik dacht eentje/ een groot. Hij komt hier/ zij komt hier ja. | I have/ I have three sister. I thought one/ one big. He comes here/ she comes here yes. |
| (session 20) | | |

| (13) ERG: | Zij/ zijn vader zij zegt/ hij zegt tegen mij "Honderd gulden nou betalen tweehonderd gulden volgend jaar". | She/ his father she says/ he says to me "Pay hundred guilders now two hundred guilders next year". |
| (session 13) | | |

| (14) ERG: | Dan daar ook baas. Zij/ hij zegt tegen mij "Vanaf negen uur komt hier". | Then there also boss. She/ he says to me "From nine o'clock comes here". |
| (session 16) | | |

Table 6.5: Pronominal 3rd role reference by Ergün

CYCLE 1	s1	s2	s3	s4	s5	s6	s7	s8	s9	Total	English
Subject:											
Sg: hij	-	-	4	2	3	13	4	8	28	62	he
hij (=zij)	-	-	-	-	-	-	-	-	4	4	he (=she)
zij	-	-	-	-	-	1	-	-	-	1	she
Possess:											
Sg: zijn X	-	-	-	-	-	1	-	-	-	1	his X

CYCLE 2	s10	s11	s12	s13	s14	s15	s16	s17	s18	Total	English
Subject:											
Sg: hij	-	6	34	23	46	45	21	21	130	326	he
hij (=zij)	3	-	-	1	-	2	-	-	9	15	he (=she)
ie	-	-	-	2	-	-	-	-	-	2	he
zij	1	2	4	3	1	1	-	-	9	21	she
zij (=hij)	-	-	-	1	-	-	1	-	1	3	she (=he)
haar (=zij)	-	-	-	-	-	-	-	-	1	1	her (=she)
Object:											
Sg: hem	-	-	1	-	2	-	-	1	4	8	him
'm	-	-	-	-	-	-	-	1	1	2	him
haar	-	-	-	-	-	-	-	-	3	3	her
zij (=haar)	-	-	-	1	-	-	-	-	-	1	she (=her)
Possess:											
Sg: zijn X	1	-	-	-	-	-	-	-	-	1	his X
zijn X (=haar)	-	-	-	1	-	-	-	-	-	1	his X (=her)
haar X	-	-	-	-	-	-	-	-	1	1	her X
hij X (=zijn)	-	-	1	-	-	-	-	-	-	1	he X (=his)
hem X (=zijn)	-	-	-	-	1	-	-	-	-	1	him X (=his)
van hem X	-	-	-	-	-	-	-	-	3	3	of him X
X van hem	-	-	-	-	-	-	-	-	1	1	X of him
X van haar	-	-	-	-	-	-	-	-	1	1	X of her
van haar X	-	-	-	-	-	-	-	-	1	1	of her X
Pl: X van ons (=hun)	-	-	-	-	-	-	-	-	1	1	X of us (=them)

CYCLE 3	s19	s20	s21	s22	s23	s24	s25	s26	s27	Total	English
Subject:											
Sg: hij	34	37	21	30	20	7	29	9	65	252	he
hij (=zij)	8	4	-	1	-	2	-	3	6	24	he (=she)
ie	-	-	-	-	1	-	-	-	-	1	he
zij	4	4	-	5	-	-	-	7	4	24	she
zij (=hij)	-	-	-	-	1	-	-	-	-	1	she (=he)
ze	1	-	-	-	-	-	1	-	-	2	she
Object:											
Sg: hem	1	-	-	3	-	-	4	2	8	18	him
hem (=haar)	-	-	-	1	-	-	-	2	1	4	him (=her)
'm	1	-	1	-	-	-	-	-	-	2	him
haar	-	-	-	2	-	-	-	1	1	4	her
Pl: hun	-	-	-	1	-	-	-	-	-	1	them
Possess:											
Sg: van hem X	2	-	1	5	1	1	3	1	15	29	of him X
X van hem	-	-	-	-	-	-	1	-	-	1	X of him
X van haar	-	-	-	2	-	-	-	-	4	6	X of her
van haar X	-	-	-	-	-	-	-	-	1	1	of her X

Finally, be it only once, the form *haar* ('her') is probably generalized in subject function:

(15) ERG: Hij wil niet die haar is dood he.   He does not want that her is dead right.
     (session 18)

In object function the object form *hem* ('him') and the form *haar* ('her') are used standardlike relatively late compared to the pronouns in subject function. The masculine pronoun *hem* ('him') appears earlier and is more frequent than the feminine pronoun *haar* ('her'). Occasionally, Ergün uses the reduced object form *'m* ('him') in object function. The pronoun *hem* ('him') is generalized for gender (see sequence 16).

(16) ERG: Die/ die meisje zegt/ oh nee ik zeg   That/ that girl says/ oh no I say
            tegen hem "Woont jij hier?".   to him "Does you live here?"
     (session 26)

Ergün generalizes (in session 13) the subject form *zij* ('she') in object function before the form *haar* ('her') is used standardlike (in session 18):

(17) N: Waarom niet?   Why not?
     ERG: Weet ik niet. Vraag maar zij.   I don't know. Ask she.
     (session 13)

In possessive function the possessive pronouns are used infrequently. The form *zijn* ('his') appears first. In cycle 2 this form is generalized for gender. However, we also find that the subject pronoun *hij* ('he') and the object pronoun *hem* ('him') are used in possessive function. It is very striking that in cycle 3 no pronominal form is used attributively to a noun in the function of a possessive pronoun. Typical examples of phrases with which in different stages of acquisition Ergün expresses a possessive relationship can be found in sequences (18)-(22).

(18) ERG: Zij en zij/ zijn vrouw komt dan. En nog   She and she/ his wife then comes. And
            een keer man/ nog eentje man daar.   another time man/ one more man there.
     (session 6)

(19) ERG: Zij/ zijn vader zij zegt/ hij zegt tegen   She/ his father she says/ he says to
            mij "Honderd gulden nou betalen,   me "Pay hundred guilders now,
            tweehonderd gulden volgend jaar".   two hundred guilders next year".
     (session 13)

(20) ERG: Als daar/ daar blijven dan moet soldaat   If there/ there stay then must soldier
            doen, dan komt hier terug. Omdat van   do, then comes back here. Because of
            hem vrouw hier woont.   him wife lives here.
     (session 23)

(21) ERG: Ja sjaal is van hem oog komt he.   Yes scarf is of him eye comes right.
     (session 27)

(22) ERG:	En die van haar vader is	And that of her father has been
	dood geschieten.	shot dead.
	(session 27)	

In the course of time, Ergün more and more often uses the pronouns *hem* ('him') and *haar* ('her') in combination with the preposition *van* ('of') in a *"van*-Pro-N" construction. Possessive relationships are encoded by placing the constructions *van hem* ('of him') and *van haar* ('of her') in both pre- and post-position with respect to the forms which refer to the possessed entities. It appears that Ergün has a special preference for pre-position, which deviates from standardlike use. Because the forms *hem* ('him') and *haar* ('her') are used in combination with the preposition *van* ('of'), the same pronouns can be used in object function as well as in possessive function. This might explain that the masculine possessive pronoun *zijn* ('his') no longer occurs in later sessions.

3rd role plural

Ergün never uses plural reference in subject function. In sequence (23) Ergün takes the homonym form *zij* ('she/they') to be the singular form, while the native speaker encodes plural reference.

(23) N:	Wat eten ze?	What do they eat?
ERG:	+ Jullie?	+ You?
N:	Ja.	Yes.
ERG:	Nee\	No\
N:	\Nee zij zij.	\No they they.
ERG:	Zij?	She?
N:	Ja.	Yes.
ERG:	+ Welke zij? Die meisje?	+ Which she? That girl?
	(session 12)	

In object function one instance of the pronoun *hun* ('them') can be found, in session 22:

(24) ERG:	Ik heb tegen hun gezegd/ tegen	I have told to them/ told to
	haar gezegd. Dit is meisje. Haar	her. This is girl. Told
	gezegd. Zij is elke/ elke avond	her. She is every/ every evening
	ik wij/ wij hebben vasten he.	I we/ we have fasting right.
	(session 22)	

Also in possessive function only one instance can be found: generalization of the 1st role pronoun *ons* ('us'). This use is given in sequence (25).

(25) ERG:	Achter komt van ons/ + van haar	Comes behind of us/ + of her
	of van hem.	or of him.
	(session 18)	

6.3.3 MOHAMED

Table 6.6: Pronominal 3rd role reference by Mohamed (cycles 1 and 2)

CYCLE 1		s1	s2	s3	s4	s5	s6	s7	s8	s9	Total	English
Subject:												
Sg:	hij	29	24	77	21	37	121	-	15	75	399	he
	hij (=zij)	-	-	4	9	-	-	-	-	-	13	he (=she)
	zij	-	-	-	-	-	1	-	-	5	6	she
Pl:	zij	-	-	-	-	-	-	-	1	-	1	they
	hij (=zij)	-	2	1	7	1	-	-	1	1	13	he (=they)
	hullie	-	-	-	-	-	-	-	-	1	1	they
	hunnie	-	-	-	-	-	-	-	-	1	1	they
Object:												
Sg:	hem	1	7	-	7	-	-	1	4	14	34	him
	hij (=hem)	-	-	1	-	-	4	-	-	-	5	he (=him)
	haar	-	-	-	-	-	-	-	-	1	1	her
	zij (=haar)	-	-	-	-	1	-	-	-	1	2	she (=her)
Pl:	hem (=hun)	-	-	-	-	1	-	-	-	-	1	him (=them)
Possess:												
Sg:	zijn X	-	-	1	-	-	-	-	-	2	3	his X
	zijn X (=haar)	-	-	-	-	-	-	-	-	1	1	his X (=her)
	hij X (=zijn)	1	-	10	-	2	8	-	-	1	22	he X (=his)
	zij X (=zijn)	-	-	1	-	-	6	-	-	-	7	she X (=his)
	hij X (=haar)	-	-	-	-	-	4	-	-	1	5	he X (=her)
	zij X (=haar)	-	-	-	-	-	-	-	-	3	3	she X (=her)

CYCLE 2		s10	s11	s12	s13	s14	s15	s16	s17	s18	Total	English
Subject:												
Sg:	hij	4	5	55	9	23	132	30	44	221	523	he
	hij (=zij)	-	-	-	-	-	2	-	-	1	3	he (=she)
	ie	-	1	-	-	-	-	-	1	3	5	he
	zij	5	10	-	1	-	6	1	5	19	47	she
	ze	-	-	-	-	-	-	-	-	2	2	she
Pl:	zij	-	8	-	-	-	-	-	-	-	8	they
	ze	-	-	-	-	-	-	-	1	-	1	they
	hij (=zij)	-	1	-	2	-	-	3	1	-	7	he (=they)
	hun	-	4	-	-	-	-	-	-	2	6	them (=they)
	hullie	-	6	-	-	-	-	-	-	-	6	they
Object:												
Sg:	hem	1	1	4	-	4	23	5	7	31	76	him
	haar	1	4	-	1	-	-	-	-	8	14	her
Pl:	hun	-	1	-	-	-	-	-	1	-	2	them
Posses.:												
Sg:	zijn X	-	-	1	-	-	-	-	-	-	1	his X
	jouw (=zijn)	-	-	1	-	-	-	-	-	-	1	your X (=his)
	hem X (=zijn)	-	1	3	-	-	3	-	-	5	12	him X (=his)
	X van hem	-	-	7	2	1	2	6	1	1	20	X of him
	hem X (=haar)	-	-	-	-	-	1	-	-	-	1	him X (=her)
	haar X	2	-	-	-	-	-	-	-	-	2	her X
	X van haar	-	1	-	1	-	2	-	-	-	4	X of her

Table 6.6 (cont.): Pronominal 3rd role reference by Mohamed (cycle 3)

CYCLE 3		s19	s20	s21	s22	s23	s24	s25	s26	s27	Total	English
Subject:												
Sg:	hij	26	138	26	18	21	55	21	37	129	471	he
	ie	-	54	10	6	-	14	6	2	13	105	he
	zij	12	12	-	7	-	4	3	3	10	51	she
	ze	-	1	-	-	-	-	-	-	-	1	she
	ie (=ze)	-	-	-	-	-	3	1	-	1	5	he (=she)
Pl:	ze	-	-	-	-	-	-	1	-	-	1	they
	hun	1	3	-	1	1	-	10	1	3	20	them (=they)
Object:												
Sg:	hem	2	50	4	10	5	17	2	8	39	137	him
	'm	1	1	-	-	-	-	-	-	-	2	him
	haar	3	4	-	4	6	3	-	-	7	27	her
Pl:	hem (=hun)	-	1	-	-	-	-	-	-	2	3	him (=them)
	hun	-	-	-	2	1	-	4	2	5	14	them
Possess:												
Sg:	'm X (=z'n)	1	-	-	-	-	-	-	-	-	1	him X (=his)
	zijn X	-	-	-	-	-	-	-	-	1	1	his X
	hem X (=zijn)	1	3	3	-	-	3	-	2	5	17	him (=his)
	hij X (=zijn)	1	-	-	-	-	-	-	-	-	1	he (=his)
	X van 'm	-	1	-	-	-	-	-	-	-	1	X of him
	X van hem	-	10	5	-	-	-	-	-	3	18	X of him
	haar X	-	-	-	1	-	2	-	-	-	3	her X
	van haar	-	-	-	-	1	-	-	-	-	1	of her
	X van haar	-	-	-	-	4	-	-	-	-	4	X of haar

3rd role reference

The pronominal 3rd role references which were used by Mohamed in the 27 sessions are given in Table 6.6.

3rd role singular

Mohamed uses 3rd role pronouns far more frequently than the two Turkish informants. In subject function the masculine pronoun *hij* ('he') already occurs frequently from session 1 onwards. The feminine pronoun *zij* ('she') appears somewhat later, in session 6. In contrast to Ergün and Mahmut, Mohamed never generalizes the feminine pronoun *zij* ('she') for masculine reference. What he regularly generalizes, is the form *hij* ('he') for male and female reference, as for example in sequences (26) and (27).

(26) N: Wat doet dat meisje?   What is that girl doing?
      MOH: Hij/ hij eten misschien de soep.   He/ he maybe eating the soup.
      (session 3)

(27) MOH: Toen hij die/ die meisje he ook wakker.   Then he that/ that girl eh also awake.
      (session 18)

From session 17 onwards Mohamed regularly uses the reduced pronoun *ie* ('he'). It is worth noting that this pronoun often occurs as a post-verbal enclitic in combination with another subject form in pre-verbal position. Typical examples are given in the following sequences:

(28) MOH: Ja toen daar loopt/ liept/ loopt   Yes then there walks/ walked/ walks
             een turk he. Hij zien die vrouw.   a turk right. He see that woman.
             Toen hij gaat ie naar haar he.   Then he goes he up to her right.
      (session 20)

(29) MOH: Volgende dag.   Next day.
      N: Ja.   Yes.
      MOH: Hij gaat ie naar groot gat   He goes he to big hole
             beetje heel groot. Hij fluiten.   little very big. He whistle.
             Komt die groot slang. Heeft ie   Comes that big snake. Has he
             verkocht voor duizend guld.   sold for a thousand guild.
      (session 20)

(30) N: En dan?   And then?
      MOH: Ja toen die meisje is ie weg en hij ook.   Yes then that girl he is gone and he too.
             Toen + ja over uh + tien dagen zij   Then + yes in er + ten days she
             heeft hem gezien.   has seen him.
      (session 27)

As in sequence (30) Mohamed sometimes in the 3rd cycle uses the form *ie* ('he') for female reference.

In object function it is striking that the object form *hem* ('him') is already used regularly from session 1 onwards, while the subject form *hij* ('he') also fulfils this function in cycle 1. In the first cycle the form *zij* ('she') is still generalized in object function too. However, from cycle 2 onwards no generalizations of subject pronouns in object function can be found. The object pronouns *hem* ('him') and *haar* ('her') are used standardlike and have taken up a steady place in the pronoun system. Mohamed uses these pronouns regularly and relatively frequently. Occasionally, also the reduced form *'m* ('him') occurs.

In possessive function Mohamed sporadically uses the forms *zijn* ('his') and *haar* ('her') standardlike. In cycle 1 Mohamed prefers the subject forms *hij* ('he') and *zij* ('she') in possessive function. Some examples are given in sequences (31)-(34).

(31) MOH: Die klein jongen hij naam is uh karl.   That little boy he name is er karl.
      (session 3)

(32) N: Je woont er alleen.   You live there alone.
      MOH: Alleen, maar uh vrouw + zij   Alone, but er wife + she
             ook woont bij hij ouders.   also lives with he parents.
      (session 6)

(33) MOH: Hij zegt van uh hij/ zij meiske of   He says er he/ she girl or
             hij vrouw "Ik nou/ ik uh/ + ik gaan   he wife "I now/ I er/ + I go
             naar/ naar ander land".   to/ to other country".
      (session 6)

(34) N: Waar zijn de kinderen nu?   Where are the children now?
     MOH: Ja die jong bij +/ bij tante/ bij   Yes that boy with +/ with aunt/ with
             tante. Die meisje zij *oncle* he/   aunt. That girl with she *uncle* eh/
             bij zij oom/ bij hij.   with she uncle/ with he.
     N: Zijn.   His.
     MOH: Oom.   Uncle.
     (session 9)

Mohamed uses the forms *hij* ('he') and *zij* ('she') instead of the form *haar* ('her') for reference to a woman as possessor (see sequence 34). He also uses the subject form *zij* ('she') instead of *zijn* ('his').

In cycles 2 and 3 subject pronouns are no longer generalized in possessive function (with the exception of *hij* 'he' in session 19). For expressing this function Mohamed now regularly uses the object form *hem* ('him') and the form *haar* ('her'). Typical examples of pronouns in possessive function are given in sequences (35)-(40).

(35) N: En uh waarom wilt u ze hier   And er why would you like
             halen?   to bring them here?
     MOH: Ja moet uh die meisje kom   Yes that girl has to come
             uh bij zijn moeder helpen he.   er to his mother help right.
     (session 9)

(36) MOH: En toen hij praat met hem vrouw of meisje.   And then he talks with him wife or girl.
     (session 15)

(37) MOH: Moet hij uh/ moet hij hem vader helpen.   Must he er/ must he help him father.
     (session 21)

(38) MOH: Toen die vriend van hem doet ie die   Then that friend of him does he turn that
             licht uit.   light off.
     (session 20)

(39) MOH: Toen hij thuis die vader van hem   Then he home that father of him
             was ie kwaad op hem.   was he angry with him.
     (session 25)

(40) MOH: Toen die vrouw van hem   Then that woman of him
     N: Ja.   Yes.
     MOH: is ook blij.   is also happy.
     (session 27)

Like Ergün, Mohamed in later sessions also encodes possessive relationships mainly with the forms *hem* ('him') and *haar* ('her'). By doing so the possessive pronoun *zijn* ('his') is forced into a secondary role. A remarkable difference between the two informants seems to be that Ergün places the forms *hem* ('him') and *haar* ('her') in pre-position in combination with the preposition *van* ('of'), while Mohamed prefers post-position (compare Ergün's sequences 18-22 with Mohamed's sequences 35-40).

3rd role plural

For plural references in subject function Mohamed starts off generalizing the masculine singular form *hij* ('he') in session 2. He keeps doing this regularly in cycle 1 (see sequence 41) and cycle 2 (see sequence 42).

(41)	MOH:	In marokko elke hm + hm allemaal	In morocco every um + um all
		jongens heb uh zeven jaar.	boys have er seven year.
	N:	Ja.	Yes.
	MOH:	Hij gaan naar school.	He go to school.
	N:	Ja.	Yes.
	MOH:	Eerste/ eerste jaar.	First/ first year.
	N:	Ja.	Yes.
	MOH:	Hij arabisch lezen.	He read arabic.
	(session 2)		

(42)	MOH:	Ja waarom die mensen verzekering als	Yes why those people insurance if
		hij dood ben?	he am dead?
	(session 16)		

In cycles 1 and 2 Mohamed occasionally uses the full form *zij* ('they') and the reduced form *ze* ('they') standardlike. In addition, the dialect forms *hunnie* ('they') and *hullie* ('they') can occasionally be observed in cycles 1 and 2. In this respect Mohamed's metalinguistic reflections in session 11 are illuminating (see sequence 43).

(43)	MOH:	Ja ik weet. Is uh ik he	Yes I know. Is er I eh
	N:	Ja.	Yes.
	MOH:	is *ana*.	is *I*.
	N:	Hm.	Um.
	MOH:	Jij is *nta*. Hij is *huwa*.	You is *you*. He is *he*.
	N:	Ja.	Yes.
	MOH:	Zij is *hiya* he	She is *she* er
	N:	Ja.	Yes.
	MOH:	is *hiya*.	is *she*.
	N:	Ja.	Yes.
	MOH:	Wij is *ḥna*.	We is *we*.
	N:	Ja.	Yes.
	MOH:	Uh jullie is *ntuma*.	Er you is *you*.
	N:	Ja.	Yes.
	MOH:	Uh hullie	Er they
	N:	Ja nee.	Yes no.
	MOH:	is *huma*.	is *they*.
	N:	Ja is niet [goed]	Yes is not [correct]
	MOH:	[of *hum*]	[or *they*]
	N:	Nee zij is/	No she<they> is/
	MOH:	Hm.	Um.
	N:	zij is *hum* of *huma*. <..>	she<they> is *she* or *they*. <..>
	MOH:	Ik een keer met/ met jongens in/	I once with/ with boys in/
		marokkaans jongens in oisterwijk he.	moroccan boys in oisterwijk right.
		Hij allemaal hebben hier acht jaar	He all have eight years here
		en uh tien jaar. En ik vraag "Zij is	and er ten year. And I ask "She<they> is

voor niet men/ een mens niet hier he?".   for not peo/ one man not here right?".
N: Ja.   Yes.
MOH: Maar die jongens zeg "Moet jij zeg   But those boys say "Must you say
    hullie niet zij".   they not she<they>".
(session 11)

In cycle 3 the object form *hun* ('them') takes over the subject function for plural reference. Although, strictly speaking, this is no standardlike use, it becomes more and more frequent in native spoken Dutch (see Chapter 4). An example of this use by Mohamed is given in sequence (44).

(44)   MOH: Ja ik vind hier he iets stoms he   Yes I find er something stupid here er
    bijvoorbeeld als hun zien + ja +   for example if them see + yes +
    jongens of met/ met zwart haar dan   boys or with/ with black hair then
    zeggen "stom turk".   say "stupid turk".
(session 25)

In object function for plural reference, the generalized use of the singular object form *hem* ('him') and the standardlike use of the plural form *hun* ('them') can be observed:

(45)   MOH: Ik heb aan hun allemaal gezegd wat   I have told them all what
    moet hun doen.   must them do.
(session 27)

6.3.4   FATIMA

3rd role reference

The form-function relationships of the pronouns used by Fatima for 3rd role reference are given in Table 6.7. Compared to the other three informants Fatima refers relatively less frequently with pronominal means to a man or a woman in 3rd role.

3rd role singular

With Fatima the acquisition of forms within the 3rd role paradigm develops considerably more slowly than with Mohamed and Ergün.

In subject function Fatima does not use the subject pronouns *hij* ('he') and *zij* ('she') until relatively late. Gender generalizations only concern the masculine pronoun *hij* ('he'). An example is given in sequence (46).

(46)   FAT: Ja maaike zeg uh/ uh/ + "Ik komt uh   Yes maaike say er/ er/ + "I come er
    + +"/. Hij zegt "Ik kom tilburg".   + +"/. He says "I come tilburg".
(session 11)

Table 6.7: Pronominal 3rd role reference by Fatima

CYCLE 1	s1	s2	s3	s4	s5	s6	s7	s8	s9	Total	English
Subject:											
Sg: hij	-	-	-	-	-	-	-	-	1	1	he
Possess:											
Sg: haar X	-	-	-	-	-	-	-	-	1	1	her X
jouw X (=zijn)	-	-	-	-	-	3	-	-	-	3	your X (=his)
jouw X (=haar)	-	-	-	-	-	-	-	-	1	1	your X (=her)
Pl: haar X (=hun)	-	-	-	-	1	-	-	-	-	1	her X (=their)

CYCLE 2	s10	s11	s12	s13	s14	s15	s16	s17	s18	Total	English
Subject:											
Sg: hij	-	-	-	-	-	-	1	-	1	2	he
zij	-	-	-	2	-	-	-	1	-	3	she
hij (=zij)	-	1	-	1	-	-	-	-	-	2	he (=she)
haar (=zij)	-	-	-	-	1	-	-	-	-	1	her (=she)
Pl: jullie (=zij)	-	3	-	-	-	-	-	-	1	4	you (=they)
Possess:											
Sg: haar X	-	1	-	5	1	3	4	4	1	19	her X
haar X (=zijn)	-	-	3	-	-	-	-	-	2	5	her X (=his)
jouw X (=zijn)	-	-	1	-	-	-	-	-	-	1	your X (=his)
jouw X (=haar)	-	-	-	-	-	-	-	1	-	1	your X (=her)

CYCLE 3	s19	s20	s21	s22	s23	s24	s25	s26	s27	Total	English
Subject:											
Sg: hij	-	2	9	4	1	29	2	4	27	78	he
zij	-	-	1	-	-	1	-	1	3	6	she
hij (=zij)	-	-	-	3	1	-	-	7	4	15	he (=she)
Pl: jullie (=zij)	-	-	-	1	-	-	-	-	4	5	you (=they)
Object:											
Sg: hem	-	1	-	-	-	-	-	-	-	1	him
hij (=hem)	-	3	1	1	1	1	-	-	3	10	he (=him)
haar	-	-	-	-	-	1	-	-	-	1	her
zij (=haar)	-	-	-	1	-	2	-	-	-	3	she (=her)
hij (=haar)	-	-	-	-	-	1	-	-	-	1	he (=her)
Pl: hun	-	-	-	-	1	-	-	-	-	1	their
Possess:											
Sg: hij X (=zijn)	-	-	1	-	-	-	-	-	-	1	he X (=his)
X van hij	-	-	1	-	-	-	-	-	-	1	X of he
haar X	-	-	-	-	-	1	-	-	-	1	her X
haar X (=zijn)	-	1	2	-	-	1	-	-	-	4	her X (=his)
jouw X (=zijn)	-	-	-	-	-	1	-	-	-	1	your X (=his)
jouw X (=haar)	-	-	-	-	-	1	-	-	-	1	your X (=her)

In object function pronouns are used just as late as in cycle 3. The object forms *hem* ('him') and *haar* ('her') both occur only once. Especially the subject forms *hij* ('he') and *zij* ('she') are generalized in object function (see sequence 47 and 48).

(47) FAT: Ik zeg voor hij "Die melk ander".   I say for he "That milk other".
       (session 22)

(48) FAT: Ja die uh + buurvrouw.   Yes that er + woman nextdoor.
     N: Ja.   Yes.
     FAT: Nou die brief kom voor haar/ voor zij. Now that letter come for her/ for she.
     (session 24)

In possessive function Fatima's use of the feminine form *haar* ('her') is striking. This form appears early, even before the subject form *zij* ('she'), and it occurs relatively often. Several times Fatima generalizes the pronoun *haar* ('her') by using it to refer to a man as possessor. Examples of this use are given in the following sequences:

(49) FAT: Ja die vader ook boos met uh +   Yes that father also angry with er +
            haar jongen.   her boy.
     (session 12)

(50) FAT: Die man uh   That man er
     N: Ja?   Yes?
     FAT: auto kocht. Nou haar vrouw uh kom.   bought car. Now her wife er come.
     (session 18)

The masculine form *zijn* ('his'), however, does not occur in any of the 27 sessions. Only the subject form *hij* ('he') is generalized in possessive function (see sequence 51).

(51) FAT: Hij vader zeg voor uh + + zoon "Jij   He father say for er + + son "You
            morgen".   tomorrow".
     N: "Niet fietsen".   "Not cycle".
     FAT: "Niet fietsen".   "Not cycle".
     (session 21)

Finally, also the 2nd role pronoun *jouw* ('your') is used regularly for 3rd role reference in possessive function. This phenomenon has been discussed in Chapter 5.

3rd role plural

Fatima occasionally generalizes the 2nd role pronoun *jullie* ('you') for plural reference in subject function (see Chapter 5). In object function the form *hun* ('them') can be found once:

(52) FAT: Ik uh hun bel van marokko.   I er them phone from morocco.
     (session 23)

In possessive function the form *haar* ('her') is used for plural reference. This form is used remarkably early (as early as session 5):

(53) FAT: Die mensen veel geld^ koopt van uh +   Those people much money^ buy of er +
            haar kinder.   her children.
     (session 5)

6.3.5   THE SHADOW INFORMANTS

The findings of the core informants will be checked against empirical data derived
from the shadow informants (cf. Chapter 5). Table 6.8 gives a simple frequency list
of the pronominal forms used by the shadow informants.

Table 6.8: Overview 3rd role pronouns used by the shadow informants

	Osman (57,495)	Abdullah (32,648)	Hassan (61,312)	Husseyn (65,983)	Total	English
hij	837	645	972	1,558	4,012	he
ie	11	2	45	7	65	he
zij	159	39	9	254	461	she/they
ze	64	13	28	13	118	she/they/them
hem	54	28	365	56	503	him
'm	10	3	2	2	17	him
haar	48	3	31	84	166	her
zijn	33	16	20	126	195	his
hun	-	1	-	6	7	their/them

The limitations of the kind of information given in Table 6.8 on the pronoun use by
the shadow informants were already discussed in the previous chapter. With respect
to forms used for 3rd role reference some homonyms have been scanned for non-
relevant meanings; excluded are those cases in which the form *haar* means "hair" and
the form *zijn* means "to be".

6.4   RESULTS

In Section 6.1 a set of predictions were presented which will be tested on the basis
of the pronominal preferences of the core and shadow informants. The first prediction to be tested was directed towards the full-reduced distinction in the Dutch pronoun system:

P1   Full forms are acquired before reduced forms

This prediction is confirmed. As with the forms in the 1st and 2nd role paradigms,
the 3rd role paradigm shows an overall dominance of full forms in the learner varieties of both the core and shadow informants. Although with one of the Moroccan
informants a striking appearance of the reduced form *ie* ('he') can be noted in the
cycle 3 sessions.

    In testing the predictions the same procedure is followed as in Chapter 5, i.e.
(dis)confirming evidence is provided by (1) the standardlike and formulaic use of a
pronoun, and (2) the generalized use. For the core informants the first moment of
standardlike and non-formulaic use of a form can be derived from their pronoun
profiles presented in the previous sections. For the shadow informants a form-func-

tion analysis was carried out until the first instance of standardlike appearance was found. The acquisition orders of pronouns within the 3rd role paradigm are given in Table 6.9.

Table 6.9: Order of acquisition 3rd role pronouns (standardlike use)

	Turkish Mahmut	Ergün	Osman	Abdullah	Moroccan Mohamed	Fatima	Hassan	Husseyn
CYCLE 1								
s1	-	-	-	-	hij	-	hij	-
	-	-	-	-	hem	-	-	-
s2	-	-	-	hij	-	-	-	hij
	-	-	-	-	-	-	-	haar (p)
s3	hij	hij	hij	-	-	-	zijn	zij (pl)
	-	-	zij (sg)	-	zijn	-	-	zijn
s4	zij (pl)	-	ze (pl)	-	-	-	hem	zij (sg)
	-	-	-	-	-	-	ie	-
s5	-	-	-	zij (sg)	-	-	-	-
	-	-	-	hem	-	-	-	-
s6	-	zij (sg)	-	zijn	zij (sg)	-	-	hem
	-	zijn	-	-	-	-	-	-
s7	-	-	-	-	-	-	-	-
s8	zij (sg)	-	-	ie	zij (pl)	-	ze (pl)	-
s9	-	-	hem	haar (p)	haar (o)	hij	haar (p)	-
	-	-	-	-	-	haar (p)	-	-
CYCLE 2								
s10	-	-	ie	-	haar (p)	-	ze (sg)	-
	-	-	-	-	-	-	zij (sg)	-
s11	-	-	-	-	ie	-	zij (pl)	-
	-	-	-	-	hun (o)	-	-	-
s12	-	hem	'm	-	-	-	-	-
	-	-	zij (pl)	-	-	-	-	-
s13	-	ie	ze (sg)	-	-	zij (sg)	-	'm
s14	-	-	haar (o+p)	zij (pl)	-	-	-	-
s15	-	-	-	-	-	-	-	-
s16	-	-	-	-	-	-	haar (o)	-
s17	-	'm	-	-	ze (pl)	-	-	hun (o)
s18	-	haar (o+p)	-	-	ze (sg)	-	-	-
CYCLE 3								
s19	-	ze (sg)	-	-	'm	-	-	ze (sg)
s20	-	-	zijn	-	-	hem	-	-
s21	-	-	-	-	-	-	-	-
s22	-	hun (o)	-	ze (pl)	-	-	-	haar (o)
s23	-	-	-	-	-	hun (o)	-	ie
s24	-	-	-	-	-	haar (o)	-	-
s25	-	-	-	-	-	-	-	-
s26	-	-	-	-	-	-	-	-
s27	haar (p)	-	-	-	-	-	-	ze (pl)

(s = subject; o = object; p = possessive; sg = singular; pl = plural)

In the next sections the predictions made with respect to dimensions in the 3rd role paradigm will be tested.

6.4.1 NUMBER

P4   Singular forms are acquired before plural forms

Results of testing this prediction on the basis of standardlike use are given in Table 6.10. The same conventions are used as in Chapter 5, i.e. "+ +" indicates that the prediction is confirmed, "– –" that it is contradicted, "+–" indicates that the members of a pair are acquired simultaneously, and "··" indicates lack of evidence.

Table 6.10: Testing the order of acquisition on the number dimension (3rd role)

P4 Singular	before	Plural	Turkish				Moroccan			
			Mah.	Erg.	Osm.	Abd.	Moh.	Fat.	Has.	Hus.
hij	before	zij (pl)	+ +	+ +	+ +	+ +	+ +	+ +	+ +	+ +
zij (sg)	before	zij (pl)	– –	+ +	+ +	+ +	+ +	+ +	+ +	– –
hem	before	hun (o)	··	+ +	+ +	+ +	+ +	+ +	+ +	+ +
haar (o)	before	hun (o)	··	+ +	+ +	··	+ +	– –	+ +	– –
zijn	before	hun (p)	··	+ +	+ +	+ +	+ +	··	+ +	+ +
haar (p)	before	hun (p)	+ +	+ +	+ +	+ +	+ +	+ +	+ +	+ +

Table 6.11 gives the number of generalizations that can be observed in the learner varieties of the core informants.

Table 6.11: Generalizations for number (3rd role)

Form	Function	Generalization	Mahmut	Ergün	Mohamed	Fatima	Total
hij	zij	Sg. > Pl.	1	-	20	-	21
hem	hun	Sg. > Pl.	-	-	2	-	2

On the whole, the prediction that singular forms are acquired before plural forms is confirmed. However, there are two exceptions: (1) Mahmut and Husseyn use the homonym form *zij* ('she/they') earlier in plural function than in singular function, (2) two Moroccan informants acquire the singular object form *haar* ('her') later than the plural object form *hun* ('them').

As can be derived from Table 6.11, one informant (Mohamed) in particular generalizes singular forms for plural reference, i.e. the object form *hem* ('him') and the subject form *hij* ('he'). Note that in the previous chapter Mohamed was the only informant who within the 2nd role paradigm generalized the singular form *jouw* ('your') for plural reference.

6.4.2 GENDER

P6 Masculine forms are acquired before feminine forms
P12 The gender dimension will be easier for Moroccan learners than for Turkish learners of Dutch.

Results of testing these predictions on the basis of standardlike use are given in the following table:

Table 6.12: Testing the order of acquisition on the gender dimension (3rd role)

P6 Masculine	before	Feminine	Turkish Mah.	Erg.	Osm.	Abd.	Moroccan Moh.	Fat.	Has.	Hus.
hij	before	zij (sg)	+ +	+ +	+ –	+ +	+ +	+ +	+ +	+ +
hem	before	haar (o)	··	+ +	+ +	+ +	+ +	+ +	+ +	+ +
zijn	before	haar (p)	– –	+ +	– –	+ +	+ +	– –	+ +	– –

The generalized use on the gender dimension that can be observed in the learner varieties of the core informants is given in Table 6.13.

Table 6.13: Generalizations for gender (3rd role)

Form	Function	Generalization	Mahmut c1	c2	c3	Ergün c1	c2	c3	Mohamed c1	c2	c3	Fatima c1	c2	c3	Total
hij	zij	Msc. > Fem.	-	8	-	4	15	24	13	3	-	-	2	15	84
	haar	Msc. > Fem.	-	-	-	-	-	-	5	-	-	-	-	1	6
zij	hij	Fem. > Msc.	1	-	-	-	3	1	-	-	-	-	-	-	5
	hem	Fem. > Msc.	1	-	-	-	-	-	-	-	-	-	-	-	1
	zijn	Fem. > Msc.	-	-	-	-	-	-	7	-	-	-	-	-	7
hem	haar	Msc. > Fem.	-	-	-	-	-	4	-	1	-	-	-	-	5
zijn	haar	Msc. > Fem.	-	-	-	-	1	-	1	-	-	-	-	-	2
haar	zijn	Fem. > Msc.	-	-	-	-	-	-	-	-	-	-	5	4	9

For the subject pronouns prediction 6 is confirmed: the masculine pronoun *hij* ('he') is acquired before the feminine pronoun *zij* ('she'). Gender generalizations mostly concern generalized use of the masculine pronoun *hij* ('he') for feminine reference. This can be observed for all core informants. In contrast, generalization of the feminine pronoun *zij* ('she') for masculine reference can only observed for the Turkish core informants.

Also, for the object pronouns prediction 6 is confirmed: the masculine form *hem* ('him') is used standardlike before the feminine form *haar* ('her'). As can be derived from Table 6.13, only the masculine form is generalized for gender.

With respect to the pronouns in possessive function prediction 6 is disconfirmed by four out of eight informants (see Table 6.12).

All in all, in accordance with prediction 6, the conclusion is that within the 3rd role paradigm masculine forms are acquired before feminine forms. However, prediction 12 is disconfirmed: the findings do not suggest that the gender dimension is easier for the Moroccan learners than for the Turkish learners of Dutch. In addition, it can be noted that for the gender dimension most commonly generalized use in both directions can be found. So, although masculine pronouns seem to be acquired before feminine pronouns, this does not imply that the masculine forms are more likely to be generalized for gender than the feminine forms. In this respect it can be noted that Fatima, the only female informant, is also the only one who frequently generalizes the feminine form *haar* ('her') for gender (see Table 6.13).

6.4.3 CASE

P7 Subject forms are acquired before object forms
P8 Subject forms are acquired before possessive forms
P9 Forms in object function are acquired before forms in possessive function
P10 The case dimension will be easier for Turkish learners than for Moroccan learners of Dutch

Results of testing these predictions on the basis of standardlike use are given in Table 6.14.

Table 6.14: Testing the order of acquisition on the case dimension (3rd role)

			Turkish				Moroccan			
			Mah.	Erg.	Osm.	Abd.	Moh.	Fat.	Has.	Hus.
P7	Subject	before	Object							
	hij	before	hem	++	++	++	++	..	++	++	++
	zij (sg)	before	haar (o)	++	++	++	++	++	++	++	++
	zij (pl)	before	hun (o)	++	−−	++	++	++	−−	++	++
P8	Subject	before	Possessive							
	hij	before	zijn	++	++	++	++	++	++	++	++
	zij (sg)	before	haar (p)	++	++	++	++	++	−−	−−	−−
	zij (pl)	before	hun (p)	++	..	++	++	++	..	++	++
P9	Object	before	Possessive							
	hem	before	zijn	..	−−	++	++	++	++	−−	−−
	haar (o)	before	haar (p)	−−	+−	+−	−−	++	−−	−−	−−
	hun (o)	before	hun (p)	..	++	..	..	++	++	..	++

The generalized use on the case dimension that can be observed in the learner varieties of the core informants is given in Table 6.15.

Table 6.15: Generalizations for case (3rd role)

Form	Function	Generalization	Mahmut c1	c2	c3	Ergün c1	c2	c3	Mohamed c1	c2	c3	Fatima c1	c2	c3	Total
hij	hem	S > O	1	2	-	-	-	-	5	-	-	-	-	11	19
	zijn	S > P	-	1	3	-	1	-	22	-	1	-	-	1	29
	haar (o)	S > O	-	-	-	-	-	-	-	-	-	-	-	1	1
	haar (p)	S > P	-	-	-	-	-	-	5	-	-	-	-	-	5
zij	hem	S > O	1	-	-	-	-	-	-	-	-	-	-	-	1
	zijn	S > P	-	-	-	-	-	-	7	-	-	-	-	-	7
	haar (o)	S > O	-	-	-	-	1	-	2	-	-	-	-	3	6
	haar (p)	S > P	-	-	-	-	-	-	3	-	-	-	-	-	3
hem	zijn	O > P	-	-	-	-	4	29	-	12	17	-	-	-	62
haar	zij	O/P > S	-	-	-	-	1	-	-	-	-	-	1	-	2
zij	hun	S > O/P	-	2	-	-	-	-	-	-	-	-	-	-	2

Prediction 7 is confirmed. There is a clear dominance of subject forms. In fact, prediction 7 is only disconfirmed by the order of acquisition of the forms *zij* ('they') and *hun* ('them'), observed with two out of eight informants (see Table 6.14). All core informants generalize subject forms in object function, Mohamed in particular. Only two instances of generalized use of the form *haar* ('her') in subject function can be observed.

Prediction 8, which states that subject forms are acquired before possessive forms, is confirmed for all four Turkish informants. Interestingly enough, for the Moroccan informants this prediction is only partly confirmed: three informants acquire the homonym for *zij* ('she'/'they') relatively late in subject function for singular reference.

With respect to prediction 9 a diffuse picture emerges. On the basis of the information presented in Table 6.14, the conclusion is that prediction 9 is disconfirmed: object forms are not acquired before possessive forms.

Finally prediction 10, with the exception of *zij* (sg) - *haar* (p) the observations do not confirm that the case dimension will be easier for Turkish than for Moroccan learners of Dutch.

However, there is a complicating factor in that pronouns used as "object of preposition", e.g. *geef het boek aan hem* ('give the book to him') can also be used in possessive function, e.g. *dat boek van hem* ('that book of him'), in particular when they are used in combination with the preposition *van* ('of'). In other words, there is a conflation between the set of object forms and the set of possessive forms. A detailed account of the decision made in the analysis was given in the previous chapter (in Section 5.2). In the pronoun profiles of the four core informants this conflation was dealt with by making a subdivision between three categories: (1) forms in object function not encoding possession, (2) forms in possessive function used without the preposition *van* ('of'), and (3) forms in possessive function used together with *van* ('of') in pre- or post-position. This subdivision made it possible to pinpoint within both the 1st role and 3rd role paradigms a remarkable difference between two core informants.

It appears that Ergün, a Turkish core informant, increasingly uses the object pronoun *hem* ('him') in a "*van*-Pro-N" construction, while Mohamed, a Moroccan informant, increasingly uses this form in a "Pro-*van*-N" construction. This observation calls for cross-learner evidence from the shadow informants. Table 6.16 gives the singular object/possessive forms which are used in non-subject function with or without the preposition *van* ('of'). Note that the generalized use of subject pronouns in object/possessive function is not taken into account, nor are generalizations for number and gender.

Table 6.16: Object/possessive forms used in non-subject function

		Turkish				Moroccan				
		Mah.	Erg.	Osm.	Abd.	Moh.	Fat.	Has.	Hus.	Total
Object:	hem	-	30	34	13	247	1	197	54	576
	haar	-	7	23	-	42	1	9	6	88
Possess:	zijn X	2	3	35	16	6	-	21	104	187
	hem X	-	1	4	7	30	-	91	-	133
	van hem X	-	32	9	8	-	-	-	-	49
	X van hem	-	2	3	-	38	-	75	1	119
	haar X	1	1	4	2	5	31	1	75	120
	van haar X	-	2	-	-	-	-	-	-	2
	X van haar	-	7	1	-	8	-	1	-	17

Table 6.16 shows that besides Ergün the two Turkish shadow informants also use "*van*-Pro-N" constructions. They start using this construction in later sessions: Osman from session 12 onwards and Abdullah from session 19 onwards. Sequences (54)-(57) give examples for these informants.

(54) OSM: Hij drinkt alleen koffie. Maar hij   He only drinks coffee. But he
            blijf drie uur of vier uur café +   stays three hours or four hours cafe +
            van hem moeder en vader snapt niet he.   of him mother and father does not
     (session 20)   understand right.

(55) OSM: Hij zegt "Rij maar hier weg". En van   He says "Drive away from here". And of
            hem moeder is kwaad op politieagent.   him mother is angry with police officer.
     (session 27)

(56) N: Waarom is die jongen daar?   Why is that boy there?
     ABD: Daar is die fiets van die jongen.   There is that bicycle of that boy.
     N: Hmhm   Uh-huh.
     ABD: Van hem fiets kapot denk ik voorkant.   Of him bicycle broken down I think front
     (session 21)   side.

(57) ABD: Dit is van onze kerstboom.   This is of our cherry tree.
     N: Zaten er ook kersen in?   Were there any cherries on it?

ABD:	Ja moet uithalen he?		Yes must pick eh?
N:	Ja.		Yes.
ABD:	Andere huis meebrengen.		Other house bring along.
N:	Oja heb je mee/ heb je uitgehaald?		Oh yes did you/ did you pick them?
ABD:	Nou zitten van de osman. Van hem thuis.		Now sit of the osman. Of him house.
N:	Die boom? In de tuin van osman?		That tree? In the garden of osman?

(session 23)

Ergün occasionally uses the possessive pronoun *zijn* ('his'). In later sessions he replaces this form by a "*van*-Pro-N" construction. In contrast, Osman and Abdullah, frequently use the possessive pronoun *zijn* ('his'), alongside the "*van*-Pro-N" construction.

It is striking that with the Moroccan informants the "*van*-Pro-N" construction can never be observed. Hassan resembles Mohamed in the frequent use of the "N-*van*-Pro" construction. Hassan uses this construction regularly from session 9 onwards. Some examples are given in sequences (58) and (59).

(58)	HAS:	En dan die kwam bij vriend van hem.	And then that came to friend of him.
		Die wil slaap bij vriend van hem.	That wants to sleep with friend of him.
	N:	Ja.	Yes.
	HAS:	Maar vriend van hem hij zegt tegen	But friend of him he says to
		hem "Moet jij uh weg uit huis".	him "Must you er go from house".
	(session 12)		

(59)	HAS:	Veel mensen.	Many people.
	N:	Ja.	Yes.
	HAS:	Die was daar kijken. Die was tot bij	That was looking there. That was to at
		die mensen. Dan was zo binnen kijken.	those people. Then was so looking inside.
		Dan zien de vriend van hem. De hoofd	Then see the friend of him. The head
		van hem staat daar en de arm van hem	of him stands there and the arm of him
		staat daar.	stands there.
	(session 16)		

Both Mohamed and Hassan also use the object pronoun *hem* ('him') frequently without the preposition *van* ('of'). In contrast, Husseyn never uses the object pronoun *hem* ('him'), but he sticks remarkably frequently to the possessive pronoun *zijn* ('his').

6.5   CONCLUSIONS

On the basis of the analyses presented so far, it is now possible to go into the research questions specified in Section 6.1.

I   Which set of forms is used in early learner varieties and what are the referential functions of these forms?

As was observed for the 1st and 2nd role paradigms a dominance of full forms can be found. Some informants also use the reduced form *ie* ('he'). With Mohamed and Ergün in particular this form can be observed in later sessions.

On the number dimension an overall-dominance of singular forms over plural forms emerges. With one Moroccan informant, Mohamed, a strong generalized use of the masculine form *hij* ('he') for plural reference was found.

On the gender dimension an overall-dominance of masculine forms over feminine forms emerges. Gender generalizations go in both directions, i.e. masculine forms are used for feminine reference, and feminine forms are used for masculine reference.

On the case dimension two observations can be made. Firstly, there is an overall-dominance of subject forms over object and possessive forms. Subject forms are also generalized in object/possessive function whereas the reverse does not occur. Secondly, the object form *hem* ('him') occurs frequently and is generalized regularly in possessive function.

II   How is this initial set expanded over time in subsequent stages of language acquisition?

The acquisition of the Dutch pronoun system by Turkish and Moroccan adults (with the focus on the core informants) reveals a growth in size as well as in variety: over time 3rd role reference occurs more often and with more different forms.

The following general principles apply to the acquisition order of forms within the 3rd role paradigm:
- Singular forms are acquired before plural forms.
- Subject forms are acquired before object/possessive forms.
- Masculine forms are acquired before feminine forms.

The first two principles, addressing the number and case dimensions respectively, were also found to apply to the 1st/2nd role paradigms (see Chapter 5).

It is difficult to specify a more precise uniform order of acquisition for the pronominal forms within the 3rd role paradigm. This can only be done if the non-subject pronouns *hem* ('him'), *haar* ('her'), and *zijn* ('his') are left out. The order of acquisition which is evidenced for all core/shadow informants is given in Table 6.17.

Table 6.17: Order of acquisition 3rd role forms

EARLY	hij	-->	zij	-->	hun	LATE

A more detailed picture can be derived from the pronoun profiles of the core informants. Besides, for each of them the order of acquisition observed within each of the three paradigms can be combined.

Mahmut and Fatima

The observed order of acquisition within the 1st/2nd and 3rd role paradigms for Mahmut and Fatima are given in Table 6.18.

Table 6.18: Order of acquisition for Mahmut and Fatima (1st/2nd/3rd role)

Mahmut				Fatima			
	1st	2nd role	3rd role		1st	2nd role	3rd role
s1	ik	-	-	s1	ik	-	-
s3	-	jij	hij	s1	-	jij	-
s4	mijn	-	zij (pl)	s2	mijn	-	-
s6	mij	-	-	s5	mij	-	-
	-	-	-	s5	-	jullie (s)	-
s8	-	-	zij (sg)		-	-	-
s11	-	jullie (s)	-		-	-	-
	-	-	-	s7	-	jou	-
	-	-	-	s8	-	jullie (o)	-
	-	-	-	s9	-	-	hij
	-	-	-		-	-	haar (p)
s16	wij	-	-	s10	wij	-	-
	-	-	-	s13	-	-	zij (sg)
s17	-	jouw	-	s14	-	jouw	-
s25	-	jou	-		-	-	-
s25	ons (o)	-	-	s19	ons (o)	-	-
	-	-	-	s20	-	-	hem
	-	-	-	s23	-	-	hun (o)
s27	-	-	haar (p)	s24	-	-	haar (o)

It appears that for the 3rd role paradigm less striking similarities can be observed than for the 1st/2nd role paradigms. The differences centre around the number dimension.

As can be derived from Table 6.18 Mahmut already from the early sessions onwards uses pronouns for 3rd role reference. He enters the 3rd role paradigm on the number dimension, i.e. *hij* ('he') and *zij* ('they'). It is a reasonable conjecture that the encoding of number within the 1st/2nd role paradigms proceeds relatively unproblematic (cf. Chapter 5).

In contrast, with Fatima only 3rd role pronouns can be observed after she has acquired most of the forms within the 1st role and 2nd role paradigms. She starts with the number dimension within the 2nd role paradigm and next generalizes the plural 2nd role form *jullie* ('you') for 1st role reference and 3rd role reference respectively (cf. Chapter 5). In fact, Fatima appears to use the homonym form *zij* ('she'/'they') exclusively for feminine reference. This form is never used by Fatima for plural reference.

Ergün and Mohamed

The observed orders of acquisition within the 1st/2nd role and 3rd role paradigms for Ergün and Mohamed are given in Table 6.19.

Table 6.19: Order of acquisition for Ergün and Mohamed (1st/2nd/3rd role)

Ergün				Mohamed			
	1st	2nd role	3rd role		1st	2nd role	3rd role
s1	ik	jij	-	s1	ik	jij	hij
	-	-	-	s1	ons (o)	-	hem
s2	mijn	-	-	s1	mijn	-	-
s3	mij, wij	-	hij	s2	mij, wij	-	-
s3	-	jullie (s)	-	s3	-	jullie (s+o)	zijn
	-	-	-	s5	ons (p)	-	-
s6	-	jou	zij (sg)	s6	-	jou	zij (sg)
s6	-	-	zijn		-	-	-
s7	-	jouw	-	s6	-	jouw	-
s8	ons (p)	-	-	s8	-	-	zij (pl)
s11	ons (o)	-	-		-	-	-
s12	-	-	hem		-	-	-
s18	-	-	haar (o+p)	s9	-	-	haar (o)
	-	-	-	s11	-	-	hun (o)
s22	-	-	hun (o)		-	-	-
	-	-	-	s26	-	jullie (p)	-

Compared to the 1st/2nd role paradigm, the order of acquisition evidenced for Mohamed and Ergün within the 3rd role paradigm shows fewer similarities. In early sessions the differences mainly concern the case dimension, i.e. Mohamed's early use of the form *hem* ('him'), and Ergün's early use of the possessive pronoun *zijn* ('his'), which disappears in favour of the form *hem* ('him'). Or to put it more precisely: in later stages of acquisition Ergün increasingly uses "*van*-Pro-N" constructions.

III   How can learner preferences be explained?

The degree of perceptual saliency is responsible for the late acquisition of reduced forms and turns out to be a stronger determinant than frequency. Nevertheless, the relative frequency of full forms in spoken Dutch corresponds with the early acquisition of singular, masculine, and subject forms, compared to plural, feminine, and object/possessive forms respectively.

Fatima's rather strange use of the feminine form *haar* ('her') is intriguing. She uses this form in relative early sessions and she is the only one who generalizes this form for masculine reference. Perhaps frequency also plays a role here. An analysis carried out by Broeder (1989b) of a corpus of native spoken Dutch (i.e. the corpus external native use by De Jong 1979, see Chapter 4) revealed that Dutch men relatively more often use masculine pronouns and that Dutch women relatively more often feminine ones. This has also been observed by Thavenius (1983:101,181) for native speakers of English.

The frequency effect has been focussed on in a number of studies which investigated the relationship between L2 input and L2 acquisition (see Gass & Madden 1985). The most recurrent finding was indeed that there is a positive correlation between the frequency of a specific form in the target language input and the order in which learners produce it in their output. Larsen-Freeman (1985) points out two problems with respect to these so-called correlation studies: (1) items of a learner variety were often analysed disregarding their function and contextual use, (2) the normative comparison was not always made against native speaker data from the same interactions. In the present study attention has been paid to both problems. In addition it should be noted that the conclusion that frequency is a determinant of language acquisition does not simply mean that the learner has a kind of in-built counter which enables him to estimate the relative frequency of forms. There are two aspects of frequency: on the one hand the relative need for the learner to use a specific item, and correspondingly, the relative number of times the learner is confronted with a specific item.

In order to explore the potential effects of the source language of the informants, the model of paradigm formation was developed further: a Turkish-based paradigm and a Moroccan Arabic-based paradigm for the Dutch pronoun system were assumed. However, in the learner varieties of Dutch no clear traces were found of substantial source language related differences in the encoding of gender and case. There was no evidence for the blocking of specific forms within a Turkish/Moroccan Arabic-based paradigm. Nevertheless, a paradigm model consisting of different dimensions and levels provided a systematic account of what at first sight appeared to be rather strange instances of pronoun use.

Finally, a remarkable difference between the Turkish and Moroccan informants groups emerged. With the Turkish informants there was a preference for the "*van*-Pro-N" construction while the Moroccan informants preferred the "N-*van*-Pro" construction. This is especially clear in the 3rd role paradigm (where cross-learner evidence was provided by the shadow informants). Also in the 1st role paradigm this is a difference between Ergün (Turkish) and Mohamed (Moroccan). This "difference in directionality" in the encoding of the possessive relationship will be further investigated in Chapters 7 and 8.

6.6   CROSS-LEARNER AND CROSS-LINGUISTIC EVIDENCE

This chapter concludes the first area of investigation in the present study: talking about people and the use of pronouns. The observations and findings of the previous three chapters will be related to investigations on (1) adult language acquisition, (2) child language acquisition, and (3) pidgin and creole languages. The aim is to find cross-learner and cross-linguistic evidence for the pronominal preferences observed in our L2 learner varieties.

Studies of pronouns in L2 acquisition are relatively scarce. For child L2 acquisition there is a study by Felix (1981) focussing on English school children learning German. For adult L2 acquisition there are the studies by Klein & Rieck (1982) on German learner varieties of Italian and Spanish adults; Huebner (1983) on a Hmong (Laos) learner of English; Véronique (1984) and Giacobbe (1987) on French learner varieties of Moroccan and Spanish learners respectively, and Broeder, Extra & Van Hout (1986) on two of our core informants (i.e. Mahmut and Mohamed).

There are a lot more studies of pronouns in L1 acquisition. Important syntheses and research overviews are given by Clark (1978), Böhme (1983), and Chiat (1986). Attempts to make abstractions over the available empirical investigations on pronouns in language acquisition are hindered by several biases. Böhme (1983:37-38) points at the following complications with respect to the L1 studies on possessive pronouns, which hold for studies on personal pronouns as well:
- Most studies yield only information about 1st and 2nd role singular pronouns, due to a Piagetian interest in some early studies in the development of the "self" and in the beginnings of the differentiation between "Ego and Alter".
- Contextual and extra-linguistic information concerning the use of specific pronouns is scarce.
- Most studies deal with English as the target language.

However, bearing in mind these limitations, the available L1/L2 acquisition data may still provide useful information concerning developmental aspects of pronoun systems. In addition, special attention will be paid to relevant observations made in a number of studies on child L1 acquisition of Dutch, in particular Kaper (1985) and Schaerlaekens & Gillis (1987).

A number of investigations on pronouns in pidgin and creole languages will occasionally be related to the findings of the present study. A pidgin language is a reduced second language used as a medium of communication between people who do not share another language. Pidgins develop from simple to more complex systems as communicative requirements become more demanding. A pidgin becomes a creole language when it is adopted as a first language of a new generation of speakers (cf. Mühlhäusler 1986:5). Of particular relevance is the work by Mühlhäusler & Harré (1990). Their survey of pronouns in pidgin and creole studies is impressive. It is a source of inspiration and offers many suggestions for further research. A serious problem with their study, however, is the abundance of speculations which are not empirically based.

With respect to investigations on child L1-English, Chiat (1986) gives an overview of the order in which pronouns are acquired. Naturalistic as well as experimental studies on personal pronouns are discussed. On the basis of Chiat's (1986) survey of child L1-English and studies on child L1-Dutch (in particular Schaerlaekens & Gillis 1987), the following conclusions can be presented on the order in which pronouns are acquired in L1 acquisition of English and Dutch:
(1)   Children start off with a fairly predictable subset of pronouns which do not constitute a natural class. These are 1st role singular, subject form, i.e. *I* and *ik* ('I'), followed by 2nd role, i.e. *you* and *jij* ('you').
(2)   The set of possessive pronouns is normally acquired a little later than the set of personal pronouns, but also in the order 1st-2nd-3rd role.
(3)   Sporadic use of pronouns often precedes more systematic and frequent use: initially the distribution of pronouns is limited to specific contexts.

(4)   When pronouns first emerge, generalizations between different personal pronouns rarely occur.

These observations suggest at least some similarities to the pronoun preference observed in the adult L2 learner varieties of Dutch focussed upon in the present study: 1st role forms before 2nd role forms, and subject forms before object forms. In addition, some differences can be noted between the order patterns of pronouns in child L1 acquisition of English/Dutch compared to adult L2 acquisition of Dutch. For the adult informants in the present study, striking similarities in the order of acquisition could be observed within the 1st/2nd role paradigms, and to a lesser extent also within the 3rd role paradigm; sporadic use does not normally precede systematic use, and after the first appearance of a form, on most pronoun dimensions generalizations do not disappear.

Below, cross-learner and cross-linguistic data with respect to the pertinent dimensions and characteristics of the pronoun system will be discussed successively.

Emphasis

A remarkable observation in the L2-Dutch learner varieties focussed on in the present study is the overall-dominance of full pronouns over reduced pronouns, despite the relatively high frequency of reduced forms in spoken Dutch. This was evidenced for 1st/2nd role reference and also for 3rd role reference, although with respect to the latter a regular use of the reduced form *ie* could be found with some informants.

The reduced-full distinction is a highly language specific property of Dutch pronouns. Nevertheless, in adult L2-German learner varieties of Spanish and Italian adults, and L2-French learner varieties of Spanish adults, similar observations have been made. Klein & Rieck (1982) and Giacobbe (1987) observed an early appearance and overextended use of full instead of reduced forms. In addition, mirrorlike evidence is provided by investigations on pidgin and creole languages, in which "unstressed pronouns of lexically related languages are typically lost" (Mühlhäusler & Harré 1990:262).

Surprisingly, the reduced full-distinction emerges rather differently in child and adult learner varieties of Dutch. Compared with children, adult learners clearly use reduced pronouns less often. For example, Kaper (1985) found many instances of reduced pronouns. Some examples for his son Hans are given in sequences (60)-(62).

(60) HAN: Ga je af, mij toel.   Go you down, me chair.
      (Hans, age 2;4)

(61) HAN: Nou zijn we allemaal een jasje uit.   Now we all are a jacket off.
      (Hans, age 2;7)

(62) HAN: Ze hebben een beetje heleboel meer   They (i.e. the bunnies) have got
              gekregen.   a little lot more.
      (Hans, age 4;0)

As yet, no systematic investigation has been carried out of the difference between adults and children in the acquisition of the reduced-full distinction. In trying to explain this difference between children and adults one can only speculate. The degree of perceptual saliency, i.e. the degree to which segments attract attention in the speech stream, might be a crucial factor. Perceptual saliency of a form depends on (1) its position in the utterance, and (2) prosodic features. In particular with respect to these properties adult L2 learners may have some L1-based preferences which might be a disadvantage in acquiring Dutch, i.e. they are used to a specific order of words to be pronounced in a specific way.

In spoken Dutch the reduced-full distinction coincides with the distribution of forms in the utterance. The underlying word order in Dutch is (S)ubject-(O)bject-(V)erb with a Verb-second rule for main clauses. This basic word order pattern most commonly corresponds with the distribution of the full subject/object pronouns. Model (1991:213,279) notes that the distribution of reduced pronouns, which he calls enclitics, differs from the basic, canonical distribution of nominal devices and full pronouns. Empirical studies carried out by Jansen (1981) and Van Hout (1989) for two different corpora of native spoken Dutch seem to confirm the typical position of reduced pronouns. Their analyses reveal that subject pronouns most commonly occur in the unmarked and unstressed position after the finite verb in main clauses.

A general finding in studies on L1 transfer is that L1 prosody is one of the most resistant aspects of the source language for which transfer to the target language can be noted, even in advanced stages of L2 acquisition (cf. Ellis 1985:40). Adult L2 learners of Dutch may be hindered by the L1-based prosodic features which do not take into account such systematic differences. In contrast, children already in a very early acquisition stage take advantage of the information provided by prosodic features in the speech stream (e.g. contrastive stress for the agent, and intonation patterns).

Role
A crucial condition for a standardlike use of 1st/2nd role pronouns is that the basic referent point is taken into account, i.e. the pronoun has to be produced and used relative to the point of view of the speaker. This is the speech role function of a pronoun. Whereas adult language learners are aware of the speech role function, this has to be discovered by children.

In studies on child language acquisition the phenomenon of pronoun reversal has been related to the "egocentrism of children" in early acquisition stages. The general observation is that 1st role singular pronouns are produced relatively early and that 2nd role singular pronouns are understood relatively early (e.g. Clark 1978, Loveland 1984, and Chiat 1986). As a result, children use 2nd role pronouns for self-reference and 1st role pronouns for reference to the addressee. A nice illustration for this is provided by the following observation which I made for my daughter Sanne:

(63) M: Is deze beker van jou?   Is this cup of you?
      SAN: Nee niet van jou, van sanne.   No not of you, of sanne.
      (Sanne, age 2;4)   < pointing to herself >

This sequence was followed by the parents' explanation of the meaning of *mij* ('me')
and *jou* ('you'). It was obvious that Sanne did not understand this and the explanation confused her. Interestingly, the next day while I was playing with her in the
sandbox, the following exchange took place:

(64) F: Goed gedaan peter.   Well done peter.
                                                  < referring to himself >
      SAN: Papa is peter. Mama is kaan,   Daddy is peter. Mommy is karin
            Sanne is jou.   Sanne is you.
      (Sanne, age 2;4)

Systematic reversal of 1st/2nd role pronouns in child L1 acquisition of Dutch is
reported for example by Van der Geest (1974) and De Vooys (1916), see sequences
(65) and (66) respectively.

(65) MAR: Dit jouw melk?   This your milk?
      (Mark, age 2;0)   < =Is this my milk? >

(66) V: Zeg eens ik, nelly is ik.   Say I, nelly is I.
      NEL: Nee. Nelly is niet ik. Nelly is jij! No. Nelly is not I. Nelly is you!
      (Nelly, age 2;6)

Other observations of pronoun reversal in Dutch have been made by Kaper
(1985:93), who noted inconsistent self-reference. Some examples of 2nd role for 1st
role pronoun reversal (*je* 'you' meaning *mij* 'me') are given in the following
sequences:

(67) ERI: Mama bij je komen.   Mama (must) come to you.
      (Erik, age 2;10)

(68) HAN: Hij zit naast je.   He is sitting beside you.
      (Hans, age 2;6)

An instance of 1st role for 2nd role pronoun reversal (*mij* 'my' meaning *jouw* 'your')
is given in the following sequence:

(69) ERI: Hier zitten, mama! Op me schoot.   (I will) sit here, mama! On my lap.
      (Erik, age 3;6)

As more investigations on pronoun reversal by children were made, a more differentiated explanatory picture emerged. Chiat (1986) noted that in most studies reversed
use of a pronoun is observed always in concord with adultlike pronoun use. Moreover, a discrepancy was found between production and comprehension. For example,
in Chiat (1982), a case study of a two-and-a-half-year old boy acquiring English,

inconsistent adultlike vs. reversed production was found next to consistent, adultlike comprehension of 1st role pronouns and production of 2nd role pronouns. A number of studies (e.g. Charney 1980, Chiat 1985,1986) which focussed on those children who systematically reversed pronouns stressed pragmatic factors of pronoun acquisition. Loveland (1984) conjectures that it is often undifferentiated, unanalysed forms and/or cases in which the child repeats the pronoun in the interlocutor's directly preceding question, in which pronoun reversal occurs. Sequence (70) is an example given by Loveland (1984).

(70) Adult: Where are your shoes?
    Child 2: There's your shoes.
            <pointing to her own>

In this sequence pronoun reversal may be caused by the process of interaction, not necessarily by the "egocentrism of the child". In this respect these types of role generalization resemble the generalized use of *jouw* ('your') observed in the present study in the L2 learner varieties of the Moroccan informants.

    In adult L2 acquisition one would not expect to find pronoun reversal because their cognitive development may be considered to be completed in this respect. This is indeed confirmed by the adult learner varieties observed in the present study: pronoun reversals of 1st/2nd role pronouns occur very infrequently. Moreover, they always concern the generalized use of 2nd role pronouns, in particular the forms *jouw* and *jullie*, which are also generalized for 3rd role reference.

    The generalized use of the 2nd role pronouns for 1st role and 3rd role references can be found in particular with Moroccan learners of Dutch. A preliminary analysis I carried out for the French learner varieties of Moroccan informants revealed some comparable cases in which 2nd role pronouns are generalized for 3rd role reference. An example is given in sequence (71):

(71) N: Et comment est-ce qu'il rencontre   And how does he meet
            cette femme?   that woman?
    ABD: La femme?   The woman?
    N: Hmhm.   Uh-huh.
    ABD: C'est pas ça + + + par exemple il a   It not that + + + for example he has
            trouve le femme.   find the woman.
    N: Oui.   Yes.
    ABD: Le/ le ton pere de elle il mort.   The/ the your father of her he died.
    (Abdelmalek, session 3.5)

Number
    With respect to the number dimension for both 1st role and 2nd role paradigms as well as the 3rd role paradigm an overall-dominance of singular forms over plural forms was found in the learner varieties.

    This is in line with findings from other language acquisition studies. There is general consensus in the investigation of both L1 and L2 acquisition processes that in early stages singular forms are acquired before plural forms (cf. Baron & Kaiser

1975, Bol & Kuiken 1986, Klein & Rieck 1982). In addition, several studies report that singular forms are generalized for plural reference. Klein & Rieck (1982) observed in German learner varieties of Spanish and Italian adults that there is not only a predominance of singular forms, but also a generalized use of singular forms for plural reference, i.e. the subject pronoun *ich* ('I') is used to refer either to the speaker alone or to the speaker and some other people, instead of the target form *wir* ('we'). Moreover, circumventions have been reported in which the singular pronoun is doubled, e.g. *you and you* in child L1 acquisition of English (cf. Huxley 1970) and *he is and he* for "they are" in adult L2 acquisition of English (cf. Butterworth & Hatch 1978).

Number seems to be a relatively less prominent dimension of pronoun systems in learner varieties, which is only differentiated after other dimensions in the pronoun system (in particular case and gender) have been differentiated.

This is in line with observations made for pidgin and creole languages. Mühlhäusler & Harré (1990:262) conclude that a comparison of pidgins and creoles with their lexical source languages reveals that "number differences are typically not signalled in early stages of pidginization".

Status

In the present study only a few instances of the V-form *u* ('you') were observed in the learner varieties of Dutch. These instances most commonly occurred in unanalysed wholes, e.g. *wat zegt u?* ('pardon?'). The status dimension has not been investigated in language acquisition studies in great detail. This can partly be explained by an Anglo-Saxon bias in these studies: the status dimension is not lexicalized in the English pronoun system.

With respect to child L1 acquisition of Dutch it is anticipated that the use of T-forms and V-forms largely depends on the conventions which exist within a family. In this respect it is worth mentioning that findings by Vermaas (1990) indicate that over the last decades the V-form *u* ('you') for addressing parents has been disappearing in Dutch families in favour of the forms *je* ('you') and *jij* ('you').

With respects to pidgin and creole languages Mühlhäusler & Harré (1990:262) note that "social deixis such as honorific pronouns is reduced but can emerge relatively quickly under appropriate social conditions".

Gender

In the Dutch learner varieties of the Turkish and Moroccan adults observed in the present study, an overall-dominance of masculine forms over feminine forms emerges. In addition it turned out that gender generalizations go in both directions, i.e. masculine forms are used for feminine reference, and feminine forms are used for masculine reference. Difference in encoding conventions between the source languages of the informants did not affect the acquisition of forms on the gender dimension in the 3rd role paradigm.

These findings seem to be in line with observations made for children acquiring Dutch. In fact, the same conclusion is presented by Schaerlaekens & Gillis

(1987:130-131) in their survey of studies on child L1-Dutch. Appel & Lalleman (1989) note the same phenomenon for L2-Dutch of Turkish children (Total=15, mean age 11;10). Sequence (72) is an example from Appel & Lalleman (1989).

(72) CHI: Maar toen het vrouw naar het kassa   But when the woman had gone to the
            honderd gulden betalen.   cash-register he had to pay a hundred
            En zij kon zijn portemonnee niet   guilders. And she could not find his wallet.
            vinden. Dus hij zegt "Ik heb mijn   So he says "I left my wallet
            portemonnee thuis vergeten".   at home".

With respect to child language acquisition a complicated interaction emerges between (1) the natural, extra-linguistic basis for the encoding devices, e.g. distinguishing between the concepts "man/boy" and "woman/girl" and, (2) linguistic properties of the target system (e.g. phonetic similarity, adjective-noun agreement). Mastering the conceptual notion of gender seems to affect in children the acquisition of the encoding devices. This is suggested by investigations on child L1 acquisition, for example, for English (e.g. Chiat 1986, Mills 1986), for Icelandic (Mulford 1985), and German (e.g. Mills 1986). Interestingly, children are inclined to generalize the pronouns for their own sex. Girls generalize the feminine pronouns relatively more often and earlier, whereas boys prefer the masculine pronouns (cf. Mills 1986:104, Chiat 1986). Adult language learners are of course familiar with the conceptual "man-woman" distinction, so in this respect one would expect no differences between men and women when acquiring a language. The observation in the present study made for Fatima with the form *haar* ('her') might be indicative of an intriguing difference between masculine and feminine language learners.

Case
    With respect to the case dimension in the pronoun system in the observed L2 learner varieties of Dutch an overall-dominance of subject pronouns over object and possessive pronouns emerges. Subject forms are acquired before object/possessive forms, and they are also generalized in non-subject function.
    These findings of the present study are in line with other investigations on adult L2 learner varieties. Nominative case forms are often used as the "unmarked forms", covering oblique cases (e.g. object and possessive) as well (cf. Perdue 1984:145). This has for example been observed in L2 learner varieties of German (Klein & Rieck 1979), English (Huebner 1983:197 and Butterworth & Hatch 1978), Dutch (Broeder, Extra & Van Hout 1986,1989), and French (Giacobbe 1987). Interestingly, again a difference between child and adult language acquisition can be noted with respect to the type of case generalization.
    Although for child L1 acquisition Tanz (1974) suggested that case errors in English are always in the direction of object forms, a more differentiated picture can be derived from observations made by Chiat (1981,1986). There is a clear discrepancy between the 1st role pronoun *I* and the other pronominal forms. Chiat (1981) observed instances of objective *he, she, we,* and *they* but not of objective *I*.

For child L1 acquisition of Dutch a similar picture seems to emerge as for child L1 acquisition of English. The investigations for child L1 acquisition of Dutch reveal that for 1st role reference the object pronoun *mij* ('me') is frequently generalized, whereas for 2nd role reference the subject pronoun *jij* ('you') is generalized (note that in the English pronoun system there is homonymy with the subject/object form *you*).

For 1st role reference a number of studies report that Dutch children generalize the object pronoun *mij* ('me') in subject function (see Schaerlaekens & Gillis 1987:129-130 for further references). Sequences (73) and (74) are examples given by Van Ginneken (1917) and De Vooys (1916) respectively.

(73) KEE: Mij moet 't hebben.   Me must have it.
     (Keesje, age 2;7)

(74) BOY: Dat is jou, dat is mij.   That is you, that is me
     (age 3;6)   <looking at pictures>

In contrast, case generalizations of the subject pronoun *ik* ('I') in object function are only observed in a few children (i.e. by Kaper 1976 in specific contexts after prepositions).

For 2nd role reference the subject pronoun *jij* ('you') takes a prominent place. This form is used frequently in object function and possessive function, whereas the corresponding form *jou(w)* ('you(r)') is never used in subject function (see Kaper 1976). Note the following sequences given by Kaper (1976), Tinbergen (1919), and Van Ginneken (1917) respectively:

(75) ERI: Voor jij niet, voor mij is het.   Not for you, for me it is.
     (Erik, age 4)

(76) LUU: Ikke met jij kijke!   I look with you!
     (Luuk, age 2;7)

(77) KEE: 'k kom niet jij mete.   I don't come to measure you.
     (Keesje, age 2;6)

With respect to the case dimension a comparison between child L1-Dutch and adult L2-Dutch reveals that within the 1st role paradigm for adults a different picture emerges than the one observed for children. Within the 1st/2nd role paradigm similar observations can be made for both type of learners: in child L1-Dutch a preference for *mij* ('me') and *jij* ('you'), in adult L2-Dutch a preference for *ik* ('I') and *jij* ('you').

CHAPTER 7

REFERENTIAL MOVEMENT

In the preceding chapters on the acquisition of pronominal reference the focus was on linguistic devices for reference to people at the word level. This chapter goes into reference to people at the discourse level. It deals with the way in which adult language learners represent information linguistically in narrative discourse, i.e. reference to main/minor characters in a narrative. The area of investigation is an extension of 3rd role reference. Besides the set of pronominal forms (i.e the one focussed upon in the previous chapter), alternative encoding devices such as nominal devices and demonstratives are taken into account.

First, some basic mechanisms for structuring information about person reference in narrative discourse are discussed: the establishment, shift and maintenance of reference. After this, the research questions are specified and some predictions are formulated on the basis of a number of investigations of child and adult language acquisition. Next, an account of the investigation method is given. Finally, the results of the analyses of a number of film retellings by the core informants are discussed and a number of conclusions are formulated.

7.1   ESTABLISHMENT, SHIFT AND MAINTENANCE OF REFERENCE

Narratives as well as other types of discourse should be coherent, i.e. the expressive devices should be organized in such a way that the sequential and hierarchial structure of the information flow is reflected. The set of expressive devices for person reference consists of nominals (henceforth: full-NPs) such as *the president* and *Peter,* and pronominals (henceforth: pro-NPs) such as *he, she, this, that.* In addition to these, zero-reference (henceforth: zero-NPs) can also occur. In the latter case, the reference can be derived from the form of the verb, e.g. *arrives at the station.* The conditions for selecting the appropriate linguistic devices are complex. The linguistic representation of person reference is determined by the dynamic interplay in the discourse between explicitly expressed and implicitly presupposed information. This means that it is necessary to mark linguistically the first mention and the subsequent mentions of persons, i.e. the establishment, shift and maintenance of reference to people in the discourse.

A quantitative cross-linguistic study of the use of pronouns and NPs was carried out by Givón and his colleagues (1983,1984). The expectedness of the referent is evaluated by the notion of "topic continuity". Factors which influence the continuity of the topic are: distance (i.e. the number of clauses since the last mention), ambiguity (i.e. the number of intervening referents), and the availability of thematic information (e.g. change of subject or episode). Based on the study of a variety of languages, Givón (1984) formulates the following quantity universal: "the more predictable an entity, the smaller the amount of coding material necessary".

There is general consensus in the literature (e.g. Dubois 1980, Marslen-Wilson et al. 1982, Chafe 1987, Prince 1985) that first mention of a referent is done through full-NPs, in particular with indefinite NPs. Subsequent mentioning of a referent might be either explicit with a definite full-NP or implicit with pro-NPs or zero-NPs. This basic idea has been developed in many studies and a number of additions have been proposed (see Tomlin 1987 for further references). Special attention has been paid to the existence of "common ground" for speaker and addressee (e.g. Clark & Marshall 1981). Mutual or shared knowledge between interlocutors affects the linguistic representation of person reference in the discourse. For instance Sanders (1990) found in a small investigation of written Dutch news items that first mentioning of a person was done through a definite full-NP (instead of an indefinite full-NP). Another example, noted in a study by McGann & Schwartz (1988), is the main character status of a person in the discourse, which allows a more extensive use of implicit representation.

The exact expressive devices through which the expectedness of the referent is marked depends on the linguistic encoding system that is used, i.e. on the encoding conventions in a particular language. Between languages different types of NPs differ in the degree of obligatoriness and saliency to which they can function as markers of referential movement. For Dutch the structure presented in Table 7.1 emerges with respect to the representation of establishment, shift and maintenance of reference.

Table 7.1: Establishment, shift and maintenance of person reference in Dutch

Encoding devices		Establishment	Shift	Maintenance
Full-NPs:	indefinite NPs	+ +	– –	– –
	definite NPs (incl. proper names)	+ –	+ +	– –
Pro-NPs:	personal pronouns	+ –	+ +	+ +
	demonstrative pronouns	– –	+ –	+ +
Zero-NPs:	∅	– –	– –	+ +

("+ +" = common; "+ –" = likely; "– –" = uncommon)

In Table 7.1 a subdivision is made within the category of pro-NPs. The reason for this is that the personal pronouns contain more specific deictic information than the demonstrative pronouns. As a result of this the two types of pro-NPs may function differently in marking referential movement in the discourse. For example, in a narrative in which there are only two persons to refer to, a man and a woman, the personal pronouns *hij* ('he') and *zij* ('she') will unambiguously mark referential movement; reference through demonstrative pronouns would not be unambiguous.

In order to get a more detailed picture of the encoding in Dutch of referential movement, a narrative produced by a native speaker of Dutch (Gerald) will be investigated. Gerald was asked to retell the content of a Harold Lloyd videoclip. In this narrative establishment, shift and maintenance of person reference is marked through [E], [S], and [M] respectively. A detailed account of this analytical distinction is given in Section 7.3.2.

(1)	N:	Nou, probeer nou 's uh zo precies mogelijk te vertellen wat je gezien hebt?	Well, try to tell us as precisely as possible what you have just seen?
	GER:	Uh d'r staan +/ da ge 't eerste ziet uh/ d'r komt 'n trein voorbij. Staan op perron uh die vent [E] die [M] sta afscheid te nemen met die drie mensen vooral met dat vrouwke van h'm [E].	Er there is +/ that you see first er/ a train passes. Stands on the platform er that guy that is taking leave with those three people especially with that woman of him.
	N:	Ja.	Yes.
	GER:	Uh die moeder [E] staat d'rbij. En komt op 'n gegeven moment 'n uh/ 'n zwarte negerin [E] die [M] komt 'r aan lopen met 'n kleine [E].	Er that mother is standing near. And at a given moment there's a er/ a black negro woman that comes walking up with a little kid.
	N:	Ja.	Yes.
	GER:	Die [M] zet haar/ d'r kleine [M] neer.	That puts her/ her little kid down.
	N:	Ja.	Yes.
	GER:	Uh hij/ hij [S] had z'n kofferke op d'n hoek staan. En op een gegeven moment uh die uh die vent [E] die [M] fluit.	Er he/ he had left his suitcase at the corner. And at a given moment er that er that guy that whistles.
	N:	Ja.	Yes.
	GER:	Dat ze [S] op moeten stappen. Dus in z'n haast uh ja hij [S] kekt helemaal niet meer. In z'n haast wil ie [M] z'n koffer pakken.	That they have to get on. Being in a hurry er yes he doesn't really look anymore. Being in hurry he wants to get his suitcase.
	N:	Ja.	Yes.
	GER:	Maar neemt ie [M] die kleine [S] mee van die zwarte vrouw [S]. Hij [M] loopt 'r mee weg.	But takes he that little kid of that black woman. He walks away with it.
	N:	Ja.	Yes.
	GER:	Nou op 'n gegeven moment die zwarte vrouw [S] die [M] he in/ in de gaten. Dus die [M] loopt 'm [S] achter na.	Well at a given moment that black woman that realizes. So that goes after him.
	N:	Ja.	Yes.
	GER:	Die [M] zeg van "Hee kom 's hier uh	That says "Hey come here er
	N:	Ja.	Yes.
	GER:	kom 's hier met oewe kleine en gij het de koffer hier laten staan en dan zullen we even wisselen dan". Weten nie.	come here with your little kid and you have left the suitcase here and then we shall exchange". You know.
	N:	Ja.	Yes.
	GER:	Dus hij [S] was allemaal nog tegen dat vrouwke [S] aan 't roepen "Bedankt". En weet ik 't allemaal zo.	So he was still shouting to that woman "Thanks". Aand that sort of thing.

N:	Ja.	Yes.
GER:	Na daar komt op 'n gegeven moment 'n uh/ die trein/ die trein die rijdt weg. En komt 'n uh perd met wagen die komt 'r overgestoken (xx) zo rechtdoor.	Well at a given moment a er/ that train/ that train that drives away. And comes a er horse-drawn cart that comes crossing over (xx) straight ahead.
N:	Ja.	Yes.
GER:	Dus ∅ [M] zeg maar zo in trance zo bezig met dat vrouwke [M]. En weet ik 't allemaal.	So let's say so in trance like so busy with that woman. And God knows what.
N:	Ja.	Yes.
GER:	Dus hij [M] wil opstappen en hij/ hij [M] grijpt achter naar 'n stang. Hij [M] dacht dat 't de trein was.	So he wants to get on and he/ he grabs behind him for a bar. He thought that it was the train.
N:	Ja	Yes.
GER:	∅ [M] Stapt op die wagen.	Gets on that cart.
N:	Hm.	Um.
GER:	Nou, en toen op 'n gegeven moment uh daar komt ie [M] toch nog achter. Ja.	Well, and then at a given moment er he realizes it. Yes.
N:	∅ [M] Springt van die wagen af, ∅ [M] loopt de trein achter na en ∅ [M] springt d'r ook nog op.	Jumps off that cart, runs after the train and manages to jump on it too.

In Gerald's narrative, establishment of person reference is done exclusively through full-NPs. There are a number of definite full-NPs, i.e. *die vent* ('that guy'), *dat vrouwke van h'm* ('that wife of him'), and *die moeder* ('that mother'), and a number of indefinite full-NPs, i.e. *'n zwarte negerin* ('a black negro woman'), and *'n kleine* ('a little kid').

Shift of person reference is achieved through a number of definite full-NPs, e.g. *die kleine* ('that little kid'), *die zwarte vrouw* ('that black woman'), and *dat vrouwke* ('that woman'). In addition, a number of pro-NPs are used for reference shift, e.g. *hij* ('he'), and *die* ('that').

For maintenance of reference no full-NPs can be found. Most commonly pro-NPs are used in this function, i.e. *hij* ('he') and *(d)ie* ('that/he'). For maintenance of reference zero-NPs are also used. As a whole, the encoding of referential movement in the narrative by Gerald confirms the encoding conventions outlined for spoken Dutch in Table 7.1.

So far, the description of the representation of referential movement in narrative discourse has emphasized the linear structure of person reference in discourse, but alongside this there is also a superposed, global level on which the information in the discourse is structured and which affects the selection of expressive devices. Global marking of information has received a lot of attention in the literature. Discourse structures are captured in notions such as theme/rheme, given/new, topic/comment, foreground/background, etc. Studies on global discourse structures often lead to endless discussions and fruitless descriptive frameworks (see Clancy 1980, Van Dijk & Kintsch 1983, and Gernsbacher 1989 for an overview). However, there is one global discourse marker which is relatively unproblematic and about which there seems to be general consensus: the thematic status of the protagonist -the main character-in the narrative discourse. The survey of the literature given by McGann & Schwartz (1988) yields the following characteristic features of the main character:

1. It is usually agentive or intimately involved in causing the events that constitute the story's actions.
2. It is higher in animacy than any competing character.
3. It usually has a primary function in the story in terms of reaching a goal.
4. It almost always gets named if any characters do.
5. It is referred to more frequently than any other character.
6. It occurs in more than one scene and across more than one setting (i.e. it is not dependent upon a single setting); it is usually introduced in the initial stage (or "setting") of a narrative.

The effect of a referent's protagonist status on the linguistic representation of the information flow in narratives has been investigated systematically in a number of studies. Grimes (1978) found that anaphoric devices are distributed according to the centrality/peripheralness of the referents (see Fox 1987 for further references). In particular the interplay of local marking and global marking of information has yielded some interesting insights into the relationship between language and cognition.

A classic study of first language acquisition is the work by Karmiloff-Smith (see 1981,1987, and especially 1985). Her subjects were four-to-nine-year old children acquiring English/French as a first language (Total=170). The analyses of the children's story retelling (i.e. picture description) showed a three-phase development which in terms of global and local marking can be summarized as in Table 7.2.

Table 7.2: A developmental model for marking information in children's
story-retelling (based on Karmiloff-Smith 1985)

	Phase 1 (<5 yrs old)	Phase 2 (5-8 yrs old)	Phase 3 (>8 yrs old)
Global marking (top-down processes)	---	xxx	xxx
Local marking (data-driven processes)	xxx	---	xxx

In phase 1, the procedural phase, the behavioural output of children is mainly generated by data-driven processes. A global discourse structuring is lacking and there is no character that has protagonist status. Each output is merely juxtaposed to the previous one. This implies locally rich descriptions of pictures whereby pro-NPs and full-NPs are used deictically. A typical example of this phase, given by Karmiloff-Smith (1987), is sequence (2) derived from a story about a boy and a girl fighting over a bucket.

(2)   There's a boy and a girl. He's going fishing and she's going to make sandcastles. So
        he takes her bucket and ... she tries to grab it back and he runs off with it, so she
        sits there crying by the tree. Now he can do his fishing. He got four fish.
        (phase 1)

In phase 2, the metaprocedural phase, top-down processes control the children's narrative. They strongly monitor their flow of behaviourial output. As a result, referential expressions are used in discourse functions. Establishment of reference is done through a full-NP or a proper name. For maintenance of reference, the children search for or create a main character, the protagonist. The behaviourial output obeys a constraint which assumes pronominalization in an utterance-initial slot for the protagonist. A side-effect of the strong attention paid to the global structure of the narrative is that children give locally poor descriptions of individual pictures. Sequence (3) illustrates this phase.

(3)   There's a boy and a girl. He's going to catch fish so he takes the girl's bucket and he
        runs off and catches lots of fish.
        (phase 2)

Finally, in phase 3, a dynamic interplay between data-driven and top-down control processes can be noted in the children's narratives. They still rely on a main character constraint (or in terms of Karmiloff-Smith, a thematic subject constraint). However, occasionally also secondary characters are referred to in sentence-initial slots, with clear local marking through full-NPs. In addition to a clear overall structure, locally rich descriptions of individual pictures are given. Consider sequence (4) which is typical of the third phase.

(4)   There's a girl and a boy. The boy wants to go fishing, so he tries to get the girl's
        bucket, but the girl won't let him take it, so he grabs it out of her hand and the girl
        chases after him, but he gets away from the girl and he starts to fish while the girl
        sits there crying. He goes home smiling with four fish.
        (phase 3)

Karmiloff-Smith (1987) states that in order to get a deeper understanding of the developmental process (especially of what is the driving force behind it), a distinction should be made between behaviourial change and representational change. The phase 1 and phase 3 children behaved in very similar ways (i.e. in giving locally rich description) in contrast to those in phase 2. However, the development evidenced in the phases shows that the representations generating the narrative products are different, i.e. that the global information structuring is different.

Several recent studies of processes of language acquisition can be related to Karmiloff-Smith's work. Cross-learner and cross-linguistic evidence is provided for English by Hickmann (1982) and McGann & Schwartz (1988), for French by Kail et al. (1987), for German by Bamberg (1986,1987) and Hickmann et al. (1989), for Swedish by Strömqvist & Day (1990) and, for Turkish by Verhoeven (1988). Although in these studies the notions of local and global marking are used, they are certainly not always used in the same meaning. In fact, substantial differences can be noted in the way these notions are operationalized. If these differences are kept in mind, the following general language independent principles can be derived:

- Establishment of reference is done through full-NPs; in early stages through definite NPs, in later stages through both indefinite full-NPs and definite full-NPs.
- Shift of reference is done through full-NPs. In later stages children might assign protagonist status to a character which implies that shift of reference to this character is done through pro-NPs.
- Maintenance of reference is most commonly done through pro-NPs and incidentally through zero-NPs.

In child language acquisition certain developmental patterns over time can be distinguished. The three-phase developmental model of Karmiloff-Smith (1987) is confirmed in several studies (see Bamberg 1987). Cognitive maturation is thought to be responsible for the developmental patterns that underly the narrative products of the children. From this perspective it is interesting to have a look at adult language acquisition, because here cognitive development and language development are no longer interwoven. The child-adult comparison becomes even more interesting if the adults acquire the target language in a "childlike fashion", i.e. spontaneously, without any form of tuition. This was done by Strömqvist & Day (1990). They dealt with the development of narrative structure in child L1 and adult L2 acquisition of Swedish. Their subjects were sixteen children acquiring Swedish as a first language and five Finnish/Spanish adults acquiring Swedish as a second language spontaneously. Data for the adult learners were collected in the framework of the ESF project (see Chapter 1) and they have the same socio-biographical background as the core and shadow informants in the present study. Strömqvist & Day (1990) found the same three-phase pattern with children as Karmiloff-Smith. However, with the adults they observed a different developmental pattern. Already in an early phase, adult L2 learners accomplished a global structuring of the narrative discourse, while in a later (intermediate) phase there was a dip in performance compared to their child colleagues. On the basis of their results Strömqvist & Day (1990) conclude that language acquisition interacts with the cognitive resources that the learner brings to the acquisition task.

7.2   RESEARCH QUESTIONS AND PREDICTIONS

Adults are experienced speakers who have already mastered a full set of encoding conventions, i.e. those of their first language. Therefore, already in early stages of the acquisition process, they will aim at achieving as much as possible a global structuring of the narrative discourse. A complicating factor here is that in early stages of acquisition they necessarily only have a restricted set of encoding devices at their disposal. A protagonist strategy provides them with an excellent device to accomplish this global structure in an efficient way. As a result of this, in early stages of adult language acquisition establishment, shift and maintenance of reference to the main character will exhibit relatively little linguistic differentiation: relatively more use will be made of the presupposing, implicit encoding devices. Over time, as the adult language learners acquire a more extensive set of linguistic devices, they may opt for alternatives to the global protagonist strategy. This means that in later stages of adult language acquisition the encoding of referential movement for the main character may be more differentiated and increasingly resemble the encoding of referential movement for the minor character(s), i.e. establishment of reference through full-NPs and subsequent reference through pro/zero-NPs.

The main issue in this chapter is the way in which adult language learners encode referential movement in narrative discourse, i.e. the way they refer to the characters participating in a narrative. The research questions can be specified as follows:

I   Which expressive devices are used for establishment, shift and maintenance of person reference?
II   Which developmental pattern can be found in subsequent stages of language acquisition?
III   How can learner preferences be explained?

On the basis of the encoding conventions in Dutch (see Table 7.1 above), the findings from a number of language acquisition studies, and the fact that the focus is on adult learners, the following predictions are made:

P1   Establishment of reference is achieved:
        - in early stages through definite full-NPs;
        - in later stages through both indefinite full-NPs and definite full-NPs.

P2   Shift of reference to main character is achieved:
        - in early stages through pro-NPs;
        - in later stages through definite full-NPs.

P3   Shift of reference to minor character is achieved:
        - in early stages through definite full-NPs;
        - in later stages through pro-NPs.

P4   Maintenance of reference is achieved:
        - in early and later stages through zero-NPs or pro-NPs.

7.3   METHOD

7.3.1   INFORMANTS AND LANGUAGE ACTIVITIES

The informants in this chapter are the two Turkish core informants (Mahmut and Ergün) and the two Moroccan core informants (Mohamed and Fatima).

The language activities consist of retelling two silent Harold Lloyd movies: *At the Station* and *The New Car*.

Harold Lloyd at the Station

In the videoclip *At the Station* the following persons occur: Harold Lloyd, his fiancée, his parents-in-law, a black woman with a baby in a carry-cot, a conductor, and some travellers. Prominent objects are: the train by which Harold Lloyd is planning to leave, his suitcase, a carry-cot with a baby, and a horse-drawn cart. Harold Lloyd is standing on the platform with his fiancée and her parents. While the family are saying their goodbyes, a number of people come on the platform, among them a black woman with a baby in a carry-cot. Harold pays too much attention to his fiancée. The train is about to leave. In a hurry Harold, takes instead of his suitcase, the carry-cot with the baby that belongs to the black woman and runs to the waiting train. The woman runs after him with his suitcase. The carry-cot and the suitcase are exchanged. Then a horse-drawn cart passes alongside the train. Harold Lloyd jumps on it, but notices his mistake, and catches his train just in time.

Harold Lloyd and the New Car

In the videoclip *The new car* the following persons occur: Harold Lloyd, his fiancée, his mother-in-law, his brother-in-law, a motor-cyclist, a car-driver, and two policemen. Prominent objects are Harold's new car, a horse-drawn cart, an umbrella, a motor, another car, a fire-engine, and a lift. A new car is delivered at the house of Harold's in-laws. They admire the new car together with their curious neighbours. Then they get into the car. Harold has problems getting the car away. When they are finally on the road, a series of comic incidents occur. They get into racing games with motor-cyclists and other cars, policemen are pushed into the water. They cause traffic jams and Harold loses control of the car as it is going down a hill. In short, it is a turbulent story which Harold's new car does not survive.

Each of the four core informants saw the videoclip three times and was subsequently asked to retell its content. On average this took ten to fifteen minutes. The informants participated in this language activity in each of the three cycles, so that for each of the core informants six narratives were analysed. (Total=4x3x2=24 narratives). In cycle 1 the informants were asked to retell the film in their first language. For these activities no complete analyses will be presented. Only occasionally will some of these retellings be considered.

7.3.2 PROCEDURE IN THE ANALYSIS

Procedural steps in the encoding and analysis of the data were guided to a large extent by Bamberg (1987) and McGann & Schwartz (1988).

First, all those instances were selected where the informants refer implicitly or explicitly to the persons in the film. Excluded were: background references with unrelated comments, e.g. *weet ik niet* ('I don't know'), references in direct speech, e.g. *die vrouw zegt "hij pakt mijn tas"* ('That woman says, 'He takes my bag'), and generic references, e.g. *een man rijden is genoeg* ('one man drive is enough').

Next for each instance the relative thematic status was identified. All instances were assigned to one of the following categories:

- Establishment of reference; those instances where a character is referred to for the first time in the retelling.
- Shift of reference; those instances where another character is referred to than the one in the preceding utterance.
- Maintenance of reference; those instances where the same character is referred to as in the preceding utterance.

In order to distinguish between shift of reference and maintenance of reference the following decisions were made:

- References which occur after a reference given by the native collocutor are taken into account in that the subsequent reference by the informant is considered to be a maintained reference, e.g.

    (5) N: Wat doet die man? [E]   What does that man do?
        INF: Hij [M] trein weg gaan naar.   He train go away to.

- Instances consisting of more than one expressive device (e.g. specifications, left-dislocations) are split up into separate units, e.g.

    (6) INF: Die [E] + een man [M]. Die ouders [E],   That + a man. Those parents,
           ouders van die man of ouders van die   parents of that man or parents of that
           vrouw [M]. Zij [M] staan op station.   woman. They are at station.
           Hij [S] weg met trein.   He gone with train.

Finally, the expressive devices through which an informant refers to a character in the film are assigned to the following categories:

- Full-NP; definite NPs, e.g. *de man* ('the man') and *die man* ('that man'), indefinite NPs, e.g. *'n vrouw* ('a woman'), bare nouns, *e.g. vrouw* ('woman'), or proper names, e.g. *Harold*.
- Pro-NP; demonstratives and personal pronouns.
- Zero-NP; implicit reference which can be derived for example from the form of the verb, e.g. *komt op het station* ('arrives at the station') (i.e. the verb form is 3rd role singular).

In the analyses some methodological bias will be taken into consideration. Firstly, in the content of the silent movies there is one clear main character, Harold Lloyd, and a number of minor characters. For referring to the latter relatively more lexical variation in the full-NPs is necessary. Secondly, the episodic structure of the retelling might influence the encoding of referential movement of the characters, e.g. full-NPs are used to mark the onset of a new episode in the narrative (cf. Marslen-Wilson et al. 1982). However, in the preliminary analyses carried out by Kiewiet (1988) for the *Harold Lloyd and the New Car* retelling the episodic structure turned out to have no effect on the encoding of referential movement.

7.4   RESULTS

In this section an analysis is presented for each of the core informants separately. A detailed account is given of the way in which the informants' linguistic repertoire is employed to mark establishment, shift, and maintenance of person reference in the retellings. A distinction is made between (1) references to the main character in the film, Harold Lloyd, and (2) references to the other characters in the film, the minor characters.

In the framework of the ESF project the analyses carried out by Klein & Perdue (1991) are important for the analyses presented in this chapter. They investigated the developing structure of utterances in learner varieties. Their analyses were syntactic/ pragmatic in character, focussing on word order phenomena. For each of the four core informants they analysed three narratives: in cycle 1 a personal narrative occurring in free conversation, and in cycles 2 and 3 a retelling of a Charlie Chaplin videoclip (taken from *Modern Times*). The retellings of the videoclip took place in the same session as the *Harold Lloyd and the New Car* retellings analysed in this chapter. Although Klein & Perdue (1991) did not focus explicitly on establishment, shift and maintenance of reference, they make some relevant observations which can be related to analyses carried out in this chapter.

7.4.1 MAHMUT

Table 7.3 summarizes how Mahmut uses the linguistic devices for marking the establishment, shift and maintenance of reference to the main character vs. minor characters. There is a clear difference between the encoding devices used for the main character vs. those for the minor characters. To refer to the main character extensive use is made of pro-NPs and zero-NPs. For the minor characters an extensive use of full-NPs emerges.

Establishment of reference
    Establishment of reference to the main character is done through definite full-NPs, e.g. *die/deze meneer* ('that/this gentleman'), and through pro-NPs, e.g. *die* ('that').

Table 7.3: Overview of referential devices used by Mahmut

| | Cycle 1 | | | Cycle 2 | | | Cycle 3 | | | |
	Est.	Shi.	Mai.	Est.	Shi.	Mai.	Est.	Shi.	Mai.	Total
References to Harold:										
full-NP	1	3	7	1	-	3	1	5	4	25
pro-NP	1	8	10	1	12	18	1	25	43	119
zero-NP	-	6	18	-	5	22	-	3	24	78
References to others:										
full-NP	6	29	22	6	10	6	9	25	11	124
pro-NP	2	1	5	-	1	1	-	3	3	16
zero-NP	-	2	5	-	1	2	-	-	4	14
Total	10	49	67	8	29	52	11	61	89	376

Establishment of reference to the minor characters is done mostly through full-NPs:
bare nouns, e.g. *vrouw* ('woman'), *kindje* ('little child'), and definite full-NPs with the
determiner *die* ('that'), e.g. *die meneer* ('that gentleman'), *die schoonmoeder* ('that
mother-in-law'). Adjectival modifications of the noun seldom occur. Occasionally,
ander(-e) ('other') is used together with a noun, e.g. *andere vrouw* ('other woman').
In addition, in cycle 1, a pro-NP, i.e. *die* ('that') is used twice for establishment of
reference to the minor character. Indefinite full-NPs do not occur.

Remarkable are those instances in which the characters are established through a
pro-NP. These instances consist of the deictically used demonstrative *die* ('that'), or
die andere ('that other'), followed by a pause and a specification with a right-dislocated full-NP. A typical example is sequence (7).

(7)	N:	Uh wat zag je net?	Er what did you just see?
	MAH:	Uh charlie chaplin he.	Er charlie chaplin right.
	N:	Nee, 't is niet charlie chaplin.	No, it is not charlie chaplin.
	MAH:	Nee. Die/ die + meneer he.	No. That/ that + gentleman eh.
	N:	Ja.	Yes.
	MAH:	Die + brilmeneer. Die + meisje.	That + spectacle man. That + girl.
		Die meisje + samen woont bij die.	That girl + lives together with that.
		+ Die andere + vader moeder?	+ That other + father mother?
	N:	Hm.	Um.
	MAH:	Ja vader moeder zitten trein he.	Yes father mother are on train right.
	(session 1.6)		

Shift of reference

Shift of reference to the main character is most commonly achieved through the
use of pro-NPs, i.e. *die* ('that') and *hij* ('he'). A number of times also full-NPs and
zero-NPs are used. Over time the relative use of pro-NPs, in particular the form *hij*
('he'), increases. In cycle 3 an overall-dominance of the pro-NP *hij* ('he') emerges
instead of the use of the pro-NP *die* ('that').

In contrast, shift of reference to minor characters in early sessions as well as in
later ones is done remarkable frequently through full-NPs (bare nouns), "*deze*-N"
('this-N') and "*die*-N" ('that-N').

Maintenance of reference

For maintenance of reference the same picture emerges as with shift of reference. In addition it can be noted that in cycles 1 and 2 Mahmut relatively often uses zero-NPs for maintenance of reference to the main character.

In all sessions Mahmut opts for a protagonist strategy. Other strategies of structuring global information cannot be found in his retellings. However the frequent use of the minimal feedback items *ja* ('yes') and *he* ('eh', 'isn't it', etc.) as discourse operators is worth mentioning. These forms occur in utterance-initial and in utterance-final position respectively, where they seem to have an utterance-linking function. It is a kind of "dialogue within a monologue". Some examples of these instances are given in sequences (8) and (9).

(8)	N:	En dan. Wat doet iedereen?	So then. What does everybody do?
	MAH:	Ja moeder boos he. Moet rijden niet ouwehoeren.	Yes mother angry eh. Have to drive not talk.
	(session 1.9)		
(9)	MAH:	Ja hij hard rijden he. Ja politie gezien he.	Yes he drive fast eh. Yes seen police eh.
	N:	Ja.	Yes.
	MAH:	Andere mensen linkse kant weg.	Other people left side of road.
	(session 3.9)		

With Mahmut, Klein & Perdue (1991:193-200) analysed a personal narrative in cycle 1 and a *Modern Times* retelling in cycles 2 and 3 with respect to the encoding of referential movement. They found no clear differences between the retellings. In all three cycles mostly bare nouns are used and "*die*-N" ('that-N'). Only for the establishment of reference a noun was sometimes preceded by the numeral *een* ('one'), and only for the maintenance of reference a noun was sometimes preceded by the determiner *deze* ('this').

7.4.2 ERGÜN

Table 7.4: Overview of referential devices used by Ergün

	Cycle 1			Cycle 2			Cycle 3			
	Est.	Shi.	Mai.	Est.	Shi.	Mai.	Est.	Shi.	Mai.	Total
References to Harold:										
full-NP	-	2	2	1	1	6	2	4	4	22
pro-NP	2	15	15	-	14	34	1	15	17	113
zero-NP	-	4	16	-	1	15	-	2	22	60
References to others:										
full-NP	8	15	9	8	18	4	8	23	9	102
pro-NP	1	3	3	2	1	8	1	2	4	25
zero-NP	-	-	3	-	1	2	1	-	4	11
Total	11	39	48	11	36	69	13	46	60	333

An overview of the linguistic devices used by Ergün for marking the establishment, shift and maintenance of reference to the main character and the minor characters is given in Table 7.4. As a whole this table shows a picture similar to the one observed for Mahmut: an overall-dominance of pro-NPs for reference to the main character and an overall-dominance of full-NPs for reference to minor characters. In their analyses Klein & Perdue (1991:201-210) also found a lot of similarities between the narratives of the two Turks Mahmut and Ergün.

Establishment of reference

There is a difference between Ergün's retellings of the two videoclips. When retelling the *Station* film in cycles 2 and 3, Ergün establishes the main character as well as the minor characters several times through the deictically used demonstrative pronoun *die* ('that') in combination with a right-dislocated full-NP. A similar phenomenon was observed earlier with Mahmut. In the *Station* retellings establishment of reference is also done with the form *een*. In Dutch this form is an emphatic indefinite article ('a') as well as a numeral ('one'). Sequences (10)-(12) are taken from the *Station* retellings, in sessions 1.6, 2.6, and 3.6 respectively.

(10)	ERG:	Die kant uit nog eentje die kant uh man.	That direction another one that direction er man.
	N:	Maar zijn dat/ wie is dat meisje?	But are those/ who is that girl?
	ERG:	En daar? En die/ die man he.	And there? And that/ that man eh.
	N:	Ja.	Yes.
	ERG:	En weg gaan naar. Misschien uh duitsland en engels^ weg gaan naar. En dan zij en zij zijn vrouw twee komt dan. En nog een keer man/ nog een/ eentje man daar.	And leave for. Maybe er germany and english^ leave for. And then she and she his wife two come then. And then once more man/ another one/ one man there.
		(session 1.6)	

(11)	ERG:	Ja die een/ een meisje een/ een vrouw meisje/ meisje he?	Yes that one/ one girl one/ one woman girl/ girl eh?
	N:	Ja dat weet ik niet.	Yes that I don't know.
		\[Jij/ jij hebt 'm gezien]	\[You/ you saw it]
	ERG:	\[Enne + een jongen of man] een jongen of man.	\[And + one boy or man] one boy or man.
	N:	Ja.	Yes.
	ERG:	Ja man.	Yes man.
	N:	Ja.	Yes.
	ERG:	Een vrouw een man ook.	One man one woman too.
	N:	Ja.	Yes.
	ERG:	Die daar ook de praten he daar die man.	That there also the talk eh there that man.
		(session 2.6)	

(12)	ERG:	En dan daar komt/ een vrouw komt	And then there comes/ one woman comes
	N:	Ja.	Yes
	ERG:	met kind.	with child.
	N:	Ja.	Yes.
	ERG:	Dan + die daar staat een oud/ ouwe mensen/ ouwe man.	Then + that there standing one old/ old people/ old man.
		(session 3.6)	

In the *Car* retellings Ergün never uses indefinite full-NPs. In these retellings establishment of reference is done mostly through the use of definite full-NP "*die*-N" ('that-N') and occasionally also the construction "*van*-Pro-N" ('of-Pro-N') can be found. Note that in the previous chapters on pronominal reference the latter construction turned out to be typical of the Turkish informants. Some examples of establishment of reference in the *Car* retellings are given in the following sequence:

(13) ERG: Ja die man is die auto bestellen.   Yes that man is ordering that car.
    N: Ja.   Yes.
    ERG: Die man zegt "Komt een claxon?"   That man says "Comes a horn?"
    "Ja". En die man ook komt. Dan even   "Yes". And that man also comes. Then
    die auto rotzooi kijken. En wat voor   just look that car and junk. And
    type of + ja.   what kind of brand or + yes.
    N: Ja ja.   Yes yes.
    ERG: En dan van hem vrouw gezien. Hij gaan   And then of him wife seen. He also go
    ook naar buiten komt. Dan ja die man   outside comes. Then yes that man
    zegt "Ja die auto is van jou". Die   says "Yes that car is yours". That
    meisje zegt tegen hem "Is van mijn?"   girl says to him "Is of mine?"
    zegt "Ja". Is zo gebeurd.   says "Yes". So it happened.
    (session 2.9)

Shift of reference

Shift of reference to the main character is mostly achieved through the use of the pro-NP *hij* ('he'). Occasionally, shift of reference is marked through *die* ('that'), e.g. *die man* ('that man'), and a zero-NP. Clear differences over time were not found.

Shift of reference to the minor character is achieved mostly through the use of definite full-NPs, in particular "*die*-N" ('that-N'). In cycles 2 and 3 Ergün regularly uses the "*van*-Pro-N" ('of-Pro-N') construction. In addition, it can be noted that twice an indefinite full-NP is used for shift of reference to a minor character, i.e. *'n baby* ('a baby') and *een vrouw* ('one woman').

Maintenance of reference

In all sessions maintenance of reference to the main character is achieved relatively infrequently through full-NPs. There is an extensive use of pro-NPs and in particular of zero-NPs.

For the minor characters, however, maintenance of reference in cycles 1 and 3 is marked mostly through full-NPs and in cycles 3 mostly through pro-NPs, i.e. *hij* ('he').

One remarkable observation concerns instances in which person reference is supported through the setting of spatial frames. A typical example is sequence (14).

(14) ERG: Dan allemaal komt hier station.   Then all come here station.
    Hij praten met de meisje. <..>   He talk with the girl. <..>
    Daar ook een uh zwarte vrouw   There also one er black woman
    komt he. <..> Daar ook baby. <..>   comes eh. <..> There also baby. <..>
    Hier ook hij/ zij komt baby staan.   Here also he/ she comes standing baby.
    (session 2.6)

Similar instances can be observed with Mahmut, the other Turkish informant. For
the two Moroccan informants on the other hand, this supporting function of spatial
reference is very untypical. In the L1 retellings of the four informants these differences can also be found. Sequences (15) and (16) are taken from the retellings in
Turkish by Ergün and Mahmut, respectively.

(15) ERG: bu/   şu/   ora-ya geliyor kadın   o   da   kendi arkadaş-ı   da   geliyor.
            this/ that/ there   comes   woman   s/he too own   friend-POSS3   too comes
       (session 1.6)

(16) MAH: şimdi orada-ki   adam var   ya
            now   there-that man there is.
       (session 1.6)

In these sequences there are a number of spatial references. Corresponding
instances cannot be found in the retellings in Moroccan Arabic by Mohamed and
Fatima. In this respect compare sequences (15)-(16) and (17)-(18).

(17) MOH: žat   dik   le-mṛa   hezz-et   l-baliza   dyal-u
            came   that   the-woman   took-she   the-suitcase   of-him
       (session 1.6)

(18) FAT: ṛ-ṛažel   ǧadi   l-ši   blad   x̌-ṛa
            the-man   goes   to-some   place   other
       (session 1.6)

Finally, it can be noted that like Mahmut, Ergün uses several times (but less frequently) the minimal feedback items *ja* ('yes') and *he* ('eh', 'right', 'isn't it', etc.) as
discourse operators. Again, this phenomenon is absent in the retellings of the two
Moroccan informants.

7.4.3 MOHAMED

Table 7.5 summarizes how the linguistic devices are used by Mohamed for marking
establishment, shift and maintenance of reference to the main character and the
minor characters.

Compared with the two Turkish informants, the retellings of Mohamed contain
relatively few zero-NPs. On the other hand, Mohamed uses relatively many pro-NPs
for reference to all the characters. Within this category already in cycle 1 a differentiation is made according to gender and case through the pronouns *hij* ('he'), *zij*
('she'), *hem* ('him') and *haar* ('her'). Mohamed regularly uses the form *(d)ie*
('that/he') in post-verbal position as a clitic form. The category of full-NPs consists
of bare nouns, indefinite NPs with *een* ('one') and *'n* ('a') as determiners, definite
NPs with *die* ('that') and *de* ('the') as determiners, possessive NPs, and occasionally
full-NPs with an adjective.

Table 7.5: Overview of referential devices used by Mohamed

	Cycle 1			Cycle 2			Cycle 3			Total
	Est.	Shi.	Mai.	Est.	Shi.	Mai.	Est.	Shi.	Mai.	
References to Harold:										
full-NP	2	2	4	1	1	2	1	-	1	14
pro-NP	-	19	68	1	16	87	1	15	95	302
zero-NP	-	-	2	-	-	1	-	-	1	4
References to others:										
full-NP	11	28	19	10	20	19	9	24	16	156
pro-NP	-	4	12	-	-	17	-	1	8	42
zero-NP	-	-	1	-	-	-	-	-	-	1
Total	13	53	106	12	37	126	11	40	121	519

Especially in the early sessions Mohamed refers in more detail to family relationships that may exist between the actors in the film. As a result there is much more variation in the lexical devices that are used for a specific actor in the early sessions than there is in later sessions. Consider for example the ways of referring to the parents in the *Station* retellings. In cycle 1 Mohamed refers to these persons as follows:

(19) MOH: Dan twee ouders. Ik weet niet of   Then two parents. I do not know whether
             die ouders is ouders van meisje of   those parents is parents of little girl or
             ouders van die jongman.   parents of that young man.
      (session 1.6)

In cycle 3 we find:

(20) MOH: Hij was bij station met uh ik denk   He was at station with er I think
             met hem ouders.   with him parents.
      (session 3.6)

Establishment of reference

Mohamed clearly does not mark the establishment of reference in the same way as he does shift and maintenance of reference. All indefinite full-NPs, i.e. "*een*-N" ('one-N') and "'*n*-N" ('a-N') are exclusively used when a character is referred to for the first time in the retelling. As with Ergün, indefinite full-NPs occur relatively more often in the *Station* retellings. Sequences (21)-(23), taken from sessions 1.6, 2.6, and 3.6 respectively, give the establishment of reference to Harold and some of the minor characters in the *Station* retellings.

(21) N: Wie zijn deze mensen?   Who are these people?
     MOH: + <..> + Een uh jongman met uh hij   + <..> + One er young man with er he
           moeske of uh met zij moeske of uh vrouw. girl or er with she girl or er woman.
     N: Ja.   Yes.
     MOH: Dan uh twee + /twee ouw/ twee ouders. Then er two + /two par/ two parents.
        (session 1.6)

(22) N: Waar gaat ie over?   What is it about?
     MOH: Ja daar was een uh jongman.   Yes there was one er young man.
     N: 'n jongeman ja.   A young man yes.
     MOH: Ja met uh/ met hem meisje of uh   Yes with er/ with him girl or er
             hem vrouw.   him woman.
     (session 2.6)

(23) N: Waar ging de film over?   What was the film about?
     MOH: + + Ja over uh + 'n jongman moet op   + + Yes about er + a young man must go
             vakantie denk ik ja hij was bij   on holiday I think yes he was at
             station met uh ik denk met hem ouders.   station with er I think with him parents.
     (session 3.6)

These findings with respect to the establishment of reference are in line with the analyses of the *Modern Times* data in sessions 2.9 and 3.9 carried out by Klein & Perdue (1991:219). They also found that new referents are introduced by Mohamed through "*een*-N" ('one N'), "*n* N" ('a N'), or a bare noun.

Shift of reference
    Shift of reference to the main character is achieved most commonly through the use of pro-NPs, i.e. *hij* ('he') and *hem* ('him'), whereas for the minor characters full-NPs are used. So, in selecting expressive devices, Mohamed like the two Turkish informants, takes into account the thematic status of the actors in the retelling.
    A remarkable way of marking shift of reference is through left-dislocation with a full-NP plus a pro-NP that is a subject pronoun. Sequences (24)-(27) illustrate this phenomenon.

(24) MOH: Die jongman uh + + hij wil uh +   That young man er + + he wants er +
             gaan + naar ander stad of ander land.   go + to other city or other country.
     (session 1.6)

(25) MOH: En toen die t/ die controleur van   And then th/ that conductor of
             trein hij fluit he.   train he whistles eh.
     (session 2.6)

(26) MOH: Die ander motor hij is weg/ ander weg.   That other motor is it gone/ other way.
     (session 2.9)

(27) MOH: Ja die politie hij tegen hem "Ja moet   Yes that police officer he to him "Yes
             jullie weg".   must you go".
     (session 2.9)

A NP is placed at the beginning of the utterance followed by another NP and a verb. The second NP is co-referential with the first, left-dislocated NP. Utterances in which left-dislocation occur have the following pattern: "NP_i-NP_i-Verb-X". Instances of left-dislocation with this pattern can be found several times in cycles 1 and 2. Surprisingly, these kinds of left-dislocation do not occur in cycle 3.
    Klein & Perdue (1991:219) made similar observations for the *Modern Times* data: in cycle 2 a number of instances of left-dislocation occur, while the pattern is used

very rarely in cycle 3. They note that Mohamed particularly uses this way of encoding when the re-introduction (i.e. the shift of reference) involves topic shift.

Maintenance of reference

Mohamed seldom, if ever, refers to people only implicitly, i.e. through zero-NPs. For maintenance of reference to the main character the same observation can be made as for shift of reference: a frequent use of the pro-NPs *hij* ('he') and *hem* ('him').

For maintenance of reference to the minor characters mostly full-NPs are used: "*die*-N" ('that-N') and possessive constructions. A number of times also the pro-NPs *hij* ('he') and *zij* ('she') are used for maintained reference to minor characters.

In addition, in cycle 3 some remarkable instances of maintenance of reference can be found. The form *(d)ie* ('that'/'he') is used as a post-verbal enclitic. This results in utterances with the following pattern: "(NP_i)-Verb-$(d)ie_i$-X". The first NP position in this pattern is often left empty. Some utterances reflecting this pattern occur in sequences (28)-(30).

(28) MOH: Toen die vrouw uh loopt ie achter hem.   Then that woman er walks he behind him.
(session 3.6)

(29) MOH: Hij kijkt. Was geen koffer. Was kindje.   He looks. Was not a suitcase. Was child.
Toen heeft ie terug gegeven aan.   Then has he given back to.
(session 3.6)

(30) MOH: Toen hij loopt ie snel naar trein.   Then he walks he fast to train.
(session 3.6)

Also for reference to objects (which are not taken into account in the tables presented) similar patterns can be observed (see sequences 31 and 32).

(31) MOH: Babyreiswieg toen stond ie bij hem.   Baby carry-cot then stood he with him.
(session 3.6)

(32) MOH: Paard en wagen + komt ie achter hem.   Horse-drawn cart + comes he behind him
(session 3.6)

A similar observation is made by Klein & Perdue (1991:220). Although they note that this "doubling" of the pronoun right after the verb does not have a particular function. Klein & Perdue (1991) suspect that this construction is quite common in the variety of Dutch spoken in the local area where Mohamed lives. This is in fact confirmed by the retelling presented for Gerald in the beginning of this chapter (see sequence 1). One is inclined to assume that Mohamed simply adopts this construction from the local variety of spoken Dutch and this is what is assumed by Klein & Perdue (1991). However, with respect to the use of *(d)ie* ('that') as post-verbal enclitic a striking similarity can be observed between Mohamed's retellings in L1 and L2. Consider for example sequence (33) which is taken from Mohamed's *Station* retelling in Moroccan Arabic.

(33) MOH: hadak   ǧadi   m-safer   l-ši   blad   ula   l-ši   qent <..>
           that   goes   on-journey to-some   place   or   to-some place

           mša   baš   ye-ṭleᶜ   fe-t-tran
           went-he to   he-gets   in-the-train

           žat   dik le-mṛa   hezz-et   l-baliza   dyal-u
           came   that the-woman   took-she the-suitcase   of-him

           u leḥqe-t   ᶜli-h
           and passed-she   over-him
      (session 1.6)

Also in this Moroccan Arabic sequence instances of person reference through post-suffixes, e.g. *leḥqe-t* ('passed-she') and of left-dislocation, e.g. *dik le-mṛa* ('that the-woman') can be observed.

7.4.4 FATIMA

Table 7.6 summarizes the way in which Fatima marked establishment, shift and maintenance of reference to the main character and the minor characters.

Table 7.6: Overview of referential devices used by Fatima

| | Cycle 1 | | | Cycle 2 | | | Cycle 3 | | | |
	Est.	Shi.	Mai.	Est.	Shi.	Mai.	Est.	Shi.	Mai.	Total
References to Harold:										
full-NP	1	5	12	2	6	4	2	3	4	39
pro-NP	1	2	2	-	4	1	-	7	14	31
zero-NP	-	4	12	-	4	11	-	-	9	40
References to others:										
full-NP	5	17	7	7	15	9	6	8	16	90
pro-NP	-	-	-	-	-	3	-	3	-	6
zero-NP	-	2	8	-	-	2	-	1	1	14
Total	7	30	41	9	29	30	8	22	44	220

In cycles 1 and 2 pro-NPs are most commonly represented by the demonstrative *die* ('that'). In cycle 3 the personal pronoun *hij* ('he') is used most commonly: occasionally *zij* ('she') and *die* ('that') occur. The full-NPs are bare nouns and definite NPs. The demonstrative *die* ('that') is the only form used as determiner. Fatima never uses definite and indefinite articles as determiners, nor is the numeral *een* ('one') used as determiner.

Establishment of reference

With the exception of one instance in session 1.9, i.e. *deze* ('this'), all establishing references are realized through full-NPs: bare nouns and definite NPs with *die* ('that') as determiner.

In the *Station* retellings Fatima in all three cycles uses an almost identical set of words for establishing reference. This set of words is illustrated by sequence (34) taken from cycle 3.

(34) FAT: Ja die man uh wil naar met trein.   Yes that man er wants to go to by train.
   N: Ja.   Yes.
   FAT: Uh alles kom fam/ eh kom familie met die man.   Er everything come fam/ er come family with that man.
   N: Hm hm.   Uh-huh.
   FAT: Uh + effe wacht in die trein.   Er + wait a while in that train.
   N: In de trein?   In the train?
   FAT: Effe wacht ja.   Wait a while yes.
   N: Ja.   Yes.
   FAT: De eh/ tot trein komt.   The er/ until train comes.
   N: Ja.   Yes.
   FAT: Die man uh praat met uh haar moeder vader + vrouw.   That man er talk with er her mother father + woman.
   N: Ja.   Yes.
   FAT: + Die ander vrouw komt met eh haar dochter.   + That other woman comes with er her daughter.
   (session 3.6)

Shift of reference

Compared with the other three informants, Fatima, in cycles 1 and 2, relatively often uses full-NPs for shift of reference to the main character. A typical example is the following:

(35) FAT: Ja die ander vrouw komt met haar dochter.   Yes that other woman comes with her daughter.
   N: Ja.   Yes.
   FAT: Die man moet goed kijk. Uh wilt pakt die uh koffer. Maar ander pakt die dochter.   That man must look well. Er wants takes that er suitcase. But other take that daughter.
   (session 2.7)

Not until cycle 3 does Fatima use similar devices for shift of reference as the other informants: for the main character most commonly pro-NPs, i.e. *hij* ('he') and zero-NPs, for minor characters most commonly full-NPs.

Maintenance of reference

For maintenance of reference the same observations can be made as for shift of reference. Only in cycle 3 does Fatima make use of the possibility of reserving zero-NPs and pro-NPs for the main character.

7.5   CONCLUSIONS

In Section 7.2 three research questions of the present chapter were specified. These can now be answered on the basis of the analyses presented for the core informants.

I   Which expressive devices are used for establishment, shift and maintenance of person reference?

Establishment of reference to both the main character and the minor characters is most commonly achieved through full-NPs. These are mostly definite full-NPs in which the demonstrative *die* ('that') is used as the determiner. Occasionally, with the exception of Fatima, also indefinite full-NPs are used in which the numeral *een* ('one') is the determiner. The unemphatic indefinite article *'n* ('a') is used very infrequently (and then only by Mohamed). The two Turkish learners occasionally mark establishment of reference through a strong deictically used pro-NP with a postponed right-dislocated full-NP, e.g. *die + brilmeneer* ('that + spectacle man' meaning: "that one + the man with the glasses").
    For shift of reference the effect of the thematic status of the characters can be observed. The main character is most commonly referred to by means of pro-NPs (mostly *hij* 'he', occasionally *die* 'that'), while the minor characters are most commonly referred to by means of full-NPs (i.e. bare noun and a definite full-NP, "*die-N*" 'that-N'). In addition, it can be noted that one Moroccan informant, Mohamed, marks shift of reference through a left-dislocated full-NP with postponed subject pronoun, e.g. *die politie hij* ... ('that police officer he ...').
    The effect of the thematic status of a character can also be observed in the encoding of maintenance of reference: for the main character most commonly pro-NPs (mostly *hij* 'he', incidentally *die* 'that') or zero-NPs, and for the minor characters most commonly full-NPs (i.e. bare nouns and definite full-NPs, "*die-N*" 'that-N'). In addition, a remarkable use of *(d)ie* ('that/he') as a post-verbal enclitic can be observed with Mohamed, e.g. *hij loopt-ie* ('he walks-he').

II   Which developmental pattern can be found in subsequent stages of language acquisition?

In Section 7.2 a number of predictions were formulated with respect to the developmental pattern in the encoding of establishment, shift and maintenance of person reference. These predictions can now be tested.

P1   Establishment of reference is achieved:
        - in early stages through definite full-NPs;
        - in later stages through both indefinite full-NPs and definite full-NPs.

No supporting evidence was found for this prediction. The informants use the same set of encoding devices in all three cycles. When an informant uses an indefinite full-

NP this is done from cycle 1 onwards. Here a preference for the use of the emphatic *een* ('one') over the use of the non-emphatic *'n* ('a') emerges.

P2 *Shift of reference to main character is achieved:*
     - *in early stages through pro-NPs;*
     - *in later stages through definite full-NPs.*

P3 *Shift of reference to minor character is achieved:*
     - *in early stages through definite full-NPs;*
     - *in later stages through pro-NPs.*

These predictions are only partly confirmed. The informants do indeed mark shift of reference to the main character differently (i.e. most commonly through pro-NPs) from shift of reference to minor characters (i.e. most commonly through full-NPs). However, the difference remains the same and no developmental pattern over time can be observed. From cycle 1 onwards, Mahmut, Ergün and Mohamed use pro-NPs relatively more often for shift of reference to the main character. For Fatima this can only be observed in cycle 3.

P4 *Maintenance of reference is achieved:*
     - *in early and later stages through zero-NPs or pro-NPs.*

This prediction is confirmed for reference to the main character: implicit encoding devices are used relatively more frequently for maintenance of reference than for establishment and shift of reference. Prediction 4 is, however, disconfirmed for reference to the minor characters, for which an abundant use of full-NPs can be observed.

On the whole, no strong developmental changes over time can be observed in the encoding of referential movement. It may be interesting to note that if one compares the different retellings over time, it is obvious that in later sessions the retelling of the film takes less effort and requires fewer trials. This can be derived for example from the degree of necessary stimulations by the interlocutor, e.g. *en wat gebeurt er nu?* ('so what happens now?'), or the presence of metalinguistic comments such as *dat is moeilijk in Nederlands* ('that is difficult in Dutch').

III How can the learner preferences be explained?

In the particular case of Dutch as a second language used by Turkish and Moroccan adults some observations might point to a transfer of L1-related conventions of marking information linguistically. These findings are related to spatial reference and the use of right/left-dislocated NPs.

With the Turkish adults some instances of person reference could be noted with a typically Turkish supportive use of spatial expressive devices such as *hier* ('here') and *daar* ('there'). A similar observation was made by Verhoeven (1988) in his study of the acquisition of discourse cohesion by Turkish children.

Moreover, the Turkish informants used the deictic pronoun *die* ('that') together with right-dislocated NPs. On the other hand, Mohamed, used left-dislocated NPs. The latter construction has also been observed by De Ruiter (1989:188) in L2-Dutch varieties of young Moroccans. In Moroccan Arabic fronting of a (pro-)nominal constituent is quite common: a pronoun or noun referring to the entity in focus is placed at the beginning of the utterance, followed by a pause. The fronted constituent is co-referential with a pronoun, either independent, suffixed or signalled by verb inflection, occurring later in the same utterance (cf. Harrell 1962:161, De Ruiter 1989:175-176).

The findings in this chapter also point to the role of perceptual saliency of words in acquiring the target language. In early stages adult language learners use perceptually salient forms such as *die* ('that') and *een* ('one'), while the corresponding less salient forms, i.e. *de* ('the') and *'n* ('a') respectively, emerge only in later stages of acquisition.

A comparison of language acquisition by children and adults might reveal whether, and if so to what extent, cognitive maturation is involved in the linguistic representation of information. On the basis of the findings in the present chapter it is concluded that processes of language acquisition by adults differ from child language acquisition in the establishment, shift and maintenance of person reference: in all stages of adult language acquisition the global structuring of information is taken into account for the linguistic representation of reference to person. Also, there is no intermediate phase (cf. Karmiloff-Smith 1985, Strömqvist & Day 1990) in which attention to global information structuring results in a temporarily limited local marking of this structuring. Once a language learner (as a child) has acknowledged the need to take into account the local and global marking of information, this knowledge is also used in the task of acquiring a new linguistic system. The adult language learner is aware of the fact that information in narrative discourse has a sequential and hierarchical structure which should both be marked linguistically: the adult has at his disposal a package of language independent principles which affects the acquisition of the encoding devices for establishment, shift and maintenance of reference.

CHAPTER 8

REFERENCE TO POSSESSION

The area of investigation in this chapter is the acquisition of the possessive relationship in Dutch and German. The preceding chapters focussed on the acquisition of Dutch by the two Turkish core informants and the two Moroccan core informants. In this chapter a detailed analysis will be presented for both the core informants and the shadow informants. In addition, a cross-linguistic comparison is made by investigating the acquisition of German by Turkish and Italian adults.

First, a global account of the encoding devices for the possessive relationship in Dutch and German as the target languages and in Turkish, Moroccan Arabic and Italian as the source languages is presented. On the basis of this typological comparison, a set of predictions about the L2 acquisition process is formulated. Next, a description of the method is given: the informants, the language activities, and the procedure in the analysis. Finally, the possessive constructions found in the learner varieties are discussed and the results are abstracted into a number of conclusions.

8.1   THE POSSESSIVE RELATIONSHIP

Nobody will disagree with Seiler (1983:1) when he claims that "possession is fundamental in human life and [..] in human language". Even though the linguistic and cognitive aspects of possession have been investigated in a great number of studies, there is as yet no general consensus about their mutual interdependence (cf. Seiler 1983). A possessive relationship always involves two entities: the possessor or owner (henceforth: O) and the entity possessed, the possession (henceforth: P). Languages have a variety of linguistic devices to encode possessive relationships. In the encoding devices (henceforth: possessive constructions) O and P can be referred to through pronominal and nominal devices.

An illuminating window on the status of possession in language use is provided by focussing upon the amalgamation of (1) the order in which O and P appear in possessive constructions, e.g. *the life of Brian* vs. *Brian's life*, and (2) the intensity of the possessive relationship between O and P. The intensity is reflected in the degree of alienability, which indicates whether O and P can be associated with each other temporary or not. In an inalienable relationship O and P are permanently connected, e.g. *father's nose* or *my knee*. In an alienable relationship P is possessed optionally by O, e.g. *father's chair*.

Some examples from English can illustrate the intriguing interplay between order and intensity characteristics of possessive relationships between entities (see Quirk & Greenbaum 1973:94-100). In English there is functional similarity between the so-called "s-genitive", e.g. *the ship's anchor,* and a prepositional phrase with *of,* the so-called "of-genitive", e.g. *the anchor of the ship.* Possessive constructions with an s-genitive have OP order, whereas possessive constructions with an of-genitive have the reverse order, PO. There are usually compelling reasons for the preference for and (un)acceptability of one or the other way of encoding the possessive relationship. In this the intensity principle plays a role in that the of-genitive is chiefly used with nouns which encode an inanimate O, e.g. *the head of the school* vs. *the man's head.*

A comparison of possessive constructions in Dutch and German with those in Turkish, Moroccan Arabic and Italian shows some interesting differences and similarities. The possessive constructions in each of these languages will be discussed in detail. No exhaustive account is aimed at, however. The comparison of the five languages focusses on general typological differences and similarities. Four types of possessive constructions are distinguished on the basis of (1) nominal vs. pronominal reference to O, and (2) the order of O and P:
- Nominal PO constructions, e.g. *the book of father.*
- Pronominal PO constructions, e.g. *the book of him.*
- Nominal OP constructions, e.g. *father's book.*
- Pronominal OP constructions, e.g. *his book.*

The encoding of possession through verbs, e.g. *he has a book,* is not taken into account. Such constructions occurred only occasionally in the learner varieties dealt with in this chapter.

8.1.1 DUTCH AND GERMAN

A description of the basic aspects of the encoding of the possessive relationship in native spoken Dutch is given in Janssen (1975) and Geerts et al. (1984:197-214). Surveys of German grammar and usage are Hammer (1980), Grebe (1973) and Schwarze (1988). Some examples of possessive constructions in Dutch and German are given in Table 8.1.

Dutch and German are rather similar in the encoding of possession, the most important difference being that German has an extensive case marking system. For the PO order the following type of encoding devices can be distinguished in both languages:
(1)   PO constructions with the prepositions *van* ('of') and *von* ('of'), e.g. *het boek van de man* ('the book of the man') and *das buch von dem mann* ('the book of-the man'). In the case of pronominal reference to O in German the accep-

tability of using an object pronoun after the preposition *von* ('of') is a moot point for native speakers, e.g. *das buch von ihm* ('the book of him'). In Dutch the corresponding possessive constructions are more acceptable than in German, e.g. *het boek van hem* ('the book of him').

(2)   PO constructions with a genitive case, e.g. *das buch des mannes* ('the book of-the man'). In Dutch such constructions only occur as fixed and archaic expressions (cf. Geerts et al. 1984:712). In spoken colloquial German there is a strong tendency to avoid the genitive case, mainly by using a "von" construction with the dative case (cf. Hammer 1980:28,104), e.g. *das buch vom mann* ('the book of-the man').

Table 8.1: Possessive constructions in Dutch and German

	Construction	English equivalent
Dutch:	het boek van de man	the book of the man
	het boek van hem	the book of him
	peters boek	peter's book
	zijn boek	his book
	de man zijn boek	the man his book
German:	das buch von dem mann	the book of the man
	das buch von ihm	the book of him
	das buch des mannes	the book of-the man
	peters buch	peter's book
	sein buch	his book
	dem mann sein buch	the man his book

For the OP order the following types of possessive constructions can be distinguished in Dutch and German:

(3)   OP constructions with s-genitive, e.g. *peters boek* ('peter's book') and *peters buch* ('peter's book').

(4)   OP constructions with the attributive use of a possessive pronoun immediately preceding the noun, e.g. *zijn boek* ('his book') and *sein buch* ('his book'). In contrast to Dutch, possessive pronouns in German are declined according to gender, number and case of the noun to which they are used attributively.

(5)   OP constructions with the juxtaposition of the antecedent and a possessive pronoun for reference to O, e.g. *de man zijn boek* ('the man his book') and *dem mann sein buch* ('the man his book'). These constructions only occur in spoken language and are most commonly used for O as human beings or animals and if there is a certain familiarity with O (cf. Geerts et al. 1984:209).

As a whole, both in Dutch and in German a general encoding principle seems to be that the order of O and P depends on whether or not the preposition *van* ('of') or *von* ('of') is used. If it is, the order is PO, if not, the order is OP.

8.1.2   Turkish, Moroccan Arabic and Italian

References to grammars which were consulted for Turkish and Moroccan Arabic are given in Chapter 4 in the sections where the pronoun system in both languages was described. For Italian Lepschy & Lepschy (1986) and Schwarze (1988) were consulted. Some examples of possessive constructions are given in Table 8.2.

Table 8.2: Possessive constructions in Turkish, Moroccan Arabic and Italian

	Construction	English equivalent
Turkish:	adam-ın kitab-ı	man-GEN book-him/her
	kitab-ı	book-him/her
	o-nun kitab-ı	s/he-GEN book-him/her
	ben-im kitab-ım	I-GEN book-my
	ben-im kitap	I-GEN book
Moroccan Arabic:	waḥed le-ktab dyal ṛ-ṛažel	one the-book of the-man
	le-ktab dyal-ha	the-book of-her
	bent-ha	daughter-her
Italian:	il libro dell'uomo	the book of-the man
	il suo libro	the his/her book
	il libro suo	the book him/her
	il libro di lui	the book of him
	il libro di lei	the book of her
	mia madre	my mother

Turkish

In Turkish the order in possessive constructions is mostly OP. In these constructions O is marked through a genitive case suffix. P is marked through a possessive suffix which corresponds with O according to an agreement rule for person (role) and mostly also for number. The following types of constructions can be distinguished:

(1)   nominal OP constructions, e.g. *adam-ın kitab-ı* ('man-GEN book-him/her').
(2)   pronominal constructions in which O is encoded only through a possessive suffix, e.g. *kitab-ı* ('book-him/her').
(3)   pronominal OP constructions in which O is encoded through an attributively used free lexical pronoun, e.g. *o-nun kitab-ı* ('s/he-GEN book-him/her') and *ben-im kitab-ım* ('I-GEN book-my'). The function of the free pronoun is to accentuate O. In these possessive constructions O also has to be encoded through a possessive suffix after P. This is obligatory in standard use. For pronominal 1st/2nd role reference, however, the possessive suffix is often deleted in colloquial speech, e.g. *ben-im kitap* ('I-GEN book').

Moroccan Arabic

In contrast to Turkish, the order of possessive constructions in Moroccan Arabic is mostly PO; the reverse order is rather uncommon (see Harrell 1962:197 for some idiomatic OP constructions in Moroccan Arabic such as *mul ḍ-ḍaṛ* 'owner the-house'). Interestingly, the linguistic encoding is affected by the intensity of the possessive relationship between O and P. Most commonly the preposition *dyal* ('of') is used in possessive constructions, e.g. *waḥed le-ktab dyal ṛ-ṛažel* ('one the-book of the-man') and *le-ktab dyal-ha* ('the-book of-her'). However, in possessive relationships in which there is a kinship or close friendship relation between O and P, pronominal reference to O is regularly expressed in a construction without *dyal* ('of'). In these constructions a possessive suffix is attached to the form which encodes P, e.g. *bent-ha* ('daughter-her').

Italian

In contrast to Turkish and Moroccan Arabic, both OP constructions and PO constructions are common in Italian.

For nominal reference to O the order is mostly PO, e.g. *il libro dell'uomo* ('the book of-the man'). In these constructions a so-called "preposizione articolata" is often used, which is the amalgamation of a definite article and a preposition, e.g. *di* ('of') and *l'* ('the') amalgamated into *dell'*.

For pronominal reference to O both OP order as well as PO order is possible. The pronoun corresponds in gender and number to the device that encodes P. The gender of O is not reflected in the possessive pronoun, e.g. *il suo libro* ('the his/her book') and *il libro suo* ('the book him/her'). In order to avoid misunderstandings, the pronoun, which is a feminine or masculine object pronoun, is regularly used in a construction with PO order, e.g. *il libro di lui* ('the book of him) and *il libro di lei* ('the book of her').

Similar to Moroccan Arabic the intensity of the possessive relationship determines the way of linguistic encoding. The definite article before the possessive pronoun can be omitted in case of kinship relations, under the additional conditions of singular reference and of P not being specified through a suffix or an adjective (cf. Lepschy & Lepschy 1986:151), e.g. *mia madre* ('my mother').

8.2 RESEARCH QUESTIONS AND PREDICTIONS

The typological comparison in the previous sections shows that order and intensity characteristics of the possessive relationship do indeed operate differently in the languages compared. How and to what extent are these differences reflected in the Dutch varieties of Turkish/Moroccan L2 learners and in the German varieties of Turkish/Italian L2 learners? More precisely, the research questions of this chapter can be formulated as follows:

I   With which linguistic devices is the possessive relationship encoded in L2-Dutch and L2-German learner varieties?

II Which developmental patterns can be observed in subsequent stages of language acquisition?

III How can learner preferences be explained?

In answering these questions the focus is on order characteristics of the possessive relationship. The order in which O and P appear in possessive constructions of the languages focussed on in the present chapter is summarized in Table 8.3.

Table 8.3: The order of O and P in possessive constructions

		Dutch		German	
	Arabic		Turkish		Italian
PO constructions	+ +	+ +	− −	+ +	+ +
OP constructions	− −	+ +	+ +	+ +	+ +

(+ + = common, − − = uncommon)

With respect to the order of linguistic devices that encode O and P, Dutch, German and Italian are ambivalent in that both PO order and OP order are common. In contrast, Turkish and Moroccan Arabic have distinct preferences for a specific order of O and P. Accordingly, the following predictions are made:

P1   Moroccan L2 learners of Dutch initially prefer possessive PO constructions
P2   Turkish L2 learners of Dutch initially prefer possessive OP constructions
P3   Turkish L2 learners of German initially prefer possessive OP constructions
P4   Italian L2 learners of German have no preference for possessive constructions
     with a specific order of O and P

Can evidence for the above predictions indeed be found in L2-Dutch and L2-German varieties in different stages of the L2 acquisition process? If not, are there perhaps other factors that play a role in the learners' strategies for the encoding of the possessive relationship in a new language? Here the intensity principle enters the game. The type of possessive relationship between O and P, in particular kinship and alienability, might determine the preferences of the adult learners in the linguistic encoding of the possessive relationship, in particular with respect to the order of O and P.

8.3   METHOD

8.3.1   INFORMANTS AND LANGUAGE ACTIVITIES

The informants in this chapter are sixteen adults: four Turkish and four Moroccan L2 learners of Dutch, and four Turkish and four Italian L2 learners of German. Socio-biographical characteristics of the informants were given in Chapter 3.

The informants were asked to retell and comment on the content of a videoclip they had just seen. The videoclip was the silent movie *Harold Lloyd at the Station* (see Chapter 7). The videoclip is very suitable for eliciting different kinds of possessive relationships existing between people and objects:

Harold Lloyd:	his fiancée, his parents-in-law, his suitcase and his train.
The black lady:	her child and her carry-cot.
The fiancée:	her friend and her parents.
The father:	his wife, his daughter and his son-in-law.
The mother:	her husband, her daughter, and her son-in-law.

The four Turkish and the four Moroccan informants in the Netherlands took part in this language activity three times: in session 1.6., session 2.6 and in session 3.6. In session 1.6., three Turkish and three Moroccan informants were also asked to retell the videoclip in their mother tongue (note that for the core informants the activities were analysed in Chapter 7).

The Turkish and Italian informants in Germany also took part in this language activity three times; in session 1.3., in session 2.3., and session 3.3. In the case of Yasar (a Turkish informant) and Alese (an Italian informant), the third session did not take place.

8.3.2 PROCEDURE IN THE ANALYSIS

In the analysis of linguistic devices by means of which possessive relationships are expressed, the starting point is the learner's use. What is focussed on are form-function relationships in a particular learner variety. The main interest is the intended referential function of a form: which entities does the learner want to refer to?

The procedure in the analysis will be illustrated through the data of Osman, a Turkish learner of Dutch. Sequence (1) is the film retelling produced by Osman in session 2.6.

(1)	OSM:	Mag ik vertellen?	May I tell?
	N:	Ja jij vertelt.	Yes you tell.
	OSM:	Ja een man wachten trein	Yes a man wait train
	N:	Ja.	Yes.
	OSM:	in de station. Ja van hem familie ook. Enne die man praten met van hem vriendin of van hem vrouw. Ja enne ik denk't de man zeggen "Ik wil uh/ ik moet nou weg, dan ik kom straks, en jij moet wachten mij".	in the station. Yes of him family too. And that man talk with of him girlfriend or of him woman. Yes and I think the man say "I want er/ I have to go now, then I come later, and you have to wait for me".
	N:	Ja.	Yes.
	OSM:	Anders weet ik niet. Komt een zwarte vrouw he. Een tas leggen op de grond. Enne die jongen heeft ook een tas. Maar uh de zwarte vrouw uh tas leggen voor de andere tas. En de man uh/ ja komt/ komt andere trein. De man moet nou weg.	Otherwise I don't know. Comes a black woman right. A bag put on the ground. And that boy also has a bag. But er the black woman er put bag in front of the other bag. And the man er/ yes comes/ comes other train. The man has to go now.
	N:	Ja.	Yes.
	OSM:	Enne een keer kusje geeft aan vrouw/ uh van 'm moeder of weet ik niet wat is dat. Enne die man pakte een tas. Hij denkte "Is van mijn tas" he. En de zwarte vrouw ook zien. Enne de vrouw ook pakte van 'm tas.	And once gives little kiss to woman/ er of him mother or I do not know what is that. And that man took a bag. He thought "Is of my bag" right. And the black woman see too. And the woman also took of him

	Dutch	English
	Die andere. Enne beetje hard lopen. En treinconducteur fluit een keer. Dan trein moet weg. En hij moet hard lopen.	bag. That other one. And walk quite fast. And train conductor whistles once. Then train must leave. And he must walk fast.
N:	Ja.	Yes.
OSM:	Enne de vrouw ook komt achteraan. De vrouw zeggen "Dit is van mijn tas. Dit is van jou". Nou enne trein is weg. Komt achteraan een paardauto. Maar hij weet niet wat is dat trein of paardauto. Hij pakt die paard- auto. Enne even die kant rijden dan he. Hij kijken die is paardauto.	And the woman also comes after him. The woman say "This is of my bag. This is of you". Now and train is gone. Comes behind a horsecar. But he does not know + what is that + train or horsecar. He takes that horsecar. And for a while ride that way then right? He look that is horsecar.
N:	Ja ja.	Yes yes.
OSM:	Hij uh/ hij stoppen. Komt/ beetje hardlopen. Komt binnen trein.	He er/ he stop. Comes/ run a little. Comes into train.
N:	En was ie/ hij was op tijd? Of was ie te te laat?	And was he/ he was in time? Or was he too late?
OSM:	Hij is te laat?	He is too late?
N:	Is ie te laat?	Is he too late?
OSM:	Ja trein moet weg. Conducteur een keer fluit^ trein weg.	Yes train must go. Conductor once whistle^ train go.
N:	Maar zit ie in de trein of zit ie niet in de trein?	But is he on the train or is he not on the train?
OSM:	Straks wel. Eerst hier paardauto.	Later yes. First here horsecar.
	(session 2.6)	

The possessive constructions selected from the three sessions with Osman are given in Table 8.4. They have been ordered according to the owner referred to.

Table 8.4: Possessive constructions used by Osman (Turkish-Dutch)

Session 1.6	N	Session 2.6	N	Session 3.6	N	English equivalent
HAROLD						
hij vrouw	1					he woman
				zijn vrouw	3	his woman
		van hem vriendin	1			of him girlfriend
		van hem vrouw	1			of him woman
		van 'm moeder	1			of him mother
		van hem familie	1			of him family
				zijn familie	1	his family
		van mijn tas	1			of my bag
		van 'm tas	1			of him bag
				zijn koffer	2	his suitcase
				deze van jou	1	this of you
BLACK LADY						
mijn tas	1					my bag
		van mijn tas	1			of my bag
				tas van mijn	1	bag of mine
die kinderen mijn	1					those children mine
				deze mijn	1	this mine
hij kinderen	1					he children
				zijn kind	1	his child

For Osman the following developmental pattern can be observed:

In session 1.6, Osman generalizes in pronominal OP constructions the form *hij* ('he') for gender. This subject pronoun is used for reference to Harold as O, i.e. *hij vrouw* ('he woman), and for reference to the black lady as O, i.e. *hij kinderen* ('he children'). For 1st role reference, which occurs within quoted speech, Osman uses the possessive pronoun *mijn* ('my') in OP constructions, i.e. *mijn tas* ('my bag') as well as in PO constructions, i.e. *die kinderen mijn* ('those children mine').

In session 2.6, the possessive relationship is always encoded with pronominal OP constructions containing the preposition *van* ('of'). A non-standardlike construction "*van*-Pro-N" is systematically used for 1st role reference, e.g. *van mijn tas* ('of my bag'), and 3rd role reference, e.g. *van 'm moeder* ('of him mother').

In session 3.6, he does not use the non-standardlike OP construction "*van*-Pro-N" anymore. For 1st/2nd role reference the pronouns *mijn* ('my') and *jou* ('you') are used in PO constructions with *van* ('of'), i.e. *deze van jou* ('this of you') and *tas van mijn* ('bag of mine'). The pronoun *mijn* ('my') also occurs in a PO construction without *van* ('of'), i.e. *deze mijn* ('this mine'). For 3rd role reference the possessive pronoun *zijn* ('his') is used in OP constructions. Osman generalizes the pronoun *zijn* ('his') for reference to men and women, as sequence (2) shows.

(2)	OSM:	Ja die man pakt zijn koffer.	Yes that man takes his suitcase.
	N:	Ja.	Yes.
	OSM:	Zelf koffer. En die vrouw pakt zijn kind.	Self suitcase. And that woman takes his child.
	(session 3.6)		

8.4   RESULTS

In this section the encoding of the possessive relationship in the observed Dutch and German learner varieties will be summarized for (1) nominal PO constructions, (2) pronominal PO constructions, (3) nominal OP constructions, and (4) pronominal OP constructions, respectively.

8.4.1 NOMINAL PO CONSTRUCTIONS

All nominal PO constructions used by the adult L2 learners of Dutch and German are given in Table 8.5. Nominal PO order most commonly corresponds to the "N-Prep-N" construction. This construction is used in particular by the Moroccan learners of Dutch. An example is given in sequence (3).

(3)	MOH:	Hij weg. En dan hij/ hij pak die zoon van die zwart vrouw.	He gone. And then he/ he take that son of that black woman.
	(session 1.6)		

Table 8.5: Overview nominal PO constructions

		Possession	Owner	N	English equivalent
MOROCCAN-DUTCH:					
Fatima	1.6	vrouw	van man	1	woman of man
		man	ander vrouw	1	man other woman
		zoon	van die vrouw	1	son of that woman
		die dochter	van ander vrouw	1	that daughter of other woman
	2.6	die ander koffer	van die man	1	that other suitcase of that man
		die meisje	van die vrouw	1	that girl of that woman
Mohamed	1.6	die zoon	van die zwart vrouw	1	that son of that black woman
		ouders	van meisje	1	parents of girl
	2.6	die moeder	van die baby	1	that mother of that baby
		die ouders	van die meisje	1	those parents of that girl
Hassan	1.6	moeder en vader	van jouw vrouw	1	mother and father of your woman
		de moeder	van jouw vrouw	1	the mother of your woman
		die moeder	van jouw vrouw	1	that mother of your woman
	2.6	(de) ouders	van hem vrouw	3	(the) parents of him woman
	3.6	de ouders	van hem vrouw	1	the parents of him woman
Husseyn	1.6	de moeder en			the mother and
		de vader	van de meisje	1	the father of the girl
		de man	van de meisje	1	the man of the girl
	2.6	vriendin	van die man	1	girlfriend of that man
		de vader en			the father and
		de moeder	van die meisje	1	the mother of that girl
		de moeder	van die vriendin	1	the mother of that girlfriend
		de moeder	van die vrouw		the mother of that woman
			of die meisje	1	or that girl
		de babytje	van die zwarte vrouw	1	the baby of that black woman
		die babytje	van die zwarte vrouw	2	that baby of that black woman
TURKISH-DUTCH:					
Abdullah	3.6	tas	van de acteur	1	bag of the actor
TURKISH-GERMAN:					
Cevdet	3.3	die mutter	von das kind	1	the mother of that child
		die frau	von das kind	1	the woman of that child
		die bekannte	von die frauen	1	the acquaintances of that woman
Ilhami	3.3	in dem hande	die andere mann	1	in the hands that other man
ITALIAN-GERMAN:					
Tino	3.3	die hande	von mädchen	1	the hands of girl
		die gesicht	von seine mädchen	1	that face of his girl
		die hande	von seine mutter	1	those hands of his mother
Angelina	1.3	die koffer	die mann	1	that suitcase that man
		der mutt	die frau	1	the mother that woman
		der vater	die frau	1	the father that woman
		die mutter	die kind	1	that mother that child
		der baby	eine mutti	1	the baby a mother
Marcello	2.3	die koffer	der mann	1	that suitcase that man
		die koffer	dies mann	1	that suitcase this man
Alese	2.3	die tasche	von der mann	1	that bag of that man
	2.3	die tasche	von die mann	1	that bag of that man

The Moroccan informants use the "N-*van*-N" ('N-of-N') construction mostly in sessions 1.6 and 2.6, while it disappears in session 3.6 (with the exception of Hassan). Note that they use this construction mostly for the encoding of kinship relations (the exception is Fatima, session 2.6). Also in the German learner varieties the "N-*von*-N" ('N-of-N') construction can be observed, in particular in later sessions. An example for Cevdet is given in the following sequence:

(4) CEV: Jetzt er nimmt das kind mit. Er/ er   Now he takes the child with him. He/ he
             weiss net habe ob da/ ob der koffer   does not know have if there/ if the
             oder kind. Er weiss net das.   suitcase or child. He does not know that.
     N: Ja + + und?   Yes + + and?
     CEV: Und die mutter von das kind das hat   And the mother of that child that has
             sie gesehen.   she seen.
     (session 3.3)

The nominal PO order also corresponds to the juxtaposition of the encoding devices for O and P. These possessive constructions are used in particular by the Italian learners of German. An example for Angelina is given in sequence (5).

(5) ANG: Und E die mutter die kind   And er that mother that child
     N: Mhm.   Uh-huh.
     ANG: E *ha vi/* kuuk kuuk.   Er *has see/* look look.
     N: Ja ja.   Yes yes.
     ANG: E *e ha corso dietro* E mit E   Er *has run behind* er with er
             die koffer die mann.   that suitcase that man.
     (session 1.3)

The form *die* occurring before the second noun (e.g. in sequence 5 before the forms *kind* 'child' and *mann* 'man'), could be considered as a German determiner ('that') or as an Italian preposition ('of').

8.4.2 PRONOMINAL PO CONSTRUCTIONS

Pronominal PO constructions are relatively rare. The instances that do occur are given in Table 8.6.

Table 8.6: Overview pronominal PO constructions

		Possession	Owner	N	English equivalent
MOROCCAN-DUTCH:					
Mohamed	1.6	die *valise*	van hij	1	that suitcase of he
	2.6	die tas	van hem	1	that bag of him
		die koffer	van hem	1	that suitcase of him
TURKISH-DUTCH:					
Osman	1.6	die kinderen	mijn	1	those children my
	3.6	deze	mijn	1	these my
		deze	van jou	1	these of you
		tas	van mijn	1	bag of my

Pronominal PO constructions can only be observed in the Dutch learner varieties. Whereas native speakers would use an object pronoun after the preposition *van* ('of'), Mohamed and Osman occasionally make use of the subject pronoun *hij* ('he') and the possessive pronoun *mijn* ('my') respectively.

8.4.3 NOMINAL OP CONSTRUCTIONS

All nominal OP constructions that can be found in the learner varieties are given in Table 8.7.

Table 8.7: Overview nominal OP constructions

		Owner	Possession	N	English equivalent
TURKISH-DUTCH:					
Mahmut	3.6	vrouw	vader moeder	1	woman father mother
TURKISH-GERMAN:					
Ayse	2.3	sein verlobte	mutter	1	his fiancée mother
	3.3	die mädchens	vater und mutter	1	that girl's father and mother
Cevdet	1.3	seine frau	gesicht	2	his woman face
	2.3	kind(s)	mutter	2	child's mother
		seins sohns	frau	1	his son's woman
Ilhami	3.3	der mann sein	tasch	1	the man his bag
		von die frauen	tasch	1	of that woman bag
ITALIAN-GERMAN:					
Marcello	3.3	von die frauen	koffer	1	of that woman suitcase
		die neger frau	koffer	1	that negro woman suitcase
		die frau	gesicht	1	that woman face

In the learner varieties of Dutch nominal OP constructions are only used once by a Turkish informant, Mahmut, who in session 3.6 refers with *vrouw vader moeder* ('woman father mother') to "the parents of the woman".

In the German learner varieties of the Turkish informants some constructions with the s-genitive can be noted. Ilhami and Marcello also use the construction "*von-die-*N" ('of-that-N'):

(6) ILH: Dann der/ der mann geht jetzt weg der   Then the/ the man goes away now he
            muss jetzt in dem zug E steigen einsteigen.   must now get er on the train get in.
            Dann die frau hat ge/ E   Then the woman has se/ er
            gesehen sein tasch war hier und   seen his bag was here and
            sein/ E von die frauen tasch in dem/   his/ er of that woman suitcase in the/
            de/ in dem hande die andere mann.   the/ in the hands that other man.
       (session 3.3)

As can be seen in sequence (6) the possessive pronoun *sein* ('his') is repaired into a possessive construction with *von* ('of').

An interesting development can be observed with Cevdet. Consider the following sequence from session 1.3:

(7) CEV: Ja der macht E seine frau gesicht und   Yes he makes er his woman face and
seine der macht hand seine frau gesicht.   his he makes hand his woman face.
(session 1.3)

In this sequence Cevdet uses the possessive pronoun *sein* ('his') in conformity with standardlike conventions. In addition it can be noted that there is a possessive relationship between *seine frau* ('his woman') as O and *gesicht* ('face') as P. Now compare sequence (8) which is taken from session 3.3, 15 months later.

(8) CEV: Der mann hat iie frau E ins gesicht   The man has him woman er in the
angefast.   face touched.
(session 3.3)

Two aspects of the development over time in Cevdet's language use are interesting. Firstly, the possessive relationship between *frau* ('woman') and *gesicht* ('face') as observed in session 1.3 is replaced in session 3.3 by a construction with the preposition *in* ('in'). Secondly, in session 1.3 the standardlike possessive pronoun *seine* ('his') is used. In contrast, in session 3.3 Cevdet use the form *iie* which might imply a generalization of the object form *ihm* ('him'). The peculiarity of this form will be discussed more in detail in the next section.

8.4.4 PRONOMINAL OP CONSTRUCTIONS

Pronominal OP constructions are used frequently by all informants. The instances are summarized in Table 8.8. For each pronominal variant the form-function relationship is taken into account. With respect to the pronominal OP constructions in the Dutch learner varieties a number of learner preferences have already been discussed in Chapters 5 and 6. However, the form-function analysis in Table 8.8 includes more informants. The preferences of the Dutch shadow informants confirm the picture that emerges from the earlier chapters. However, a comparison of Dutch and German learner varieties reveals a number of interesting differences.

1st role pronominal reference
Both in Dutch and in German learner varieties the 1st role possessive pronouns *mijn* ('my') and *mein* ('my') respectively, are used in conformity with standardlike conventions. However, two types of non-standardlike pronominal OP constructions can be observed in the Dutch learner varieties which are absent in the German learner varieties.

First, the use of a 1st role object pronoun instead of a 1st role possessive pronoun. In the Dutch varieties of one Turkish and three Moroccan informants the object pronoun *mij* ('me') is used instead of the possessive pronoun *mijn* ('my'). In particular Husseyn's preference for object pronouns can be noted. In sessions 1.6 and 3.6 Husseyn uses *mij babytje* ('me little baby') and *mij koffertje* ('me little suitcase').

*Table 8.8: Overview pronominal references in OP constructions**

Dutch	Turkish Mah.	Erg.	Osm.	Abd.	Moroccan Moh.	Fat.	Has.	Hus.	Total	English
1ST ROLE										
mijn X	3	3	1	5	-	5	-	2	19	my X
van mijn X	-	2	2	1	-	-	-	-	5	of my X
mij X (=mijn)	-	-	-	1	3	-	1	5	10	me X (=my)
2ND ROLE										
jouw X	-	2	-	-	-	1	1	2	8	your X
uw X	-	-	-	1	-	-	-	-	1	your X
jij X (=jouw)	1	-	-	-	-	-	-	-	1	you X (=your)
3RD ROLE (MSC.)										
zijn X	-	1	6	1	-	-	2	15	25	his X
hem X (=zijn)	-	-	-	1	6	-	13	1	21	him X (=his)
van hem X	-	1	3	4	-	-	-	-	8	of him X
van 'm X	-	-	2	-	-	-	-	-	2	of him X
hij X (=zijn)	3	-	1	-	5	-	-	-	9	he X (=his)
zij X (=zijn)	-	-	-	-	6	-	-	7	13	she X (=his)
haar X (=zijn)	-	-	-	-	-	1	-	3	4	her X (=his)
jouw X (=zijn)	-	-	-	-	-	4	10	2	16	your X (=his)
3RD ROLE (FEM.)										
haar X	-	-	-	1	1	2	1	6	11	her X
hem X (=haar)	-	-	-	-	1	-	3	-	4	him X (=her)
zijn X (=haar)	-	-	1	-	-	-	1	-	2	his X (=her)
hij X (=haar)	-	-	1	-	3	-	-	-	4	he X (=her)
zij X (=haar)	-	-	-	-	-	-	-	3	3	she X (=her)
jouw X (=haar)	-	-	-	-	-	1	-	2	3	your X (=her)
mijn X (=haar)	-	-	-	-	-	1	-	-	1	my X (=her)

German	Turkish Ays.	Yas.	Cev.	Ilh.	Italian Ang.	Mar.	Tin.	Ale.	Total	English
1ST ROLE										
mein X	6	2	8	3	2	1	4	5	31	my X
2ND ROLE										
dein X	1	-	4	-	-	-	2	-	7	your X
iie X (=ihr)	2	-	-	-	-	-	-	-	2	your X (=your)
3RD ROLE (MSC.)										
sein X	25	17	29	12	5	43	33	13	177	his X
iie X (=sein)	5	-	8	-	-	-	-	-	13	him X (=his)
ihr(e) X (=sein)	1	-	-	-	-	-	-	2	3	her X (=his)
mein X (=sein)	-	-	-	-	-	-	1	-	1	my X (=his)
3RD ROLE (FEM.)										
ihre X	1	-	-	1	1	-	-	2	5	her X
iie X (=her)	7	-	3	-	-	-	-	-	10	her X (=her)
sein X (=ihr)	-	1	5	2	-	4	6	3	21	his X (=her)
sua X (=ihr)	-	-	-	-	1	-	-	-	1	*his* X (=her)

* in the German learner varieties the pronouns *ihm* and *ihr(e)* are mostly pronounced as "iie"

The absence in the German learner varieties of the generalized use of the object pronouns, that is *mir* ('me') or *mich* ('me'), may be an effect of the larger phonetic distance between object and possessive forms in standard German.

A second type of pronominal OP construction which is of interest is the construction "*van-mijn*-N" ('of-my-N'). This construction can only be found in the Dutch learner varieties of the Turkish informants. It appears that in later stages three Turkish informants prefer to encode the possessive relationship with the non-standardlike construction "*van-mijn*-N" ('of-my-N'), while in an earlier stage they used the standardlike construction "*mijn*-N" ('my-N'). This development can be illustrated with data from Ergün. Sequence (9) shows that in session 2.6 Ergün refers to "the bag of Harold" and "the baby of the woman" with *mijn tas* ('my bag') and *mijn baby* ('my baby') respectively.

(9) ERG: Dan hij is zo de baby halen.   Then he is so the baby taking.
  N: Ja.   Yes.
  ERG: Hij zegt/ hij uh/ hij denkt   He says/ he er/ he thinks
     "Ik mijn tas". Denk ik he.   "I my bag". I think right.
  N: Ja.   Yes.
  ERG: Hij is de baby gaat weg. Die ander vrouw He is the baby goes away. That other
     zien "Hee hee wachten of uh mijn baby". woman see "Hey hey wait or er my baby".
  (session 2.6)

In session 3.6, which took place nine months later, Ergün uses the non-standardlike "*van-mijn*-N" ('of-my-N') construction, i.e. *van mijn zoon* ('of my son') and *van mijn tas* ('of my bag'). This can be seen in sequence (10).

(10) ERG: Baby vast. Die j/ die man dacht Baby tight. That y/ that man thought
     "Van mijn tas". Vlakbij daar staan he "Of my bag". Near there stands er
     die kleine/ ja kleine jongen of meisje. that little/ yes little boy or girl.
  N: Hm.   Um.
  ERG: En dan die/ die jongen pakken met tas. And then that/ that boy take with bag.
     Hij is weg. Die hij komt/ daar komt He is gone. That he comes/ there comes
     een vrouw "En waar/ waar ga naar toe? a woman "And where/ where going to?
     Van mijn/ van mijn/ ja van mijn zoon Of my/ of my/ yes of my son
     of". + Ja dan weet ik niet.   or". + Yes then I do not know.
  (session 3.6)

It appears that the construction "*van-mijn*-N" ('of-my-N') which is so typical in L2-Dutch of Turkish adults can never be observed in L2-German of Turkish adults.

2nd role pronominal reference

With respect to the pronominal OP constructions used for 2nd role reference a "*van-jouw*-N" ('of-your-N') construction never occurs, not even in the Dutch varieties of the Turkish informants.

In the Dutch varieties of the Moroccan informants the standardlike construction "*jouw*-N" ('your-N') can be observed more often (see Chapter 5 for a detailed discussion).

Formality is marked in the Dutch learner variety by Abdullah, a Turkish informant, through the V-form *uw* ('your'):

(11) ABD: Maar komte + ander vrouw. Hij kijkt   But comes + other woman. He looks
              de + nee "Mij baby is weg". En hij   the + no "Me baby is gone". And he
              pakte hem tas.   took him bag.
       N: Ja.   Yes.
       ABD: Hij gaat achter. Zij/ zij zegt "Dit is   He goes after. She/ she says "This is
              mij baby, hier is uw tas". Dan uh de   me baby, here is your bag". Then er the
              man pakt zelf tas maar de trein is weg.   man takes self bag but the train is gone.
       (session 2.6)

In the German varieties, Ayse, a Turkish informant, uses the V-form *iie* ('your') for formal 2nd role reference. Note that *iie* stands for the native form *ihr* ('your'):

(12) AYS: Der wollte einsteigen und sie hat + E   He wanted to get on and she has + er
              wie sagt man dass streien oder?   how do you say that fight or?
              Ja und der/ sie sagt "Iie koffer ist   Yes and the/ she says "Your suitcase is
              hier. Warum nehmen sie mein baby?".   here. Why do you take my baby?".
       (session 3.3)

3rd role pronominal reference

Differences between the Dutch and German learner varieties can be observed in particular with the pronominal OP constructions for 3rd role reference.

Firstly, there is the generalized use of subject pronouns in possessive OP constructions. This use can only be observed in the Dutch learner varieties (see the pronoun profiles of the Dutch core informants presented in Chapter 6). Sequence (13) contains some examples from session 3.6 with Husseyn, one of the Moroccan shadow informants.

(13) HUS: Zij zit achter die jongman +   She sits behind that young man +
              met uh zij kinder of zij baby.   with er she children or she baby.
       N: Hmhm.   Uh-huh.
       HUS: Zij/ zij/ zij/ zij of haar baby?   She/ she/ she/ she or her baby?
       N: +   +
       HUS: Haar of zij?   Her or she?
       N: Ja wat is 't haar of zijn?   Yes what is it her or his?
       HUS: Haar?   Her?
       N: Haar?   Her?
       HUS: Ha/ nee zij baby.   He/ no she baby?
       N: Zijn baby.   His baby.
       HUS: Haar baby haar baby.   Her baby her baby.
       N: <laughs>.   <laughs>.
       HUS: Haar babytje.   Her little baby.
       (session 3.6)

Secondly, there is the use of an object pronoun in OP constructions. In the Dutch learner varieties the use of the object pronoun *hem* ('him') instead of the possessive pronoun *zijn* ('his') is very frequent. The construction "*van-hem*-N" ('of-him-N') is used by all Turkish informants except Mahmut. The use of this construction is preceded by the standardlike construction "*zijn*-N" ('his-N') in an earlier session. This is illustrated in sequences (14) and (15), with Abdullah, taken from sessions 2.6 and 3.6 respectively,

(14) ABD: Die man heeft 'n vriendin. + +   That man has a girlfriend. + +
              Zijn moeder en vader is ook daar.   His mother and father is also there.
          (session 2.6)

(15) N: Waar gaat de film over?   What is the film about?
     ABD: Ja + die acteur he. Ik weet niet naam.   Yes + that actor eh. I do not know name.
     N: Ja.   Yes.
     ABD: Van hem familie wacht op uh station.   Of him family wait at er station.
          (session 3.6)

In the German varieties of the Italian informants the use of the object pronoun *ihm* ('him') instead of the possessive pronoun *sein* ('his') cannot be found (see Table 8.8). In the German varieties of two Turkish informants, Cevdet and Ayse, however there seem to be some instances in which a 3rd role object pronoun, that is the form *iie*, is used for possessive reference. Some examples derived from Cevdet are given in sequence (16).

(16) N: Erzählst du mir was passiert ist?   You tell me what has happened?
     CEV: Ja so eine familie sind am bahnhof.   Yes so a family are at the station.
     N: Mhm.   Um.
     CEV: Und + und E der sohn fahrt   And + and er the son is leaving for
              irgendwo ab und er will E abschieden   somewhere and he wants er say farewell
              von iie vater und mutter. Und   to him father and mother. And
              iie frau ist auch da und + der/ der   him woman is also there and + the/ the
              zug ist gekommen.   train has come.
              Und + E und der vat E/ vater hat   And + er and the fath er/ father has
              gesagt zu sein sohn "Und der zug ist   said to his son "And the train is already
              schon dort du muss jetzt gleich gehen". there you must now go immediately".
              (Oder) und + und die (für) die mutter   (Or) and + and the (for) the mother has
              hatte etwas mit iie mann gesprochen so talked about something with her man and
              und der sohn auch mit iie frau und +   and the son also with him woman and +
              und der sohn hatte iie mutti geküsst.   and the son has him mother kissed.
          (session 2.3)

In sequence (16) there are indeed several instances of generalized use of the object pronoun, i.e. *iie vater und mutter* ('him father and mother'), *iie frau* ('him woman'), and *iie mutti* ('him mother'). In these constructions a native speaker of German would use the possessive pronoun *sein* ('his'). It seems as if with the form *iie* used by Ayse and Cevdet two types of generalizations are collapsed: (1) the generalized use of the object pronoun (compare the standard form *ihm* 'him'), and (2) the generalized use of the feminine pronoun for masculine reference (compare the standard form *ihr* 'her'). As can be derived from sequence (16), at the same time, pronouns are used standardlike, i.e. *sein sohn* ('his son') and *iie man* ('her man'). It appears that in the German learner varieties of Cevdet and Ayse the gender of P influences the selection of the pronoun that refers to O. An example of this use with Ayse is given in sequence (17).

(17) AYS: Der mann hat sein mü/ E mütze genommen.   The man has taken his ca/ er cap.
Dann der tragt mütze und der hat   Then he wears cap and he has
gelacht. Später sieht iie verlobte.   laughed. Later sees < him/her> fiancée.
Sie ist traurig. Sie sieht so traurig aus.   She is sad. She looks so sad.
(session 2.3)

In this sequence Ayse refers to "the man" as O with the masculine pronoun *sein* ('his') attributive to a masculine noun, i.e. *mütze* ('cap'), and with the form *iie* ('him/her') attributive to a feminine noun, i.e. *verlobte* ('fiancée').

A close examination of the pronominal OP constructions in the Dutch/German varieties of all informants strongly suggests that the gender of P is of influence on the selection of the pronoun that refers to O: a masculine 3rd role pronoun is more likely to be generalized for gender if P is a woman, and a feminine pronoun if P is a man.

There are also instances of pronoun reversal. In the Dutch varieties of the Moroccan informants some instances can be found where the 2nd role pronoun *jouw* ('your') is used for 3rd role reference. This phenomenon was discussed in Chapter 5. On the basis of the form-function analysis presented in Table 8.8 one might conclude that in the German learner varieties the generalized use of a 2nd role pronoun, i.e. *dein* and *ihr*, for 3rd role reference does not occur. Note, however, that in standard German the pronoun *ihr* can be used for 2nd role reference ('your') as well as for 3rd role reference ('her'). Therefore, generalizations in German learner varieties, in contrast to generalizations like *jouw* ('your') in Dutch learner varieties, cannot always be detected simply. Consider for example in sequence (18) Ayse's use of the pronominal OP constructions *iie mutter* and *iie baby*.

(18) AYS: Schnell laufen und der hat diese wagen   Walk fast and he has taken this cot
genommen nicht E seine koffer sondern   not er his suitcase but
[E die baby]   [er that baby]
N: [E nicht/ nicht] seinen koffer?   [er not/ not] his suitcase?
AYS: Ja sondern/ sondern das baby hat er   Yes but/ but the baby has he taken.
genommen.
N: Ach mhm.   Ah uh-huh.
AYS: Und später hat E iie mutter gesehen der   And later has er < her/your> mother seen
hat iie baby und der/ die frau hat geschreit.   he has < her/your> baby and the/ the
Ich weiss es nicht. Dann der mann hat   woman has screamed. I do not know. Then
gehört. Dann später sie haben umgetauscht.   the man has heard. Then later they have
(session 2.3)   exchanged.

If we take into consideration the use of *jouw* ('your') in the Dutch varieties of the Moroccan informants it is possible that a similar use can be observed in the pertinent OP constructions used by Ayse in German.

8.5 CONCLUSIONS

We now return to the central research questions that were formulated in Section 8.2. The conclusions focus on general patterns and abstract over individual, informant-specific preferences.

I   *With which linguistic devices is the possessive relationship encoded in L2-Dutch and L2-German learner varieties.*

An overview of the number of possessive constructions used by each group of learners is given in Table 8.9.

Table 8.9: Overview of possessive constructions

| L2 | Dutch | | German | | |
L1	Moroccan	Turkish	Turkish	Italian	Total
PO order:					
Nominal PO constructions	26	1	4	12	43
Pronominal PO constructions	3	4	-	-	7
OP order:					
Nominal OP constructions	-	1	9	3	13
Pronominal OP constructions	122	48	143	128	441
Total	151	54	156	143	504

Nominal PO constructions are most commonly represented by "N-Prep-N", with the preposition *van* ('of') in Dutch, e.g. *die moeder van die baby* ('that mother of that baby') and the preposition *von* ('of') in German, e.g. *die mutter von das kind* ('the mother of that child'). These constructions can be observed in particular in the Dutch varieties of the Moroccan learners.

Pronominal PO constructions cannot be found in the German learner varieties. In the Dutch learner varieties these constructions are rare and can only be observed with one Turkish and one Moroccan learner, e.g. *die tas van hem* ('that bag of him').

Nominal OP constructions are most commonly represented by juxtaposition of nominal devices. In the Dutch varieties only one instance of this construction can be found, i.e. *vrouw vader moeder* ('woman father mother'). In the German varieties a number of instances of these constructions can be observed in which some Turkish learners occasionally use the s-genitive, e.g. *kinds mutter* ('child's mother').

All four groups of learners have a strong preference for pronominal OP constructions, represented by "Pro-N". In the Dutch learner varieties object pronouns are used instead of possessive pronouns, e.g. *hem vrouw* ('him woman') with the Turkish informants and *van hem vrouw* ('of him woman') with the Moroccan informants. For 3rd role reference also subject pronouns are used instead of possessive pronouns, e.g. *hij kinder* ('he children'). In addition, it can be concluded that the observed gender generalizations strongly suggest that in both Dutch and German learner varieties (1) a masculine pronoun is more likely to be generalized for gender if P is a woman, and (2) a feminine pronoun is more likely to be generalized for gender if P is a man.

Turkish learners of Dutch use the OP construction "Prep-Pro-N" for 1st/3rd role reference and Moroccan learners of Dutch generalize the 2nd role pronoun *jouw* ('your') for 3rd role reference. These findings for the Dutch learner varieties confirm the conclusions drawn in Chapters 5 and 6 on pronominal reference. It is remarkable, however, that the type of generalized use of pronominal OP constructions found in the Dutch learner varieties cannot be found in the German learner varieties. In the latter varieties a generalized use of the form *iie* can be observed. In this form a number of target language functions are merged: (1) 2nd role formal reference (cf. *Ihr* 'your'), (2) 3rd role feminine reference (cf. *ihr* 'her'), and (3) 3rd role masculine reference (cf. *ihm* 'him').

II   Which developmental patterns can be observed in subsequent stages of language acquisition?

Over time a number of developmental changes can be observed for the Dutch learner varieties. These changes are clearest in the generalized use of subject and object pronouns in possessive constructions. Over time this generalized use decreases.

On the basis of the source language systems of the informants, a number of predictions were formulated about their preferences for L2 constructions with a specific order of O and P.

P1   Moroccan L2 learners of Dutch initially prefer possessive PO constructions

This prediction was confirmed. With the Moroccan learners of Dutch an extensive use of nominal PO constructions, i.e. "N-*van*-N" constructions, can be observed in sessions 1.6 and 2.6. This type of nominal PO constructions disappears in session 3.6.

P2   Turkish L2 learners of Dutch initially prefer possessive OP constructions

With the Turkish L2 learners of Dutch there is indeed a strong preference for pronominal OP constructions, i.e. "*van*-Pro-N" constructions. However, in contrast to what was predicted, this preference emerges only in later stages of the acquisition process. In early acquisition stages, Turkish L2 learners of Dutch use the standard-like pronominal OP construction "Pro-N" for 1st/3rd role reference, e.g. *mijn tas* ('my bag') and *zijn vrouw* ('his woman'), while in later stages they use the non-standardlike construction "*van*-Pro-N", e.g. *van mijn tas* ('of my bag') and *van hem familie* ('of him family').

P3   Turkish L2 learners of German initially prefer possessive OP constructions

On the basis of the preference of the Turkish L2 learners in the Dutch varieties, one would expect similar preferences of Turkish L2 learners in German varieties. These are not found, however, so that prediction 3 is disconfirmed.

P4   Italian L2 learners of German have no preference for possessive constructions with a specific order of O and P

The Italian L2 learners do not seem to have a preference for possessive constructions with a specific order of O and P. Although with two Italian informants the construction "Det-N-Det-N" can be found in the early stages, e.g. *die koffer die mann* ('that suitcase that man') which seems to be directly related to an Italian construction with a "preposizione articolata", e.g. *il libro dell'uomo* ('the book of-the man').

III   How can learner preferences be explained?

The focus of this chapter was to establish to what extent learner preferences in the encoding of the possessive relationship can be explained through order preference for O and P in possessive constructions in the pertinent source systems. The intensity of the relationship between O and P (in particular +/- kinship) was considered to be a potential determinant of the way of linguistic encoding. In two of the source languages, Moroccan Arabic and Italian, intensity had an effect on the type of possessive construction. However, in the L2-Dutch and L2-German varieties observed, the intensity of the possessive relationship between O and P appears to have no effect on the manner of expression. A differentiated picture emerges in that traces of L1 are the result of the interplay between (1) linguistic properties of both the L1 system and the L2 system, and (2) the stage of the acquisition process. The Dutch and German learner varieties will be discussed successively.

The Dutch learner varieties

In spoken Dutch the "N-*van*-N" construction is rather similar to the "N-*dyal*-N" construction in Moroccan Arabic. It is therefore not surprising that the "N-*van*-N" construction can be observed early and frequently in the learner varieties of the Moroccan informants. In contrast, for the Turkish informants, for whom there is not such a strong correspondence between an L1 construction and an L2 construction, L1 order preferences pop up in later stages of the acquisition process with the "*van*-Pro-N" construction.

The same type of L1-related order preferences was found in investigations by Broeder & Extra (1988,1991) on the acquisition of word formation devices. We observed a mirror-image division between the Turkish and Moroccan learners of Dutch according to different principles in their respective source languages.

The Turkish core informants made more use of both standardlike and innovative "left-branching" (head-final) devices, e.g. *sigarettenwinkel* ('cigar shop'), *winkelbaas* ('shop owner'), *broodbaas* ('breadboss') instead of standardlike *bakker* ('baker'), and *moslimkerk* ('moslim church') instead of standardlike *moskee* ('mosque'). For kinship reference, the Turkish informants used possessive OP constructions such as *vader zus* ('father sister' for "aunt"), *vader broer zoon* ('father brother son' for "cousin") and *zuster dochter* ('sister daughter' for "niece").

Mirror-wise, the Moroccan core informants made more use of innovative "right-branching" (head-initial) devices than the Turkish learners, e.g. *winkel van sigaret* ('shop of cigars'), *baas van winkel* ('boss of shop'), *boek van baby* ('book of baby'), and *fabriek van boten* ('factory of ships'), instead of *sigarettenwinkel* ('cigar shop'), *winkelbaas*, ('shop owner'), *baby-boek*, (book of baby'), and *scheepswerf* ('ship yard'), respectively. For kinship reference in Dutch, these informants preferred PO constructions such as *broer van vader* ('brother of father'), *vrouw mijn oom* ('wife my uncle'), and *dochter van tante* ('daughter of aunt').

The German learner varieties

In the German learner varieties only minor L1-related traces can be observed in the word-for-word translation of the L1 construction "Det-N-Det-N" with two Italian informants in early stages of acquisition. An intriguing point is, of course, why the "*von*-Pro-N" construction can hardly be observed in the German varieties of Turkish L2 learners. A possible explanation might be that they were already advanced learners compared with the Turkish learners of Dutch. Note, however that in the Dutch learner varieties the construction "*van*-Pro-N" appeared in later stages of acquisition. This could clearly be derived from the pronoun profiles of Ergün and Mahmut presented in Chapters 5 and 6. The explanation of the absence of the construction "*von*-Pro-N" construction in the German learner varieties of the Turkish learners might be that the German possessive pronouns *sein* ('his') and *mein* ('my') are relatively transparent in comparison to the Dutch equivalents *zijn* ('his') and *mijn* ('my').

In Dutch the form *zijn* is a possessive pronoun ('his') as well as a verb ('to be'). In addition, within the 3rd role pronoun paradigm *zijn* ('his'), is phonetically rather close to the homonym *zij* ('she/they'). The learner might assume, incorrectly, that these forms are semantically related in the same way as the forms *mij* ('me') and *mijn* ('my') within the 1st role pronoun paradigm.

In German the form *sein* is also a homonym ('his' and 'to be'). However within the German pronoun paradigms the forms *sein* ('his') and *mein* ('my) are more transparent compared to Dutch, i.e. *sein* ('his') vs. *sie* ('she/they'), and *mein* ('my') vs. *mir* ('me'), *mich* ('me').

In the German learner varieties observed in this chapter the pronoun *sein* ('his') is indeed used frequently (see Table 8.8). In addition, as was concluded in Chapter 6, in the Dutch learner varieties *zijn* ('his') indeed turns out to be problematic for the L2 learners of Dutch. In specific intermediate stages the Turkish as well as the Moroccan Arabic informants strongly favour the object pronoun *hem* ('him') in possessive constructions. In spoken Dutch the object form *hem* ('him') is frequently used in combination with the preposition *van* ('of'). This causes problems for the Turkish informants, because they are not used to prepositions. These forms do not exist in Turkish. In contrast, the Moroccan informants are supported in the acquisition of the preposition *van* ('of') by the strong correspondence with the Moroccan Arabic form *dyal* ('of'). The result is that Moroccan L2 learners of Dutch use *van* ('of') in standardlike PO constructions, e.g. *boek van hem* ('book of him') and *boek van mij* ('book of me'), and that Turkish L2 learners of Dutch use *van* ('of') in non-standard-like OP constructions, e.g. *van hem boek* ('of him book') and *van mij boek* ('of me book').

The analysis by Broeder et al. (1988:84) supports the assumption that preposi-tions are difficult for L2 learners with a Turkish source system. In their quantitative analysis of the distribution of word classes (such as nouns, verbs, prepositions) in all the L2 learner varieties observed in the ESF project (see Chapter 1), no clear target/source language-related effect was found. However, Turkish learners of Dutch and German, and Finnish learners of Swedish used fewer prepositions than the other learners of these target languages.

CHAPTER 9

CONCLUSIONS AND OUTLOOK

During the early stages of language acquisition, learner varieties necessarily consist of a restricted set of linguistic devices which learners have to use as efficiently as possible in daily interactions with native speakers of the target language. The questions relevant to this study are: how do adult language learners start out encoding person reference, how does their repertoire develop, and why do they make the choices they make?

Two Turkish adults (Mahmut and Ergün) and two Moroccan adults (Mohamed and Fatima) were followed over time, from the first stages of their untutored L2 acquisition of Dutch over a period of almost two-and-a-half years at intervals of approximately one month. Cross-learner and cross-linguistic comparisons were made through analyses of L2-Dutch by two Turkish adults (Abdullah and Osman) and two Moroccan adults (Hassan and Husseyn). In addition, some analyses were presented of L2-German by four Turkish and four Italian adult immigrants.

The unifying thread in this study is a combination of a description of (1) the form-function relationships of encoding devices for talking about people, and (2) how the learner preferences can be explained in subsequent stages of the L2 language acquisition process. A global distinction was made between properties of the source system, properties of the target system, and the interaction of these two systems.

The area of investigation is the acquisition of linguistic devices for reference to person at the levels of word and discourse. At the word level the study focussed on pronominal reference, i.e. the use of subject, object, and possessive pronouns (Chapters 4-6) and the encoding of the possessive relationship (Chapter 8), while at the discourse level it focussed on the establishment, shift and maintenance of person reference (Chapter 7).

In this chapter the findings of the present study are put into a broader perspective. The preferences of our adult learners will be discussed in terms of specific learner type characteristics and source/target system characteristics of language development.

9.1   PRONOMINAL REFERENCE

In many languages the pronoun system constitutes a delimited and fixed set of referential devices. Being a closed class, it is in keeping with the idea of a paradigm representing a set of related linguistic encoding devices. Table 9.1 shows a paradigm
model for 1st, 2nd, and 3rd role pronominal reference in Dutch.

Table 9.1: Paradigm model for 1st, 2nd, and 3rd role pronominal reference

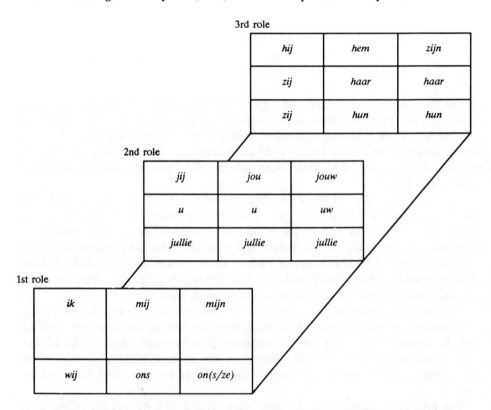

An overwhelming dominance of full forms was observed for the three paradigms in
the L2-Dutch varieties of Turkish and Moroccan adults. Although reduced forms
occur frequently in native spoken Dutch and in the input the informants were confronted with, these forms rarely occurred in the observed L2-Dutch varieties. Within
the 2nd role paradigm the infrequent use of intended V-forms, viz., the reduced
form *je* ('you') and the full form *u* ('you'), was worth noting.

Occasionally, a conflation between the 1st role, 2nd role, and 3rd role paradigms
was observed. It always concerned instances in which a 2nd role pronoun is used for
1st/3rd role reference. This use emerged in particular with the Moroccans.

On the number dimension of the three paradigms, there was evidence for an overall-dominance of singular forms over plural forms.

On the case dimension an overall-dominance of subject forms over object and possessive forms was observed. Subject forms were also generalized in non-subject function, while the reverse, i.e. generalized use of object/possessive pronouns in subject function, was not found. In addition, it appeared that the object forms *mij* ('me') and *hem* ('him') were regularly generalized in possessive constructions with the preposition *van* ('of'), e.g. *van hem boek* ('of him book') and *van mij boek* ('of me book').

On the gender dimension within the 3rd role paradigm, an overall-dominance of masculine forms over feminine forms emerged. Gender generalizations went in both directions, i.e. masculine forms were used for feminine reference, and feminine forms were used for masculine reference.

The following general acquisition principles were observed within the paradigms for the full pronouns:

Role: 1st role forms are acquired before 2nd role forms.
Number: Singular forms are acquired before plural forms.
Case: Subject forms are acquired before object/possessive forms.
Gender: Masculine forms are acquired before feminine forms.

These general principles were specified further through the acquisition order of pronominal forms/functions within the three paradigms. The acquisition order of the full forms was derived from the first moment of standardlike and non-formulaic use. The observed orders are summarized in Table 9.2.

Table 9.2: Order of acquisition of pronouns

1st ROLE:	ik	-->	mijn	-->	mij	-->	wij	-->	on(s/ze)
2nd ROLE:	jij	-->	jullie	-->	jou(w)				
		\-->	jou(w)	-->	jullie				
3rd ROLE:	hij	-->	zij	-->	hun				

Within the 1st role paradigm the access route taken by the informants was the case dimension. They first filled in the singular level in the order: subject, possessive, object. Next, the plural level was filled in. Interestingly, differences between the Turkish and Moroccan informants emerged when they started working on the homonym *ons* ('us/our') of the 1st role paradigm. Here, the Turkish informants followed the same order as for the singular level, i.e. subject, possessive, object, while the Moroccan informants followed the order of subject, object, possessive.

Within the 2nd role paradigm a less coherent picture emerged. All informants used the subject form *jij* ('you') relatively early. With respect to the next form that was acquired, a difference emerged between the informants: for some Turkish/ Moroccan informants the order *jullie-jou(w)* ('you(r)') was observed, whereas for others the reverse order appeared. In fact, the order of acquisition revealed that within the 2nd role paradigm both access routes, case and number, were taken by the informants. The differences between the informants did not point to source language-related determinants.

Within the 3rd role paradigm it was difficult to specify a precise order of acquisition. This could only be done if the non-subject forms *hem* ('him'), *haar* ('her'), and *zijn* ('his') were left out.

Looking at the process from a communicative point of view, the interplay between dimensions and levels is exactly what one would expect. For 1st role reference (i.e. reference to the speaker) and 2nd role reference (i.e. reference to the addressee), the person spoken about can be derived from the communicative act itself. It is important to be able to know and to express whether someone does, undergoes, or possesses something. This accounts for the early differentiation of the entries on the case dimension. When the acquisition task in this dimension has been completed, attention can be paid to the differentiation of the number dimension. In contrast, for 3rd role reference it is important first of all that the person in question is identified. As a result, a small differentiation of the gender and number dimensions precedes the full differentiation of the case dimension. When the identification of a person in 3rd role can be adequately expressed, attention is paid to whether the person in 3rd role does, undergoes, or possesses something. This implies a differentiation of the case dimension.

The source system

In order to explore the effect of properties of the source system, the model of paradigm formation was developed further. It was assumed that there would be a Turkish-based paradigm and a Moroccan Arabic-based paradigm for the Dutch pronoun system. However, in the acquisition order of the pronominal forms/functions no clear traces of paradigm formation on the basis of the source system were found. It turned out that the developmental set of personal and possessive pronouns constituted a fairly homogeneous subset in the learner variety which were not easily penetrated by properties of the source system.

Nevertheless, there was some evidence which suggested that the extensiveness of encoding for a specific dimension in the source system was present in the background. There were few of these traces, but they were very striking. Of particular interest was Fatima's use of the Moroccan Arabic feminine gender suffix -*a*. Fatima used the word *oma*, which literally means "grandma" in Dutch, but her expressive device actually consisted of the bilingual combination *oom-*a**, i.e. "wife of uncle" (meaning "aunt"). This phenomenon emerged as one of the rare examples of direct source language influence: i.e. the standard Dutch kinship term *oom* (male reference) was combined with Moroccan Arabic -*a* (female suffix). Such use of *om*a** obviously will lead to misunderstandings, as can be observed in sequence (1) where Fatima showed family photos to her native interlocutor.

(1) FAT: Uh haar zus van mijn moeder.   Er her sister of my mother.
     N: Zus van je moeder?   Sister of your mother?
     FAT: Ja.   Yes.
     N: Met allemaal kindertjes   With all little children
     FAT: van deze.   of these.
     N: Ja.   Yes.
     FAT: Amal.   Amal. < =proper name of aunt>
     N: Ja.   Yes.
     FAT: Van haar dochter/ uh zoon   Of her daughter/ er son
           deze van dochter deze uh.   these of daughter these er.
     N: Ja.   Yes.
     FAT: Mijn neef.   My cousin.
     N: Neef ja.   Cousin yes.
     FAT: Ja oom-*a* kind van oom-*a*.   Yes uncle-*a* child of uncle-*a*.
     N: Kind van?   Child of?
     FAT: *Mon oncle*   *My uncle*
     N: Ja van jouw oom ja + ja   Yes of your uncle yes + yes
           leuk oom-*a* als vrouwelijk   funny uncle-*a* as the feminine form
           van oom ja + 't kind van je/   of uncle yes + the child of your/
           + jouw neef ja jouw neefje.   + your cousin yes your little cousin.
     (session 1.5)

Fatima's use of this feminine suffix -*a* is discussed in more detail in Broeder & Extra's (1991) study on the acquisition of kinship reference in the L2 learner varieties of the Dutch core informants. A similar example of Fatima's "code-mixing" was the use of *doctor-*a** for reference to a female doctor in Dutch.

There were two major differences in pronoun reference between the Turkish and Moroccan informants that suggested we may be dealing with properties of the source system. First, there was the use of the 2nd role pronoun *jouw* ('your'). The Moroccans in particular also used this form for 1st/3rd role reference. It was difficult to find a single conclusive explanation for this phenomenon. It is probably a combination of several properties of the source system. The Moroccans may be inclined to take the form which refers to the possessor and that which refers to the possessed entity as one unit. In the initial stages *jouw* ('your') is part of an unanalysed whole in some types of possessive relationships, in particular where kinship is involved, e.g. *jouw moeder* ('your mother') and *jouw man* ('your husband/man'). In the course of the interaction it is usually clear who the possessor is. Besides, the interactional context itself promotes the use of 2nd role pronoun reversal by providing the opportunity for reprisive behaviour (cf. Broeder & Vasseur 1988). This would also explain why pronoun reversal of 1st role forms was not observed.

A second difference observed between the two groups concerned constructions in which the preposition *van* ('of') was used. The Turkish informants had a preference for the "*van*-Pro-N" construction, the Moroccans preferring the "N-*van*-Pro" construction. This clearly emerged in the 3rd role paradigm (where cross-learner evidence was provided by the shadow informants). With Ergün (Turkish) and Mohamed (Moroccan) this difference also occurred in the 1st role paradigm. This "difference in directionality" was subjected to a closer analysis in the investigations on referential movement and the encoding of the possessive relationship.

The target system

There was a positive relationship between the frequency of sets of pronouns in the input and the order in which learners produced them in the output. The relative frequency of subject, masculine, and singular forms corresponded to the early acquisition of these forms in comparison with object/possessive, feminine, and plural forms, respectively. However, frequency did not affect the order of acquisition of reduced vs. full forms. Although reduced forms occurred frequently in native spoken Dutch and in the input the informants were confronted with, these forms were rarely observed in the Dutch learner varieties. The different use of reduced and full pronouns in the Dutch learner varieties revealed that what appears frequently in the target language does not necessarily appear early in language acquisition processes if competitive principles play a role. Here, a difference between adults and children acquiring Dutch as the target language can emerge: compared to adults, children appear to be more sensitive to reduced forms. The degree of perceptual saliency, i.e. the degree to which segments attract attention in the speech stream, might be a crucial factor. Perceptual saliency of a form depends on (1) its position in the utterance and (2) prosodic features. The distribution of reduced pronouns in the utterance differs from the basic, canonical distribution of nominal devices and full pronouns. In particular with respect to these properties adult L2 learners might have some L1-based preferences which do not take into account such systematic differences. In contrast, children at a very early acquisition stage take advantage of the information provided by prosodic features in the speech stream.

9.2   REFERENTIAL MOVEMENT

In the second part of this study the focus was on the structuring of information in narrative discourse: i.e. establishment, shift, and maintenance of reference.

The findings suggested that processes of language acquisition in adults differed from those in children. In all stages of adult language acquisition the global structuring of information was taken into account for the linguistic representation of reference to person. Also, there was no intermediate phase (cf. Karmiloff-Smith 1985, Strömqvist & Day 1990) in which attention to global information structuring resulted in a temporarily limited local marking of this structuring. Once a language learner (as a child) has acknowledged the need to take into account the local and global marking of information, this knowledge is also used in the task of acquiring a new linguistic system. The adult language learner is aware of the fact that information in narrative discourse has a sequential and hierarchical structure. This awareness is exploited from the early stages onwards.

In our analysis only minor developmental patterns over time could be found: from the beginning advantage was taken of the opportunity to refer to the protagonist (the main character) with implicit devices. Differences in subsequent stages of acquisition concerned the set of encoding devices. This set differed from standardlike use: e.g. definiteness was not marked through (in)definite determiners; instead, the demonstrative pronoun *die* ('that') was often used.

The source system

With respect to the encoding of referential movement, there were some traces of L1-related conventions. The findings were related to spatial reference and the use of right/left-dislocated NPs.

With the Turkish L2 learners a number of instances of person reference could be noted with a typically Turkish supportive use of spatial expressive devices such as *hier* ('here') and *daar* ('there'). A similar observation was made by Verhoeven (1988) in his study on the acquisition of L2 discourse cohesion by Turkish children.

Moreover, the Turkish adults used the deictic pronoun *die* ('that') together with right-dislocated NPs, e.g. *die + een meisje* ('that + one girl') and *die + brilmeneer* ('that + spectacle man'). On the other hand, one Moroccan informant (Mohamed), used left-dislocated NPs, e.g. *die meisje zij* ('that girl she') and *die politie hij* ('that police he'). The latter construction has also been observed by De Ruiter (1989:188) in L2-Dutch varieties of young Moroccans. The observed use of right/left-dislocated NPs corresponded with the findings in the area of pronoun reference, i.e. the "*van*-Pro-N" construction of the Turkish informants and the "N-*van*-Pro" construction of the Moroccan informants. It should be noted that these types of constructions could not be related to the specific information status (i.e. establishment of reference, etc.) in narrative discourse.

The target system

In the encoding of referential movement the effect of the target system was reflected in the phonetic properties of words. In early stages the informants used emphatic forms such as *die* ('that') and *een* ('one'), while the corresponding reduced forms *de* ('the') and *'n* ('a') emerged only in later stages of acquisition.

9.3   POSSESSIVE REFERENCE

The third part of this study dealt with the encoding of the possessive relationship. The main issue was to what extent learner preferences can be explained through order preference of (O)-wner and (P)-ossession in possessive constructions of the source systems. The hypothesis was that the intensity of the relationship between O and P (in particular +/- kinship) would be a potential determinant of the way in which the relationship was encoded linguistically.

First, a comparison of linguistic and conceptual properties of the source and target systems was made, which revealed remarkable differences and similarities in the order of O and P in possessive constructions. Moreover, it turned out that in particular languages the type of possessive relationships (intensity) also affected the selection of the encoding devices. Next, a cross-linguistic excursion was made through highly comparable L2-German varieties of Turkish and Italian adults.

The target system

All four groups of learners showed a strong preference for pronominal OP constructions, represented by "Pro-N". In the L2-Dutch varieties object pronouns were used instead of possessive pronouns, e.g. *hem vrouw* ('him wife') instead of *zijn vrouw* ('his wife'). For 3rd role reference also subject pronouns were used instead of possessive pronouns, e.g. *hij kinder* ('he children'). In addition, it was found that Turkish learners of Dutch used the OP construction "Prep-Pro-N" for 1st role and for 3rd role reference (see below), and that Moroccan learners of Dutch generalized the 2nd role pronoun *jouw* ('your') for 3rd role reference. Gender generalizations strongly suggested that in both L2-Dutch and L2-German (1) a masculine pronoun is more likely to be generalized for gender if P is a woman, and (2) a feminine pronoun is more likely to be generalized for gender if P is a man. In the L2-German varieties a generalized use of the form *iie* was observed. In this form a number of target language functions were merged: (1) 2nd role formal reference (cf. *Ihr* 'your'), (2) 3rd role feminine reference (cf. *ihr* 'her'), and (3) 3rd role masculine reference (cf. *ihm* 'him'). An intriguing question was why "*von*-Pro-N" constructions were never observed in the German varieties of Turkish L2 learners. In the Dutch varieties of Turkish L2 learners the construction "*van*-Pro-N" appeared in later stages of acquisition. The explanation of the absence of the "*von*-Pro-N" construction in the L2-German of the Turkish learners might be that the German possessive pronouns *sein* ('his') and *mein* ('my') are relatively easy to acquire in comparison to the Dutch equivalents *zijn* ('his') and *mijn* ('my'). In Dutch the form *zijn* is a possessive pronoun ('his') as well as a verb ('to be'). In addition, within the 3rd role pronoun paradigm, *zijn* ('his') is phonetically rather close to the homonym *zij* ('she/they'). The learner might assume, incorrectly, that these forms are semantically related in the same way as the forms *mij* ('me') and *mijn* ('my') within the 1st role pronoun paradigm (compare *mijn boek* 'my book' vs. *boek van mij* 'book of me'). In German the form *sein* is also a homonym ('his' and 'to be'). However, within the German pronoun paradigms the forms *sein* ('his') and *mein* ('my) are more transparent compared to Dutch, i.e. *sein* ('his') vs. *sie* ('she/they'), and *mein* ('my') vs. *mir* ('me'), *mich* ('me'). The additional claim was made that for Turkish L2 learners of Dutch the alternative construction with the preposition *van* ('of') is not attractive either, because prepositions do not exist in Turkish (cf. Broeder et al. 1988:84). In contrast, in the acquisition of the preposition *van* ('of'), the Moroccan informants are supported by the strong correspondence with the Moroccan Arabic form *dyal* ('of').

Nominal PO constructions were mostly represented by "N-Prep-N", with the preposition *van* ('of') in L2-Dutch, e.g. *die moeder van die baby* ('that mother of that baby'), and the preposition *von* ('of') in L2-German, e.g. *die mutter von das kind* ('the mother of that child').

Pronominal PO constructions were rare and could only be observed in the L2-Dutch varieties, e.g. *die tas van hem* ('that bag of him').

Finally, nominal OP constructions were mostly represented by juxtaposition of nominal devices. In the L2-Dutch varieties only one instance could be found, i.e. *vrouw vader moeder* ('woman father mother'). In the L2-German varieties a number of instances of this construction could be observed in which some Turkish learners occasionally used the s-genitive, e.g. *kinds mutter* ('child's mother').

The source system
 Moroccan L2 learners of Dutch initially showed a preference for possessive PO constructions: whereas in cycles 1 and 2 an extensive use of "N-*van*-N" constructions could be observed, this type of nominal PO construction disappeared in cycle 3. The "N-*van*-N" construction is similar to the "N-*dyal*-N" construction in Moroccan Arabic.
 Turkish L2 learners of Dutch showed a strong preference for "*van*-Pro-N" constructions. However, this preference emerged in later stages of the acquisition process. In early stages, they used the standardlike pronominal OP construction "Pro-N" for 1st/3rd role reference, e.g. *mijn tas* ('my bag') and *zijn vrouw* ('his woman'), whereas in later stages they used the non-standardlike pronominal OP construction "*van*-Pro-N", e.g. *van mijn tas* ('of my bag') and *van hem familie* ('of him family'). Similar preferences of Turkish L2 learners in German varieties could not be found.
 Italian L2 learners of German showed no preference for possessive constructions with a specific order of O and P. However, the "Det-N-Det-N" construction could be found with two Italian informants in early stages, e.g. *die koffer die mann* ('the suitcase the man'), and appeared to be directly related to an Italian construction with a "preposizione articolata", e.g. *il libro dell'uomo* ('the book of-the man').
 Although in some source languages (Moroccan Arabic and Italian) the intensity of the relationship has an effect on the type of possessive construction used, the intensity of the possessive relationship between O and P in the observed L2-Dutch and L2-German varieties had no effect on the way they were encoded. The empirical data on the encoding of possession did indeed point to preferences for specific possessive constructions which could be traced back to the source language systems. However, the strength of L1 influence depended on properties of the target system.

Directionality
 A remarkable area where the source and target systems interacted was directionality. In the present study the following traces of this principle surfaced repeatedly in the L2 Dutch varieties: (1) right-dislocated NPs and "*van*-Prep-N" constructions in L2-Dutch varieties of the Turkish learners, and (2) left-dislocated NPs and "N-Prep-N" constructions in L2-Dutch varieties of the Moroccan learners. The same type of source system effect was found in earlier investigations by Broeder et al. (1988), and Broeder & Extra (1988,1991) on the acquisition of word formation devices.
 Directionality (or right/left branching, modifier-head order) is a central notion in current theories on language and language acquisition. There is general consensus about the relevance of such a principle in explaining the systematic variation between languages. However, a moot point is the way in which directionality is reflected in languages. Language typological studies have recently discussed the correspondence widely believed to exist between the order of adjective-noun and the order of object-verb (see Dryer 1988, Rijkhoff 1990). In generative studies directionality is explored through the head parameter (e.g. Flynn 1989, Eubank 1989, White 1989).

The order preferences in the learner varieties observed in the present study call for extensive cross-linguistic excursions. As a final analysis in the present study one cross-linguistic excursion will be made through all the source/target language pairs dealt with in the ESF project (see Chapter 1). However, rather than adopting descriptive categories which follow from the "state-of-the-art" of a specific theoretical framework, the learner varieties of the target languages will speak for themselves.

The language activity selected for all the five target languages in the ESF project is the retelling of parts from Charlie Chaplin's film *Modern Times*. A detailed description of this language activity can be found in Klein & Perdue (1991:7-9). There are four informants per source language, and 2-3 film scenes per informant. The instances considered were the informants' referring to one specific actor in the film, the baker. Only those instances were selected which consisted of more than one lexeme, i.e. compounds and descriptions.

Table 9.3: References to the baker in Charlie Chaplin's Modern Times

L2	L1	head-final	head-initial	English equivalent
Swedish	Finnish	affärs-männen	-	sales-men
"	Spanish	-	-	-
French	Spanish	-	monsieur *del camion*	mister *of-the lorry*
		-	*el* chauffeur de la camionnette	*the* driver of the lorry
		-	le monsieur de la boulangerie	the mister of the bakery
"	Arabic	-	un monsieur la boulanger	a mister the baker
Dutch	Arabic	bakker-man	-	baker-man
		-	meneer van die winkel	mister of that shop
		-	die van brood	that of bread
		-	de baas van winkel	the boss of shop
"	Turkish	brood-baas	-	bread-boss
		die brood-man	-	that bread-man
German	Turkish	geschäfts-mann	-	shop-man
"	Italian	-	die chef der geschäft	the boss the shop
		-	die chef vom bäckerei	the boss of-the bakery
		-	der mann der brot	the man the bread
English	Italian	-	owner of the shop	owner of the shop
		-	the manager the shop	the manager of the shop
		-	the boss the shop	the boss the shop
"	Punjabi	shop-man	-	shop-man
		cake-man	-	cake-man
		shops-gaffer	-	shops-gaffer
		shop-keeper	-	shop-keeper

The preferences of the L2 learners given in Table 9.3 show how order conventions of the source systems operate in approaching the target systems. Reference to the baker in the L2-Swedish varieties of the Spanish learners was done through the single lexeme *män* ('men'). In this respect relevant observations were made by Broeder et al. (1988:114-151). They found that only the Spanish learners made use of head-initial compounds in Swedish, e.g. *en man-polise* ('a man-police') instead of *en polis-man* ('a policeman') and *säng-barn* ('bed-child') instead of *barnsäng* ('child's bed').

So, Spanish L2 learners of Swedish appear to have the same order preferences as Spanish L2 learners of French.

Similar order preferences can be derived from the expressive devices used by the learners for referring to the police car in the *Modern Times* clips (see Table 9.4).

Table 9.4: References to the police car in Charlie Chaplin's Modern Times

L2	L1	head-final	head-initial	English equivalent
Swedish	Finnish	polis bilen	-	police car$_{def}$
"	Spanish	-	bil polis	car police
		-	bilen med fràn polisen	car$_{def}$ with from police$_{def}$
French	Spanish	-	la voiture de la police	the car of the police
		-	*el* camion de la police	*the* car of the police
"	Arabic	-	le voiture di la police	the car of the police
Dutch	Arabic	-	auto (van) *police*	car (of) *police*
		-	de auto van politie	the car of police
		politie auto	-	police car
"	Turkish	politie auto	-	police car
German	Turkish	polizist wagen	-	police car
		polizei wagen	-	police car
"	Italian	-	*camion* di polizei	*car* of-the police
		-	auto (di) polizei	car (of-the) police
English	Italian	-	van for burglars	van for burglars
		-	the van of the police	the van of the police
		police car	-	police car
"	Punjabi	police van	-	police van
		police man bus	-	police man bus
		police car	-	police car

Sequence (2) illustrates that Fatima (Moroccan) is aware of the problem of acquiring word order principles in Dutch as the target language:

(2)　FAT:　Die politie uh bel van die *police*/　　　That police er bell of that *police*/
　　　　　auto *police* *ma^{c}raftshi linsebbek oeli*.　car *police* *I do not know which one
　　　(session 2.9)　　　　　　　　　　　　　　must go first*.

In the observed L2 learner varieties, directionality preferences result in systematic variation (see also Broeder et al. 1988:114-151). In this particular domain, learner preferences with respect to the acquisition of the target language system can be traced back to the interplay between the target and source language systems. Table 9.5 presents the word order preferences observed in the learner varieties.

Table 9.5: Word order preferences in L2 learner varieties

L2:		Swedish	French		Dutch		German		English	
		∧	∧		∧		∧		∧	
L1:	Finnish		Spanish	Arabic		Turkish		Italian		Punjabi
HEAD	final		initial	initial		final		initial		final

9.4   OUTLOOK

This study presented a longitudinal and cross-linguistic perspective on developing learner varieties in adult untutored language acquisition. The encoding of person reference revealed an intriguing interplay between properties of the source/target systems and the stage of the acquisition process. The variety of the target language used by the learner is dynamic and unique. This was reflected in the systematics of form-function relationships. In subsequent acquisitional stages, different traces of the source language were observed. All in all, similar preferences and developmental patterns emerged. However, for various aspects of person reference, fairly unexpected differences between the informants were seen. These differences showed that the individual learner was involved in a process of dynamic (re-)construction based on a continuous formulation and revision of hypotheses about the structure of the target language. This (re-)construction process was both accumulative and multidimensional. It went from initial to advanced or standardlike learner varieties, and it did so at different levels of the target language system.

The adults in the present study acquired Dutch without systematic formal tuition. This made it very tempting to compare them with children who acquired their mother tongue in a similar way. Unfortunately, not many studies with a longitudinal perspective like that of the present study are available, certainly not for Dutch as a target language.

In this study various attempts were made to link child language acquisition and adult language acquisition. In particular with respect to the areas of pronoun acquisition and referential movement, observations from studies on child language acquisition were taken into account.

The differences and similarities between child language acquisition and adult language acquisition could be explained through the abstract notion of "knowledge base". A knowledge base which a learner has at his disposal covers a diversity of language-dependent and language-independent aspects. The knowledge included in such a base would, for example, be that in the surrounding physical world there are masculine and feminine entities, or to put it differently, that language provides an opportunity to refer differently to men and women. A mature adult has at his disposal a knowledge base with two basic characteristics: it is comprehensive and fine-grained. In children's language acquisition processes the knowledge base is more incomplete. Parts are missing and as they grow older their knowledge base becomes more and more extensive. With each addition the base becomes more sophisticated. In adult language acquisition processes, however, the knowledge base is comprehensive from the beginning. The contours are there, but the structure is rather coarse. Some empirical observations will make the abstract notion of knowledge bases more concrete. These observations call for future research.

Pronoun reversal

The findings in this study suggested that adult language learners, in particular those with a Moroccan Arabic source system, only generalized 2nd role pronouns for

1st/3rd role reference. Adults know the basic principles of communication. Thus they are acquainted with the reference shift involved in the use of 1st role and 2nd role pronouns. In contrast to this, children generalized 1st role and 2nd role pronouns in both directions. Pronoun reversals are explained (partly) through the process of interaction, i.e. reprisive behaviour. Broeder (1987) and Broeder & Vasseur (1988) investigated reprisive behaviour in the learner varieties of the five target languages in the ESF project. We observed differences in ethnic style between adult learners with Moroccan Arabic vs. Turkish as the source systems. One of these differences in ethnic style was that Turkish communication conventions include repeating the interlocutor's utterances more frequently than Moroccan Arabic communication conventions. Further research is required to establish the precise relationship between differences in ethnic style (i.e. degree of reprisive behaviour) and the generalized use of 2nd role pronouns for 3rd role reference.

Perceptual saliency
Adults know that in a language system specific functions are encoded through specific forms. Those forms which are perceptually more salient are picked up fairly early. Children have to discover the specific function and then notice that there are several forms for encoding this function. Their perception has to become fine-grained, i.e. sensitive to subtle differences in meaning. The findings in this study showed that the adult L2 learners of Dutch had a strong preference for full forms. They rarely used reduced forms, which have a much higher frequency in native spoken Dutch. The speculation is that children acquiring Dutch are different in this respect and that they are more sensitive to the different functions related to the full-reduced distinction. One would like to know whether children are more sensitive to the convention in spoken Dutch that reduced forms can refer both to personal animates and to impersonal (in)animates, whereas full forms only refer to personal animates (or personified entities). In this respect it is worth noting that in both Turkish and Moroccan Arabic reference to non-persons is most commonly done through demonstrative pronouns (cf. Broeder 1989b).

Pronoun generalizations
In the L2-Dutch varieties of Turkish and Moroccan adults no clear traces were found of source language related differences in the encoding of gender and case in the Dutch pronoun system. In contrast, mastering the conceptual notion of gender seemed to affect in children the acquisition of the encoding devices. On the gender dimension children were inclined to generalize the pronouns for their own sex. Girls generalized the feminine pronouns relatively more often and earlier, whereas boys preferred the masculine pronouns. On the case dimension in child L1-Dutch, a preference for the object form *mij* ('me') was observed, whereas in adult L2-Dutch, a preference for the subject form *I* ('ik') emerged. Further empirical studies are required to explain the observed pronoun generalizations and to establish the relationships with the encoding of other paradigms in the source/target language systems. The work by Mühlhäusler & Harré (1990) could be a gold mine. In this respect an

extension could be made by studying the acquisition of other types of pronouns, in particular the demonstrative pronouns.

Global information structuring

The findings in this study suggested that in all stages of adult language acquisition the global structuring of information was adhered to. Unlike children, adults were aware of the fact that information in narrative discourse has a sequential and hierarchical structure and from the beginning they availed themselves of the opportunity to refer to the protagonist with implicit devices.

Word classes

Broeder et al. (1988:84) did a quantitative study on the acquisition of different types of word classes (including nouns, verbs, adjectives) for L2 learner varieties of all the target languages in the ESF project. We found that even at the start of the acquisition process adult learners used words from all classes. In this respect the lexical development of adult L2 learners appears to be quite different from the early selective patterns observed in first language acquisition by children (cf. Broeder & Voionmaa 1986). A particularly fruitful area for further research is the acquisition of prepositions and related parts of speech such as spatial adverbs. These forms recurrently provided an illuminating window on language development: (1) the use of *van* ('of') in L2-Dutch, (2) the conflation of space and person reference with the Turkish L2 learners of Dutch (see also Broeder et al. 1985,1986), and (3) the strong L1-effect found for Moroccan vs. Turkish learners of Dutch (see Broeder et al. 1988).

Directionality

A number of observations made for word formation processes in child L1 acquisition suggested that children pay attention to the differences in meaning that underly differences in word order, e.g. *dogsled* vs. *sleddog* (cf. Clark 1983, see also Golinkoff & Markessini 1980). In the present study several traces were found of a structuring mechanism labelled "directionality". A follow-up study can be done by investigating the learner varieties on the acquisition of word order preferences at different linguistic levels.

The assumption is that the child's knowledge initially only enables it to grasp a limited part of the target system, but that the elements that it can grasp are acquired thoroughly. In contrast, the adult L2 learner "knows" what to look for from the start and has some basic idea of what options are available. However, once the adult feels that he can communicate adequately, i.e. that the expression of the knowledge base in L2 is acceptable (to himself), fossilization may occur. Fossilization has never been observed over time in child L1 acquisition.

REFERENCES

Allwood, J. (ed.) (1988), *Feedback in adult language acquisition*, Strasbourg: ESF (Final Report Volume II of the European Science Foundation project "Second language acquisition by adult immigrants").

Andersen, R. (1979), Expanding Schumann's pidginization hypothesis, *Language Learning* 29, 105-119.

Andersen, R. (1983), *Pidginization and creolization as language acquisition*, Cambridge, Mass.: Newbury House.

Andersen, R. (1984), The One to One principle of interlanguage construction, *Language Learning* 34, 77-95.

Andersen, R. (1987), Models, processes, principles, and strategies: second language acquisition in and out of the classroom, (Paper presented at the SLA-FLL conference, April 3, 1987).

Anderson, S. & E. Keenan (1985), Deixis, in: T. Shopen (ed.), *Language typology and syntactic description: grammatical categories and the lexicon*, Cambridge: Cambridge University Press. p. 259-309.

Anderson, A. & S. Strömqvist (1990), *Adult L2 acquisition of gender - A cross-linguistic and cross-learner types perspective*, Göteborg: Dept. of Linguistics, Göteborg University (Gothenburg papers in theoretical linguistics 61).

Appel, R. & J. Lalleman (1989), Het Nederlands van Turkse kinderen, *Gramma* 13, 113-127.

Bamberg, M. (1986), A functional approach to the acquisition of anaphoric relationships, *Linguistics* 24, 227-284.

Bamberg, M. (1987), *The acquisition of narratives. Learning to use language*, Berlin: Mouton.

Baron, J. & A. Kaiser (1975), Semantic components in children's errors with pronouns, *Journal of Psycholinguistic Research* 4, 303-317.

Bastuji, J. (1976), *Les relations spatiales en turc contemporain*, Paris: Klincksieck.

Bates, E. & B. MacWhinney (1981), Second language acquisition from a functional perspective: Pragmatic, semantic, and perceptual strategies, in: H. Winitz (ed.)

Native language and foreign language acquisition, New York: New York Academy of Science, p. 190-214.

Bates, E. & B. MacWhinney (1987), Competition, variation and language learning, in: B. MacWhinney (ed.), *Mechanisms of language learning*, Hillsdale, N.J: Erlbaum, p. 157-193.

Becker, A., M. Carroll & A. Kelly (eds.) (1988), *Reference to space*, Strasbourg: ESF (Final Report Volume IV of the European Science Foundation project "Second language acquisition by adult immigrants").

Bhardwaj, M., R. Dietrich & C. Noyau (eds.) (1988), *Temporality*, Strasbourg: ESF (Final Report Volume V of the European Science Foundation project "Second language acquisition by adult immigrants".

Bley-Vroman, R. (1989), What is the logical problem of foreign language learning? in: S. Gass & J. Schachter (1989), *Linguistic perspectives on second language acquisition*, Cambridge: Cambridge University Press, p. 41-68.

Bloomfield, L. (1935), *Language*, London: Allen & Unwin.

Böhme, K. (1983), *Children's understanding and awareness of German possessive pronouns*, Doctoral dissertation, University of Nijmegen.

Bol, G. & F. Kuiken (1986), Het gebruik van pronomina bij kinderen van een tot vier, *Toegepaste Taalwetenschap in Artikelen* 24, 47-58

Bosch, P. (1983), *Agreement and anaphora: a study of the role of pronouns in syntax and discourse*, London: Academic Press.

Braun, F. (1988), *Terms of address: Problems of patterns and usage in various languages and cultures*, Berlin: Mouton.

Bremer, K., P. Broeder, C. Roberts, M. Simonot & M. Vasseur (1988), *Ways of achieving understanding: communicating to learn in a second language*, Strasbourg: ESF (Final Report Volume I of the European Science Foundation project "Second language acquisition by adult immigrants").

Broeder, P. (1987), *Learning to repeat to interact: learner's repetitions in the language acquisition process of adults*, Tilburg: Dept. of Linguistics, University of Tilburg (Till-paper 114).

Broeder, P. (1989a), Learning to talk about people: towards an FL syllabus for adult learners, *Language, Culture and Curriculum* 2, 31-42.

Broeder, P. (1989b), Praten over mannen en vrouwen, *Interdisciplinair Tijdschrift voor Taal- en Tekstwetenschap* 9, 51-75.

Broeder, P. (1990), Reference to people in adult language acquisition, *I.T.L. Review of Applied Linguistics* 87/88, 23-43.

Broeder, P. (1992), Possession in a new language, *Applied Linguistics* 13,2.

Broeder, P., J. Coenen, G. Extra, R. van Hout & R. Zerrouk (1985), Spatial reference in L2 Dutch of Turkish and Moroccan adult learners: the initial stages, in: G. Extra & T. Vallen (eds), *Ethnic minorities and Dutch as a second language*, Dordrecht: Foris, p. 209-252.

Broeder, P., J. Coenen, G. Extra, R. van Hout & R. Zerrouk (1986), Ontwikkelingen in het Nederlandstalig lexicon bij anderstalige volwassenen: een macro- en micro- perspectief, in: J. Creten, G. Geerts & K. Jaspaert (eds.), *Werk-in-uitvoering*.

Momentopname van de sociolinguïstiek in België en Nederland, Leuven: ACCO, p. 39-57.

Broeder, P. & G. Extra (1988), Woordvormingsprocédé's bij verwijzing naar objecten in de tweede-taalverwervingsprocessen van volwassenen, *Toegepaste Taalwetenschap in Artikelen* 30, 105-117.

Broeder, P. & G. Extra (1991), Acquisition of kinship reference. A study on word formation processes of adult language learners, *International Journal of Applied Linguistics* (to appear).

Broeder, P., G. Extra & R. van Hout (1986), Acquiring the linguistic devices for pronominal reference to persons: a cross-linguistic perspective on complex tasks with small words, in: F. Beukema & A. Hulk (eds.), *Linguistics in the Netherlands 1986*, Dordrecht: Foris, p. 27-40.

Broeder, P., G. Extra & R. van Hout (1989), Processes in the developing lexicon of adult immigrant learners, in: R. Carter & P. Nation (eds.), *Research on vocabulary acquisition: an update*, Amsterdam: Free University Press, p. 86-109 (AILA Review 6).

Broeder, P., G. Extra, R. van Hout, S. Strömqvist & K. Voionmaa (1988), *Processes in the developing lexicon*, Strasbourg: ESF (Final Report Volume III of the European Science Foundation project "Second language acquisition by adult immigrants").

Broeder, P. & C. Roberts (1988), Indications of non-understanding, in: K. Bremer et al., *Ways of achieving understanding: communicating to learn in a second language*, Strasbourg: ESF, p. 52-123.

Broeder, P. & M. Vasseur (1988), The learner's reprise of the TLS' words, in: K. Bremer et al., *Ways of achieving understanding: communicating to learn in a second language*, Strasbourg: ESF, p. 164-202.

Broeder, P. & K. Voionmaa (1986), Establishing word-class distinctions in the vocabulary of adult language learners; a cross-linguistic perspective, in: Ö. Dahl (ed.), *Papers from the Ninth Scandinavian Conference of Linguistics*, Stockholm: Dept. of Linguistics, University of Stockholm, p. 74-85.

Brown, R. & A. Gilman (1960), The pronouns of power and solidarity, in: T. Sebeok (ed.), *Style in language*, New York: Wiley.

Bühler, K. (1934), *Sprachtheorie*, Jena: Fischer (repr. Frankfurt/m: Ullstein).

Butterworth, G. & E. Hatch (1978), A Spanish-speaking adolescent's acquisition of English syntax, in: E. Hatch (ed.), *Second language acquisition. A book of readings*, Rowley, Mass.: Newbury House, p. 231-245.

Carroll, S. & J. Meisel (1990), Universals and second language acquisition, *Studies in Second Language Acquisition* 12, 201-208.

Chafe, W. (1987), Cognitive constraints on information flow, in: R. Tomlin (ed.), *Coherence and grounding in discourse*, Amsterdam: Benjamins, p. 21-52.

Charney, R. (1980), Speech roles and the development of personal pronouns, *Journal of Child Language* 7, 509-528.

Chiat, S. (1981), Context-specificity and generalization in the acquisition of pronominal distinctions, *Journal of Child Language* 8, 75-91.

Chiat, S. (1982), If I were you and you were me: the analysis of pronouns in a pronoun-reversing child, *Journal of Child Language* 9, 359-379.

Chiat, S. (1985), Children's pronouns, in: U. Wiesemann (ed.), *Pronominal systems*, Tübingen: Narr, p. 382-404.

Chiat, S. (1986), Personal pronouns, in: P. Fletcher & M. Garman (eds.), *Language acquisition: studies in first language development*, Cambridge: Cambridge University Press, p. 339-355.

Chomsky, N. (1957), *Syntactic structures*, The Hague: Mouton.

Chomsky, N. (1965), *Aspects of the theory of syntax*, Cambridge, Mass.: MIT Press.

Chomsky, N. (1981), *Lectures on government and binding*, Dordrecht: Foris.

Chomsky, N. (1986a), *Knowledge of language: Its nature, origin, use*, New York: Praeger.

Chomsky, N. (1986b), *Barriers*, Cambridge, Mass.: MIT Press.

Chomsky, N. (1988), *Language and problems of knowledge*, Cambridge, Mass.: MIT Press.

Clahsen, H. & P. Muysken (1986), The accessibility of universal grammar to adult and child learners: A study of the acquisition of German word order, *Second Language Research* 2, 93-119.

Clahsen, H. & P. Muysken (1989), The UG paradox in L2 acquisition, *Second Language Research* 5, 1-29.

Clancy, P. (1980), Referential choice in English and Japanese narrative discourse, in: W. Chafe (ed.), *The pear stories: Cognitive, cultural, and linguistic aspects of narrative production*, Norwood, N.J.: Ablex, p. 127-201.

Clark, E. (1978), From gesture to word: on the natural history of deixis in language acquisition, in: J. Bruner & A. Garton (eds.), *Human growth and development*, Oxford: Clarendonn Press, p. 85-120.

Clark, E. (1983), Convention and contrast in acquiring the lexicon, in: T. Seiler & W. Wannenmacher (eds.), *Concept development of word meaning*, Berlin: Springer Verlag, p. 67-89.

Clark, H. & C. Marshall (1981), Definite reference and mutual knowledge, in: A. Joshi, B. Webber & I. Sag (eds.), *Elements of discourse understanding*, Cambridge: Cambridge University Press, p. 10-63.

Cook, V. (1988), *Chomsky's universal grammar*, Oxford: Blackwell.

Cornish, F. (1986), *Anaphoric relations in English and French: a discourse perspective*, London: Crook Helm.

Daan, J. (1978), U en Je, *Taal en Tongval* 30, 50-75.

Davies, A., C. Cryper & A. Howatt (eds.) (1984), *Interlanguage*, Edinburgh: Edinburgh University Press.

de Jong, E. (1979), *Spreektaal. Woordfrequenties in gesproken Nederlands*. Utrecht: Bohn, Scheltema & Holkema.

Deprez, K. & G. Geerts (1976), Pronominale varianten in West-Vlaanderen, *Forum der Letteren* 17, 215-238.

Deprez, K. & G. Geerts (1977), Lexical and pronominal standardization, *Zeitschrift für Dialektologie and Linguïstik* 22.

de Ruiter, J. (1989), *Young Moroccans in the Netherlands*, Doctoral dissertation, University of Utrecht.

Deutsch, W. & F. Wijnen (1985), The article's noun and the noun's article: explorations into the representation and access of linguistic gender in Dutch, *Linguistics* 23, 793-810.

de Vooys, C. (1916), Iets over woordvorming en woordbetekenis in kindertaal, *De Nieuwe Taalgids* 10, 93-100 and 128-141.

Dryer, M. (1988), Object-verb order and adjective-noun order: dispelling a myth, *Lingua* 74, 185-217.

Dubois, J. (1980), Beyond definiteness: the trace of identity in discourse, in: W. Chafe (ed.), *The pear stories. Cognitive, cultural, and linguistic aspects of narrative production*, Norwood, N.J.: Ablex, p. 203-274.

Dulay, H. & M. Burt (1975), Creative construction in second language learning, in: M. Burt & H. Dulay (eds.), *New directions in second language learning, teaching and bilingual education*, Washington, D.C.: TESOL, p. 21-32.

Edwards, J. & W. Levelt (1987), *The observation situation as enriched input context: effects on learner repertoire and motivation to perform*, Strasbourg: ESF (working paper).

Ellis, R. (1985), *Understanding second language acquisition*, Oxford: Oxford University Press.

Eubank. L. (1989), Parameters and L2 learning: Flynn revisited, *Second Language Research* 5, 43-73.

Extra, G. (1978), *Eerste- en tweede-taalverwerving: de ontwikkeling van morfologische vaardigheden*, Muiderberg: Coutinho.

Feldweg, H. (1991), *The European Science Foundation Second Language Databank*, Nijmegen: Max-Planck-Institut für Psycholinguistik.

Felix, S. (1981), The effect of formal instruction on second language acquisition, *Language Learning* 31, 87-112.

Flynn, S. (1987), *A parameter-setting model of L2 acquisition*, Dordrecht: Reidel.

Flynn, S. (1989), The role of the head-initial/head-final parameter in the acquisition of English relative clauses by adult Spanish and Japanese speakers, in: S. Gass & J. Schachter (eds.), *Linguistic perspectives on second language acquisition*, Cambridge: Cambridge University Press, p. 89-108.

Forchheimer, P. (1953), *The category of person in language*, Berlin: De Gruyter.

Fox, B. (1987), *Discourse structure and anaphora in written and conversational English*, Cambridge: Cambridge University Press.

Gass, S. & C. Madden (eds.) (1985), *Input in second language acquisition*, Rowley, Mass.: Newbury House.

Gass, S. & J. Schachter (eds.) (1989), *Linguistic perspectives on second language acquisition*, Cambridge: Cambridge University Press.

Gass, S. & L. Selinker (eds.) (1983), *Language transfer in language learning*, Rowley, Mass.: Newbury House, p. 1-20.

Geerts, G., W. Haeseryn, J. de Rooij & M. van den Toorn (1984), *Algemene Nederlandse Spraakkunst*. Groningen: Wolters-Noordhoff.

Gernsbacher, M. (1989), Mechanisms that improve referential access, *Cognition* 32, 99-156.

Giacobbe, J. (1987), *Pronominal reference to persons. The use of subject and oblique pronouns in French by two Spanish speaker informants*. Strasbourg: ESF (working paper).

Givón, T. (1983), *Topic continuity in discourse*, Amsterdam: Benjamins.

Givón, T. (1984), Universals of discourse structure and second language acquisition, in: W. Rutherford (ed.), *Language universals and second language acquisition*, Amsterdam: Benjamins, p. 109-136.

Golinkoff, R. & J. Markessini (1980), 'Mommy sock': the child's understanding of possession as expressed in two-noun phrases, *Journal of Child Language* 7, 119-135.

Grebe, P. (1973), *Grammatik der deutschen Gegenwartssprache*, Mannheim: Duden-verlag.

Grimes, J. (ed.) (1978), *Papers in discourse*, Arlington, Texas: SIL.

Hammer, A. (1980), *German grammar and usage*, London: Edward Arnold.

Harrell, R. (1962), *A short reference grammar of Moroccan Arabic*, Washington, D.C.: Georgetown University Press.

Hatch, E. (ed.) (1978), *Second language acquisition: A book of readings*, Rowley, Mass.: Newbury House.

Hatch, E. (1983), *Psycholinguistics. A second language perspective*, Rowley, Mass.: Newbury House.

Hawkins, J. (ed.) (1988), *Explaining language universals*, London: Blackwell.

Head, F. (1978), Respect degrees in pronominal reference, in: Greenberg, J. (ed.), *Universals of human language*, Stanford: Stanford University Press, p. 151-211.

Hickmann, M. (1982), *The development of narrative skills: pragmatic and metapragmatic aspects of discourse cohesion*, Doctoral dissertation, University of Chicago.

Hickmann, M. (ed.) (1987), *Social and functional approaches to language and thought*, New York: Academic Press.

Hickmann, M., J. Liang & H. Hendriks (1989), Diskurskohäsion im Erstspracherwerb: Eine sprachvergleichende Untersuchung, *Zeitschrift für Literaturwissenschaft und Linguistik* 73, 53-74.

Huebner, T. (1983), *A longitudinal analysis of the acquisition of English*, Ann Arbor: Karoma.

Huxley, R. (1970), The development of the correct use of the subject personal pronouns in two children. in: G. Flores d'Arcais & W. Levelt (eds.), *Advances in psycholinguistics*, Amsterdam: North-Holland, p. 141-165.

Ingram, D. (1978), Typology and universals of personal pronouns, in: J. Greenberg (ed.), *Universals of human language*, Stanford: Stanford University Press, p. 213-247.

James, C. (1980), *Contrastive analysis*, London: Longman.

Jansen, F. (1981), *Syntaktische konstrukties in gesproken taal*, Amsterdam: Huis aan de drie Grachten.

Janssen, T. (1975), Possessieve konstrukties, *De Nieuwe Taalgids* 68, 1-13.

Jarvella, R. & W. Klein (1982), *Speech, place and action*, Chichester: Wiley.

Kail, M., M. Hickmann, & N. Emmenecker (1987), *Introduction de référents dans le récit: étude développementale des constraints contextuelle*, Aix-en-Provence 1987.

Kaper, W. (1976), Pronominal case-errors, *Journal of Child Language* 3, 439-441.

Kaper, W. (1985), *Child language: a language which does not exist?* Dordrecht: Foris.

Karmiloff-Smith, A. (1979), *A functional approach to child language: a study of determiners and reference*, Cambridge: Cambridge University Press.

Karmiloff-Smith, A. (1981), The grammatical marking of thematic structure in the development of language production, in: W. Deutsch (ed.), *The child's construction of language*, New York: Academic Press, p. 123-147.

Karmiloff-Smith, A. (1985), Language and cognitive processes from a developmental perspective, *Language and Cognitive Processes* 1, 61-85.

Karmiloff-Smith, A. (1987), Function and process in comparing language and cognition, in: M. Hickmann (ed.), *Social and functional approaches to language and thought*, New York: Academic Press, p. 185-202.

Karsten, G. (1939), Hem en hun als onderwerp, *De Nieuwe Taalgids* 33, 369-372.

Kiewiet, H. (1988), *Introductie en voortgezette referentie naar personen in interethnische communicatie*, MA-thesis, University of Tilburg.

Kirsner, R. (1979), Deixis in discourse: an exploratory quantitative study of the modern Dutch demonstrative adjectives, in: T. Givón (ed.), *Syntax and semantics*, New York: Academic Press, p. 355-375.

Klein, W. (1986), *Second language acquisition*, Cambridge: Cambridge University Press.

Klein, W. (1990), A theory of language acquisition is not so easy, *Studies in Second Language Acquisition* 12, 219-231.

Klein, W. & N. Dittmar (1979), *Developing grammars*, Berlin: Springer.

Klein, W. & C. Perdue (eds.) (1988), *Utterance structure*, Strasbourg: ESF (Final Report Volume VI of the European Science Foundation project "Second language acquisition by adult immigrants").

Klein, W. & C. Perdue (1991), *Utterance structure: developing grammars again*, Amsterdam: Benjamins.

Klein, W. & B. Rieck (1982), Der Erwerb des Personalpronomina im ungesteuerten Spracherwerb, *Zeitschrift für Literaturwissenschaft und Linguistik* 45, 35-71.

Klootwijk, A., J. Treffers & R. Appel (1986), Van jij naar gij: kodewisseling in het taalgebruik van Nederlandse Vlamingen, *Spektator* 15, 239-248.

Kooiman, K. (1967), Lotgevallen van hen en hun in de twintigste eeuw, *De Nieuwe Taalgids* 60, 410-413.

Kooiman, K. (1969), 'Hun = zij', *De Nieuwe Taalgids* 62, 116-120.

Lado, R. (1957), *Linguistics across cultures*, Ann Arbor: University of Michigan Press.

Larsen-Freeman, D. (1985), State of the art on input in second language acquisition, in: S. Gass & C. Madden (eds.), *Input in second language acquisition*, Rowley, Mass.: Newbury House, p. 433-444.

Lees, R. & E. Klima (1963), Rules for English pronominalization, *Language* 39, 17-28.

Lepschy, A. & G. Lepschy (1986), *Die Italienische Sprache*, Tübingen: Francke.

Levy, Y. (1988), On the early learning of formal grammatical systems: evidence from studies on the acquisition of gender and countability, *Journal of Child Language* 15, 179-187.

Lewis, G. (1967), *Turkish grammar*, Oxford: Oxford University Press.

Long, M. & C. Sato (1984), Methodological issues in interlanguage studies: an interactionist perspective, in: A. Davies et al. (eds.), *Interlanguage*, Edinburgh: Edinburgh University Press, p. 253-279.

Loveland, K. (1984), Learning about points of view: spatial perspective and the acquisition of 'I/You', *Journal of Child Language* 11, 535-556.

Lyons, J. (1977), *Semantics*, Cambridge: Cambridge University Press.

Mardin, Y. (1961), *Colloquial Turkish*, London: Routledge.

Marslen-Wilson, W., E. Levy & L. Tyler (1982), Producing interpretable discourse: the establishment and maintenance of reference, in: R. Jarvella & W. Klein (eds.), *Speech, place, and action*, Chichester: Wiley, p. 339-378.

McGann, W. & A. Schwartz (1988), Main character in children's narrative, *Linguistics* 26, 215-233.

McLaughlin, B. (1987), *Theories of second language learning*, London: Edward Arnold.

Miller, G. & P. Johnson-Laird (1976), *Language and perception*, Cambridge, Mass.: Harvard University Press.

Mills, A. (1986), *The acquisition of gender*, Berlin: Springer.

Model, J. (1991), *Grammatische analyse*, Dordrecht: Foris.

Mulford, R. (1985), Comprehension of Icelandic pronoun gender: semantic versus formal factors, *Journal of Child Language* 12, 443-453.

Mühlhäusler, P. (1986), *Pidgin and Creole linguistics*, Oxford: Blackwell.

Mühlhäusler, P. & T. Harré (1990), *Pronouns and people*, Oxford: Blackwell.

Otten, R. (1983), *Basiswoordenboek van het Marokkaans Arabisch*, Coutinho: Muiderberg.

Paardekooper, P. (1969). Aanspreekvormen in mnl. taal en tekst, *De Nieuwe Taalgids* 62, 441-455.

Paardekooper, P. (1987/1988), De rol van half- en indirekte aanspreekvormen bij het ontstaan van u enz. als ond. - en als beleefdheidsvorm I-II, *De Nieuwe Taalgids* 80, 491-511 and 81, 42-71.

Perdue, C. (ed.) (1984), *Second language acquisition by adult immigrants: A field manual*. Rowley, Mass.: Newbury House.

Pinker, S. (1984), *Language learnability and language development*, Cambridge, Mass.: Harvard University Press.

Prince, E. (1985), Fancy syntax and 'shared knowledge', *Journal of Pragmatics* 9, 65-81.

Quirk, R. & S. Greenbaum (1973), *A university of grammar of English*, London: Longman.

Rauh, G. (1983), *Essays in deixis*, Tübingen: Narr.

Rijkhoff, J. (1990), Explaining word order in the noun phrase, *Linguistics* 28, 5-42.

Robinett, B. & J. Schachter (eds.) (1983), *Second language learning*, Ann Arbor: University of Michigan Press.

Rogers, M. (1987), Learners' difficulties with grammatical gender in German as a foreign language, *Applied Linguistics* 8, 49-74.

Sanders, J. (1990), Expliciet of niet? Referentie-bepalende factoren bij personen in nieuwsberichten, *Interdisciplinair Tijdschrift voor Taal- & Tekstwetenschap* 9, 159-180.

Schaerlaekens, A. & S. Gillis (1987), *De taalverwerving van het kind*, Groningen: Wolters-Noordhoff.

Schumann, J. (1978a), *The pidginization process*, Rowley, Mass.: Newbury House.

Schumann, J. (1978b), Social and psychological factors in second language acquisition, in: J. Richards (ed.), *Understanding second and foreign language learning*, Rowley, Mass.: Newbury House, p. 163-178.

Seiler, H. (1983), *Possession as an operational dimension of language*, Tübingen: Narr.

Slobin, D. (1973), Cognitive prerequisites for the development of grammar, in: C. Ferguson & D. Slobin (ed.), *Studies of child language development*, New York: Holt, Rinehart and Winston, p. 175-208.

Slobin, D. (1985), *The cross-linguistic study of language acquisition*, Hillsdale, N.J.: Erlbaum.

Slobin, D. (1987), Thinking for speaking, *Proceedings of the Berkeley Linguistics Society* 13, 435-444.

Slobin, D. (1990), *Learning to think for speaking: native language, cognition, and rhetorical style* (Plenary lecture, International Pragmatics Conference, Barcelona, July 1990).

Storms, G. (1978), Etymologische mijmeringen, *Gramma* 2, 235-240.

Strömqvist, S. & D. Day (1990), *On the development of narrative structure in child L1 and adult L2 acquisition*, Göteborg: Dept. of Linguistics, Göteborg University (Gothenburg papers in theoretical linguistics 56).

Schwarze, C. (1988), *Grammatik der italienische Sprache*, Tübingen: Niemeyer.

Tanz, C. (1974), Cognitive principles underlying children's errors in pronominal case-marking, *Journal of Child Language* 1, 271-276.

Tarone, E. (1988), *Variation in interlanguage*, London: Edward Arnold.

Thavenius. C. (1983), *Referential pronouns in English conversation*, Lund: Liber.

Thun, H. (1985), *Personalpronomina für Sachen. Ein Beitrag zur romanischen Syntax und Textlinguistik*, Tübingen: Narr.

Tinbergen, D. (1919), Kinderpraat, *De Nieuwe Taalgids* 13, 1-16 and 65-86.

Tomlin, R. (ed.) (1987), *Coherence and grounding in discourse*, Amsterdam: Benjamins.

Tomlin, R. (1990), Functionalism in second language acquisition, *Studies in Second Language Acquisition* 12, 155-177.

Türkmen, K., M. Dorleijn & H. Lamers (1988), *Standaard Turks: een leergrammatica*, Coutinho: Muiderberg.

Underhill, R. (1976), *Turkish grammar*, Cambridge, Mass.: MIT Press.

van den Toorn, M. (1977), De problematiek van de Nederlandse aanspreekvormen, *De Nieuwe Taalgids* 70, 520-540.

van der Geest, T. (1974), *Some aspects of communicative competence and their implications for language acquisition*, Doctoral dissertation, University of Amsterdam.

van Dijk, T. & W. Kintsch (1983), *Strategies of discourse comprehension*, New York: Academic Press,

van Ginneken, J. (1917), *De roman van een kleuter*, Nijmegen: Malmberg.

van Hout, R. (1989), *De structuur van taalvariatie*, Dordrecht: Foris.

Verhoeven, L. (1988), Acquisition of discourse cohesion in Turkish, *Studies in Turkish Linguistics* 437-452 (Middle East Technical University Ankara).

Verhoeven, P. (1990), Voornaamwoordelijke aanduiding in het hedendaagse Nederlands, *De Nieuwe Taalgids* 83, 494-513.

Vermaas, J. (1990), U of jij/je zeggen tegen ouders? *Onze Taal* 59, 108-109.

Véronique, D. (1984), Apprentissage naturel et apprentissage guidé, *Le Français dans le Monde* 185, 45-52.

von Stutterheim, C. & W. Klein (1987), A concept-oriented approach to second language studies, in: C. Pfaff (ed.), *First and second language acquisition processes*, Rowley, Mass.: Newbury House, p. 191-205.

vor der Hake, J. (1911), Is de beleefdheidsvorm U 'n verbastering van Ued.? *De Nieuwe Taalgids* 5, 16-24.

White, L. (1989), *Universal grammar and second language acquisition*, Amsterdam: Benjamins.

White, L. (1990), Second language acquisition and universal grammar, *Studies in Second Language Acquisition* 12, 121-133.

Wiesemann, U. (ed.) (1986), *Pronominal systems*, Tübingen: Narr.